The Comics of
Joss Whedon

ALSO BY VALERIE ESTELLE FRANKEL

The Symbolism and Sources of Outlander*:
The Scottish Fairies, Folklore, Ballads, Magic and
Meanings That Inspired the Series* (2015)

Women in Game of Thrones*:
Power, Conformity and Resistance* (2014)

*Buffy and the Heroine's Journey:
Vampire Slayer as Feminine Chosen One* (2012)

*From Girl to Goddess: The Heroine's
Journey through Myth and Legen*d (2010)

EDITED BY VALERIE ESTELLE FRANKEL

The Comics of Joss Whedon: Critical Essays (2015)

*Teaching with Harry Potter: Essays on Classroom
Wizardry from Elementary School to College* (2013)

FROM MCFARLAND

The Comics of Joss Whedon
Critical Essays

Edited by
VALERIE ESTELLE FRANKEL

McFarland & Company, Inc., Publishers
Jefferson, North Carolina

LIBRARY OF CONGRESS CATALOGUING-IN-PUBLICATION DATA

The comics of Joss Whedon : critical essays / edited by Valerie Estelle Frankel.
   p.   cm.
Includes bibliographical references and index.

ISBN 978-0-7864-9885-7 (softcover : acid free paper) ∞
ISBN 978-1-4766-2193-7 (ebook)

1. Whedon, Joss, 1964—Criticism and interpretation.
I. Frankel, Valerie Estelle, 1980– editor.

PN6727.W445Z44 2015
741.5'973—dc23   2015019744

BRITISH LIBRARY CATALOGUING DATA ARE AVAILABLE

© 2015 Valerie Estelle Frankel. All rights reserved

No part of this book may be reproduced or transmitted in any form or by any means, electronic or mechanical, including photocopying or recording, or by any information storage and retrieval system, without permission in writing from the publisher.

On the cover: Joss Whedon, 2001, modified (Photofest); city background © 2015 Shutterstock

Printed in the United States of America

McFarland & Company, Inc., Publishers
   Box 611, Jefferson, North Carolina 28640
      www.mcfarlandpub.com

To all the *Buffy, Firefly,* and
other Whedon scholars who have so enriched
academia with classes, lessons, essays and books of analysis

Table of Contents

• • •

Preface	1

Part One: *Buffy* Comics

The Origin of a Superhero: Sacrifice, Choice and the Significance of Merrick in Buffy's Journey (Joel Hawkes)	9
Buffy Is in Bed with a Woman? Problematic and Perfect Gay and Lesbian Representation (Lisa Gomez)	19
Separate Worlds or One? Canonicity, Medium and Authorship (David Kociemba and Mary Ellen Iatropoulos)	31

Part Two: *Angel* and *Spike* Comics

"Live in the Lie for a While": Closure in *Angel: After the Fall* (Thomas Johnson)	51
The Trouble with Spike: An Examination of William the Bloody's Problematic Progression (Bryant Dillon)	60

Part Three: *Tales of the Slayers*

"So I wear pearls": Exploring Gender in *Tales of the Slayers* (Traci J. Cohen)	73
"There will be Others…Like me": The Legacy of Otherness in *Tales of the Slayers* (Kristi Pope Key)	82

Part Four: *Firefly*

Do *Serenity* Comics Forecast Our Pedagogies of Identity Construction? (Thalia M. Mulvihill and Christina L. Blanch)	93

Part Five: *Dollhouse*

Mind-Body Dualism vs. Materialism: Personal Identity in *Dollhouse: Epitaphs* (S. Evan Kreider)	109

Part Six: Dr. Horrible's Sing-Along Blog

Joss Whedon, Alan Moore and the Whole Horrible Future (Tracy S. Morris) — 121

Part Seven: Marvel's *Runaways*

Dancing in the Sky: The Value of Love in *Runaways* (Don Tresca) — 133

Part Eight: Marvel's *X-Men*

Embracing Goodness (and Colorful Costumes) Amid a World of Gray (Fernando Gabriel Pagnoni Berns and César Alfonso Marino) — 147

River Is Wolverine: Whedon Performs a Sex-Change (Melissa C. Johnson) — 155

Part Nine: Whedon's Other Comics

The Heroine's Journey from Fray to Wonder Woman (Valerie Estelle Frankel) — 165

Comic-Con, Consumerism and Chaos: Reflecting the Fans in *Last Angel in Hell, Stan Lee Meets the Amazing Spider-Man* and *Sugarshock!* (Valerie Estelle Frankel) — 180

Part Ten: *The Avengers, Agents of S.H.I.E.L.D.* and the MCU

Authorship Assembled: Joss Whedon as Promotional Auteur in Marvel's *The Avengers* (Leora Hadas) — 199

Whedon's Women and the Law: Parallels from Slayers to S.H.I.E.L.D. (Gail D. Rosen) — 209

A Guide to Buffyverse Comics — 219

Glossary — 223

Bibliography — 227

About the Contributors — 237

Index — 241

Preface

• • •

"Comics are big business. They sit at the crossroads of art and commerce. Their unique style and subject matter power Hollywood blockbusters and *New York Times* Bestsellers" (Salkowitz 2). As *Avengers* and *X-Men* dominate the big screen, the comic book medium demands attention. Comics are everywhere—bouncing around in children's action figures and Halloween costumes, waiting on the web, humming on ebook readers. It's a new era, and this century-old medium has found a new resurgence.

Joss Whedon has been writing comics for decades, from *X-Men* to of course *Buffy*. Now helming *Avengers* and *Avengers 2*, to say nothing of *Agents of S.H.I.E.L.D.*, he's a transmedia event all by himself, as he transforms bestselling comics into shows, and also bestselling shows into comics. "American comics are the product of a unique idiosyncratic industry: one that is almost entirely reliant on individual creative talent for its success" (Salkowitz 5). And who is more individual, with a style and creativity that resounds the world over, than Whedon himself?

As *Buffy, Angel, Firefly, Dollhouse,* and *Dr. Horrible* continue in comic form, there are many surprises for readers. Famed comic writer Grant Morrison notes, "The low production costs (pen and ink can conjure scenes that would cost millions of dollars of computer time to re-create onscreen) and rapid publication frequency mean that in comic books, almost anything goes" (xvi). *Angel: After the Fall* sees all of Los Angeles banished to hell with a dragon, a ghost, and dozens of demons added to the ensemble. Buffy *Season Eight* features trips to Scotland, Tibet, and Japan, along with a giant Dawn, flying Willow, and truly superpowered Buffy. By Season Ten of Buffy, vampires can fly and turn into mist or occult animals, much as Whedon originally envisioned. His *X-Men* run features a no-holds barred Danger Room (something he was forced to cut from his *X-Men* movie script) and a Kitty Pryde who phases through the entire planet. While the shows demonstrate occasional budget constraints, the comics hold nothing back.

As Morrison adds, "No idea is too bizarre, no twist too fanciful, no storytelling technique too experimental" (xvi). Like Whedon's "unusual episodes" "Hush" (B4.10), "The Body" (B5.16), "Once More with Feeling" (B6.7), or "Smile Time" (A5.14), *The Shepherd's Tale* relates Shepherd Book's history in reverse, while the Dr. Horrible comic tells prequel vignettes in first and second person to immerse readers in the Horrible world. Whedon's "Righteous" story in *Tales of the Slayers* is written as a ballad, as is Lorne's adventure in *Angel: After the Fall, First Night.* In the comic *Long Night's Journey,* Angel retells scenes from his past including a Chinese epic and a black and white twenties noir story. Whedon continues the dream episodes like "Restless" (B4.22) and "The Attic" (D2.10) with the short *Buffy* comics "Always Darkest" and "After These Messages... We'll Be Right Back!" (in Buffy *Season Eight*). The former follows Buffy's dream-wedding to skinless Warren, while the latter blends the unmade *Buffy: The Animated Series* with a dreamy return to Buffy's childhood. The wish-fulfillment *Firefly* comic *Better Days* shares these tropes, revealing characters' deepest desires. There are also new mediums as *Buffy: Season Eight* and *Astonishing X-Men* were released as motion comics. Whedon's *Sugarshock!* like *Dr. Horrible's Sing-Along Blog* began as a three-part web-production.

Aside from Whedon's own franchises, his guest writing brings new insights. During his run, Whedon invented several new X-Men (Blindfold and Armor, both empowered Asian women) and the extraterrestrial complement to S.H.I.E.L.D.: S.W.O.R.D. He sent the Runaways to 1907 to discover the secrets of their ancestry and the true meaning of being a teenager, as well as the truth behind the Skrull member Xavin's identity. His auteur brand significantly impacted his interpretations of *The Avengers* as Black Widow, tied to a chair, interrogates the thugs surrounding her and *Agents of S.H.I.E.L.D.* as Skye transforms from ingénue to superheroine.

In fact, Whedon's works were already primed for comics. His television and films display an essential "comicness" (Kaveney, *Superheroes* 201–225). Critic Kieran Tranter explains:

> In *Serenity* this "comic-ness" is evident in how the film and the television episodes were written and filmed. The dialogue is snappy, speech bubble like. Characters rapidly spar, tease and comment in short sentences before the camera jumps to another view or scene. It is as if their speech was doubly contained by a speech bubble and a frame.... In short *Serenity*'s comic book adventures do not feel out of place because the comic was already there in *Serenity*'s moving image media [284–285].

Buffy's battles take on a melodramatic quality as she whacks Glory into next week with a troll hammer, which Xander follows up with a wrecking ball. The Angel-as-Batman joke is heavy through his series, while Buffy compares herself to Clark Kent with his double lives, and the independent Power Girl. She has the coming-of-age quality of Kitty Pryde or Spider-Man, combined with the pure courage and strength of the Hulk. When in the Season Eight continuation comics she gains superpowers and attempts to outrun a speeding bullet and lift a locomotive, her readers are scarcely surprised. Her writers for this season include Brian K. Vaughan, author of Marvel's *Runaways,* Christos Gage of *Astonishing X-Men* and *The Amazing Spider-Man,* and Brad Meltzer of *Identity Crisis* and *Justice League*—these are more than *Buffy* writers penciling stories as if nothing has changed. Bill Willingham of *Fables* contributed several arcs to *Angel: After the Fall,* as did David Tischman from *American Century.*

In the comics, Whedon's characters embrace their new medium. "Generally speaking, a hero's costume (the sign of his superpowers) is linked in some (permanently visible) way with his origin" (Reynolds 49). While Buffy and her friends generally wear civilian clothes as they do on the show, her iconic white-gown-leather jacket appears again, in *Buffy: The Origin* but also in the white-gowned slayer of "Righteous." Willow dresses as if she stopped time in the musical episode, while visions of Tara show her dressed the same. Wesley returns to his original "Men's Warehouse" outfit, as Cordy's ghost bemoans ("As if he hasn't suffered enough!") (*Angel: After the Fall* 3). Villains wear costumes, from Twilight to the Siphon. Whistler too wears his trademark outfit, as if a decade hasn't passed. Whedon's X-Men return to their uniforms from the Claremont era as a statement of redefinition and his Captain America, on the big screen, makes a similar gesture.

Viewing the comics through a feminist lens is also revealing. *Buffy* critic Jennifer K. Stuller suggests examining how women are depicted—exaggerated body parts and skimpy outfits or not—as well as how they relate to other women and whether they deal with real women's issues of the time. Are the women heroines? Sidekicks? Or only clumsy stereotypes? (240). Whedon's characters earn high scores across the board. For his first, *Fray,* he insisted on a realistic, normally proportioned drawing. "I wanted a real girl, with real posture, a slight figure (that's my classy way of saying 'little boobs') and most of all a distinctive face," he explains in the comic's foreword. Wade in *Sugarshock!* is positively plump. As with the Buffy show, there's some nudity in the comics, but the men are objectified as much as Buffy or more. The Slayers of *Tales* contend with isolation and the difficulty of maintaining their gender while fighting evil in a man's world. In

Season Nine, Buffy contemplates an abortion. While some of the moments are problematic (such as Buffy's casual lesbian affair in Season Eight, Willow's salacious appearance in "Goddesses and Monsters" and Inara's new status as Mal's jobless girlfriend), the characters drive the story, with female friends and relationships. As she mourns Merrick's death in *The Origin* comic, Buffy appears a real person. And she's certainly no sidekick.

"Comics are moving in several directions at once: toward the wide-open spaces of broad transmedia saturation, digital distribution, and globalization, and toward the narrowing horizons of fannish insularity, nostalgia, and niche-art connoisseurship" (Salkowitz 5). Whedon's works of course could be said to do the same, as *Twilight* and *Vampire Diaries* fans snatch Buffy DVDs off the shelf, and motion comics and e-comics pulse through the media. *Avengers* and *Avengers 2* are winning him a new fanbase, even as his black and white *Much Ado About Nothing*, starring the "Whedon crew" of *Angel* and *Firefly* actors caters to long-time fans.

There is another important correlation between Whedon's work and comics: their reception. Popular culture throughout history has meant well-liked works of generally inferior quality, created to be enjoyable. High art is more revered and often considered more instructive or culturally valuable. While 90 percent of boys and girls in the U.S. read comic books in 1953 (establishing their popularity), they were also considered "inferior kinds of work" or often unnecessarily violent and harmful to readers' young minds (Kukkonen 114). Karin Kukkonen, author of *Studying Comics and Graphic Novels*, explains: "You expect important pieces of art in a gallery—not meaningless rubbish—because it is a place of high culture. You expect repetitive and exploitative stories in comics, because comics are a medium of pop culture" (115). A similar argument could be made for television shows, especially ones broadcast during the teen hours on Fox, WB, and UPN. While Whedon's works are celebrated and deconstructed for their artistry (especially inventive episodes like "Restless" or "The Body"), the episodes' origin on a show about a teen fighting vampires has given many of the more snobbish critics pause. Still, just as *Buffy* has broken through to become a genre of academic criticism, with journals, books, and even academic classes, comics have broken through into all these mediums of scholarship as well.

The book is divided into ten parts, each covering specific comics, series or characters. Each part is introduced with a short essay written by the editor of the collection. As a whole this collection explores Whedon's work in the comic book medium—from his original stories to his transmedia television shows, to his contributions to the preexisting Marvel franchises. Joel

Hawkes considers the artistry of the *Buffy: The Origin* comic as both a re-envisioning of the movie and a presentation of Buffy's superhero origin story. Bryant Dillon, president of Fanboy Comics, follows Spike's path as a character caught between the *Buffy* and *Angel* franchises and unable to grow past his role as Buffy's devotee thanks to shifting ownership of his character. My own essays trace the heroine's journey and the celebration of fandom in more obscure projects, such as Whedon's independent comics *Sugarshock!* and *Fray,* contribution to *Stan Lee Meets the Amazing Spider-Man,* and his unmade *Wonder Woman* script.

Some essays narrow in on the art form, examining just a few panels of comics for their artistry and symbolic meaning. Thomas Johnson does this with the Fred-Wesley arc in *Angel: After the Fall,* while Traci J. Cohen compares the subversive clothing choices and fighting styles of three gender-hybridized slayers.

On the more philosophical side, several authors tackle identity as a theme. S. Evan Kreider examines mind-body dualism in *Dollhouse: Epitaphs,* while Kristi Pope Key tackles Otherness in *Tales of the Slayers.* The *Serenity* comics are excellent for teaching identity in the classroom, as Thalia M. Mulvihill and Christina L. Blanch reveal. The problematic homosexuality of the *Buffy* comics appears in Lisa Gomez's essay—not just Buffy's sensational lesbian affair in Season Eight, but the treatment of Willow, Andrew, Billy, and other characters. Fernando Gabriel Pagnoni Berns and César Alfonso Marino from the Universidad de Buenos Aires examine the good-evil dichotomy faced in several series. Whedon's views of love and his famous celebration of the chosen family are examined by Don Tresca through Marvel's *Runaways.*

Several authors compare their favorite franchises with other comics: Tracy S. Morris sees *Dr. Horrible* as an antihero tale worthy of comics genius Alan Moore, while Melissa C. Johnson examines River Tam as a reflection of several X-Men, from Wolverine to Dark Phoenix. Gail D. Rosen compares Whedon's women, rebelling against the patriarchy in both *Buffy* and the comic book as show, *Agents of S.H.I.E.L.D.*

Of course, Whedon is known for bringing his particular mark, known as auteurism, to whatever he touches. Leora Hadas examines how the marketing of *The Avengers* utilized his brand name, while *Buffy* scholars David Kociemba and Mary Ellen Iatropoulos look at his authorship, or not, of the *Buffy* and *Serenity* comics. Most of the essays explore Whedon's themes and how they are maintained or altered from shows to comics. A few incorporate public responses to the new formats and character arcs, preserving a moment of fannish history. Across many spectrums, all of the essays celebrate Whedon's works in this new medium. As he incorporates splash pages, contrasting art styles, new talents, and of course an unlimited special effects budget, it's still the Whedonverse, but much bigger and bolder.

Through the book, episodes and comics alike are referred to by name and number: A Buffy television episode (from seasons one through seven) is shown as B2.6, meaning the episode "Halloween," the sixth episode of season two. The comic book continuations of *Buffy*, Seasons Eight through Ten, are B8, B9 and B10. Each season consists of individual comic book issues, which are then collected in larger books, so B8.1 means the first volume of the Season Eight trade paperbacks. A few essays discuss individual issues so they are shown as #3 or #4. *Buffy Season Eight* through *Ten* in italics refer to the comics, and without italics refer to the seasons, though admittedly, it's a very faint line of distinction. Of course, *Angel* is *A*, *Firefly* F, *Dollhouse* D, *Doctor Horrible* DH, and *Agents of S.H.I.E.L.D.* AS. And *ATF* refers to *Angel: After the Fall*, a comic series equivalent to *Angel* season six. Films and other comics are referred to by name.

Part One

Buffy Comics

• • •

The *Buffy* franchise began as a parody movie, achieved cult status as a TV show, then switched mediums again to continue in comic form during and after the show. As early as 1998, tie-in comics from Dark Horse appeared for the *Buffy* series. Though Joss Whedon didn't supervise directly, Doug Petrie, Jane Espenson, and other beloved Buffy writers wrote some of the individual pieces. Most comics took place synonymously with the current season. However, *Buffy: The Origin* retold the original Buffy movie, now with more of Whedon's original lines and vision for the character. Joel Hawkes begins this collection by comparing this comic to superhero origin stories and examining the nuances it adds to the show characters.

A few years after the show ended came the *Buffy: Season Eight* comics, helmed by Whedon. This 40-issue run was published by Dark Horse Comics from 2007 to 2011, with a motion comic adaptation as well. It follows Buffy as leader of thousands of Slayers across the world, though she must battle her slipping morals and several rebellious and evil slayers before, of course, the apocalypse comes once more. *Buffy: Season Nine*, 25 issues, was published 2011–2013 as Buffy and her friends battled to restore magic to a simpler world. Spin-off titles include the five-issue series *Willow: Wonderland* and *Spike: A Dark Place*. Season Ten began in 2014. Unlike tie-in comics, the continuation offers dramatic character changes, from deaths to new relationships and powers. Most of these comics are available in graphic novel trade paperbacks, including some ebook versions. A guide is printed at the end of this collection.

In this collection, Lisa Gomez and David Kociemba and Mary Ellen Iatropoulos examine fans' reactions and problematic character change in the Season Eight through Ten comics with Giant Dawn, lesbian-fling Buffy, abortion-storyline Buffy, closeted Andrew and many new creators.

The Origin of a Superhero
Sacrifice, Choice and the Significance of Merrick in Buffy's Journey

JOEL HAWKES

• • •

Slayer, Superheroes and Sacrifice

The comic book *Buffy the Vampire Slayer: The Origin* was published in three parts at the beginning of 1999, halfway through the airing of season three of the television series. The comic combines elements of the earlier 1992 *Buffy* movie and the series (1997–2003) to retell Buffy's origin story as Joss Whedon intended in his original script. Buffy now burns down the school gymnasium, an event that does not occur in the movie, but is referenced in the television show ("Welcome to the Hellmouth," B1.1); the color and tone of the comic are oddly reminiscent of a late 1990s/Whedon aesthetic, rather than the 1980s almost-pantomime feel of the movie; characters more closely resemble their television incarnations; and, in the closing moments of issue three of the comic, we connect to Sunnydale, and discover Buffy's origin tale has been retold by Buffy herself in the high school library to Rupert Giles, Willow Rosenberg, and Xander Harris. Buffy's first Watcher, Merrick Jamison-Smythe—a central figure in Buffy's inception as Slayer—also looks more like his television incarnation, despite appearing only briefly in flashback in "Becoming, Part One" (B2.21). Though changes in the comic are various, they at first seem minor and cosmetic, the "canonical" text appearing little altered from the "non-canonical" movie.

This apparent lack of major revision surprises, considering Whedon's distaste for the movie, which he claims he had "written [as a] scary film about an empowered woman," only to see it transformed by director Fran Rubel Kuzui into a "broad comedy"—a reworking that Whedon found "crushing" (qtd. in Havens 51). However, on closer reading we discover subtle but far from minor alterations in the comic, changes that restructure Buffy's birth as the Slayer, distancing Buffy from the film and aligning her with the television series, and, importantly (and fittingly for an origin tale), with the show's preoccupation with mythic origins. This central concern grows later in the television series, with the First Slayer (Sinyea) and First Evil, but is earlier located in the origin stories of its heroes and villains (e.g., Buffy, Spike, Angel, and Drusilla). The anthropologist David George discusses this sacred "in the beginning" as a central concern of religious and mythic storytelling—the genesis of good and evil, and creation myths (12)—but it is also an integral part of superhero mythology. Origin tales often define the motives, powers, and actions of such heroes. As Xander points out in the second episode of the television show, "Buffy's a superhero" ("The Harvest," B1.2). The comic finally gives Buffy the origin story that befits a hero inspired by both comic book superheroes and their older, mythical antecedents, and helps establish a criterion to which other characters on the show must adhere in order to become superheroes themselves.

So what makes a superhero? Origin tales often conform (more or less) to a template. Richard Reynolds in *Super Heroes: A Modern Mythology* lists seven steps that define the superhero genre, especially the origin story:

1. The hero is marked out from society. He often reaches maturity without having a relationship with his parents.
2. At least some of the superheroes will be like earthbound gods in their level of powers. Other superheroes of lesser powers will consort easily with these earthbound deities.
3. The hero's devotion to justice overrides even his devotion to the law.
4. The extraordinary nature of the superhero will be contrasted with the ordinariness of his surroundings.
5. Likewise, the extraordinary nature of the hero will be contrasted with the mundane nature of his alter-ego. Certain taboos will govern the actions of these alter-egos.
6. Although ultimately above the law, superheroes can be capable of considerable patriotism and moral loyalty to the state, though not necessarily to the letter of its laws.
7. The stories are mythical and use science and magic indiscriminately to create a sense of wonder [16].

Spider-Man, to whom Buffy is repeatedly compared, nicely illustrates this broad criteria, but also allows us to develop the pattern to focus on more specific aspects of the origin tale in *Buffy*: the hero-to-be receives great power (a radioactive spider bite); this power transforms, empowering but also troubling the hero (a choice must be made to use powers selfishly or for the greater good—"with great power comes great responsibility"); the hero takes on a dual identity (he is both human and superhero); and a mentor helps guide him at the start of his superhero/mythic journey, but dies/is killed (Uncle Ben). A similar pattern exists in *Buffy* film and comic: the previous Slayer dies and Buffy receives her powers; she is transformed, unsure whether to fight or flee from this new world filled with vampires; now she must be an average schoolgirl by day, Slayer at night. Merrick guides Buffy in her transformation, dying in his bid to protect her from the vampire Lothos. In the movie, inconsistencies in the origin template, and in character development, weaken the superhero mythos, but in the comic, through a consideration of Merrick, we observe a greater reconfiguration of Buffy's mythic origins.

The rewriting of Merrick's death in the comic introduces a quality (or, indeed, "superpower") that defines Buffy and other "superhero" characters on the show. Rather than being killed by the vampire Lothos (as in the movie), Merrick now kills himself in order to protect Buffy's identity. Her superhero double life begins, and an act of self-sacrifice helps birth a hero (and a show) defined by sacrifice (just as it helps us define, and understand, other superheroes like Superman and Power Girl with whom Buffy is notably compared).[1] The rewritten Merrick (a rather minor character in the Buffyverse) helps create a more carefully defined superhero Slayer, who exhibits less of the "vapidity and stereotypical femininity [that] repeatedly place her in danger" (Moss para. 2) in the movie. As Gabrielle Moss suggests, the "bubbly Valley girl" only becomes Whedon's intended feminist heroine in the show (para. 1); the comic helps rectify this uneasy transition, more clearly demonstrating the birth of a powerful superhero. Merrick's death now foreshadows the abnegations required by Buffy and others, such as Spike and Angel, to follow a hero's journey, and transcend to superhero status (origins glimpsed in the aptly titled double episode "Becoming" [B21 and 22], the only episode in which Merrick appears). Merrick's death also helps engender a Slayer that we believe capable of such heroic acts. George writes that perhaps more important than religion's obsession with origins is a search for perfection as heaven or redemption (12); in *Buffy*, sacrifice allows such a quest to take place, enabling characters to truly become super-heroic, and Buffy to become the Slayer who not only fulfills her sacred duties but transcends them, so that at the close of Season Seven, she is no longer "The Chosen One," but one among many.

Merrick

The Merrick of film, television and comic all fulfill the same function of establishing Buffy's Slayer credentials, highlighting her birthright as the Chosen One. An origin point for Buffy, Merrick gives her the knowledge and initial training needed to survive as a Slayer. It is no surprise that comic book Merrick resembles Richard Riehle, who plays the character in the series, considering Whedon's dislike for the "certain OTHER thespian who shall remain hated," Donald Sutherland, who played Merrick in the film and insisted on rewriting his own part, much to Whedon's chagrin ("Bronze VIP Archive"). Though English in the film, and American in show and comic, Merrick remains essentially the same grumpy, slightly humorless character—Buffy comments in mock surprise when he makes a joke (*Buffy* and *Buffy: The Origin*). He in turn despairs at a Slayer he finds to be "vacuous" (*Buffy* and *Buffy: The Origin*).

Sutherland's Merrick is, though, more pompous (though admittedly most Watchers are)—with an aloofness that seems to more closely align him with the coldness of Quentin Travers or ridiculousness of the young Wesley Wyndam-Pryce than, for example, Giles. While the comic book Merrick operates in a more expanded Buffyverse, with its more developed Slayer and Watcher mythology (so allowing for a greater understanding and perhaps sympathy with the character), Merrick also seems to more closely resemble the type of Watcher found in Giles. Where movie Merrick does come to respect Buffy, advising her to do things her own way—"Don't play our game," he tells her—in the comic, his advice connects to his father, a man who taught him the "subtleties" of being a Watcher that the "Council never bothered with." He now foreshadows the later need to question the Council, and becomes approachable as more of a fatherly figure passing on his own father's advice to a young Buffy. The father role is, of course, more fully embodied in Giles. In the film, Merrick describes training many Slayers before Buffy, but in the comic, he also reveals something of the emotional trauma of then seeing them "ripped apart." He even apologies for the brutality of his training methods. The Merrick of the comic thus becomes a more sympathetic incarnation of the character, and so a more fitting mentor to a powerful but caring Slayer.

Not only is the reimagined Watcher more humane; he is also, literally, more human, and this gives a greater significance to his death. In the movie, the semi-immortal Merrick dies, but each time returns with "the knowledge that [his] purpose is to prepare the Chosen One for her battle" (*Buffy*). His position shadows the mythic lineage of the Slayer (established by Merrick, and by Buffy's dreams of past Slayers, in both film and comic). Merrick's death—too easy, and almost without merit—seems a tragic waste, and also tragic in the sense that, semi-immortal, he is perhaps doomed to walk the earth until the death of the last vampire. This tragedy—but also Merrick's pomposity—compounds his final words, "The rest is...." With the half-spoken word "silence" following, Merrick cannot quite complete the phase uttered by Shakespeare's dying Hamlet. This melodrama in the film gains greater significance in the comic because a rewritten Merrick is mortal. He kills himself, without thought or pretension, to protect Buffy; he will not be reborn.

Buffy as Sacrifice and Superhero

This kind of self-sacrifice sets Buffy apart in the show, torments her, and makes her both human and more than human: a superhero. She must hide her Slayer identity and face death (and die twice in "Prophecy Girl," B1.12 and "The Gift," B5.22) to keep an unsuspecting humanity safe. Her Slayer duties also make her a social outcast on arrival in Sunnydale ("Welcome to the Hellmouth," B1.1); she cannot move away to the university of her choice ("Choices," B3.19); and she must eventually drop her studies ("Tough Love," B5.19) to take care of her "sister," Dawn—not of her blood but rather the manifestation of a mystical convergence Buffy must protect ("No Place Like Home," B5.5). Later, Buffy must work serving fast food just to support herself and sister ("Doublemeat Palace," B6.12). Her life bursts with self-denial for the benefit of others: a giving up of the self and the selfish that allows her to be the Slayer. At the same time, she must hide an empowering identity, so that just like Clark Kent she must "endure everyday humiliation in the workaday world" (Wilcox 66).

When Buffy gives up her life for her "sister," and to save the world, by closing the portal opened by Glory at the end of Season Five ("The Gift," B5.5), she completes her most selfless act. The "Gift" of this episode's title relates to Buffy's own death, as foretold by a spirit guide who appears as the First Slayer—"Death is your gift" Buffy learns ("Intervention," B5.18). Her gift is not, as Buffy fears, for killing (with the consequential loss of her "humanity") (B5.18); rather, her power comes from her humanity, and the gift is of her own life: the ultimate act of self-sacrifice.

This offering of the self aligns Buffy with comic book superheroes. Figures like Superman and Spider-Man, though superhuman, similarly gain great strength from their greater "humanity," and by the apotheosis of humanity in them: their capacity for self-sacrifice. This is evident in the superhero behavior criteria suggested by Robin Rosenberg in "Our Fascination with Superheroes": they "fight," even when "tired, burned out"; they put aside their "personal lives"; when "hard," they still make the "right decision"; and they have an "enviable" "moral compass" (14–15). They too must live double lives, giving up any chance of a "normal" existence. Buffy suitably compares herself to both superheroes in the show, referring to her "spider-sense" ("I Robot, You Jane," B1.8) and more specifically to her dual identity when she complains of turning into Clark Kent ("Never Kill a Boy on the First Date," B1.5). The comic *Spider-Man* (a repeated point of intertextuality in *Buffy* and *Angel*[2]) defines its hero by his sense of "responsibility," and Superman (the original golden-age comic book superhero), though alien, is raised as human, with his strong sense of morality learned from his adoptive American parents. Those superheroes' willingness, and Buffy's, to put others before themselves makes their other powers effective and aligns them with the no less heroic figures of older mythology, such as Prometheus, who willingly suffers to bring wisdom (and fire) to humankind, and the man-god, Christ, who offers his own life to save the world.[3]

The will to sacrifice that defines these "savior" figures creates a powerful and compulsive mythical storytelling. Merrick's now-selfless death in the comic foreshadows this heroic savior-like behavior embodied in the Slayer and offers a more mythically/narratologically-suited origin for such a superhero. Merrick kills himself to protect Buffy's secret, so emphasizing the importance of the superhero dual identity and the need to give up all for others.

The Buffy of the comic seems to learn much more from her mentor, successfully renouncing her shopping and ditzy friend lifestyle. She is also more troubled by his death than her movie counterpart—his death becomes a moment in which to ponder her options and decide what to do with her powers; she fittingly offers a prayer for Merrick—a suitable ritual in the greater ritual pattern of a superhero's birth. Comic book Buffy defeats Lothos and abandons her valley-girl life, leaving on her next adventure, while in the film she is more reliant on the male love-interest, Pike (even jumping on the back of his bike at the film's end), and more easily manipulated (in a dream-based sexual seduction) and injured by Lothos. In the film, we wonder how she has managed to survive the vampire attack; we are not convinced that she has made the decision to use her powers without regard for herself; and we remain unconvinced by her escape from her vapid schoolgirl origins, and transformation into a superhero. Comic book Merrick helps birth a far more convincing superhero.

The Origin of Sacrifice and "Becoming"

Merrick's suicide also helps foreshadow the importance of choice in *Buffy*. A figure might well receive great power or have tragedy thrust upon them; however, while that which is forced might create a powerfully mythic figure, that which is chosen—the responsibility of giving up a normal life to aid others—finally creates the superhero. In Spider-Man mythology, Peter learns his "responsibility" from his guardian (and mentor), Uncle Ben, and from his uncle's death, caused by a fleeing thief that Peter ignores. Death and tragedy—the loss of a loved one through indifference—compound the transforming effects of the spider bite, but it is the choice to help others that truly births the hero. Batman's origins begin in similar trauma, with the murder of his parents. Both *Buffy* and *Angel* make numerous references to Batman (Buffy and Angel are in many ways the "Batmans" of their respective shows).[4] Such forced beginnings (a kind of "sacrifice," itself), originate the Slayer line: located in the First Slayer, a woman forced by men into bondage and endowed with powers to battle evil: the offering of a young girl and her innocence to a cause ("Get It Done," B7.15). Buffy's personal Slayer origin mirrors this forced beginning, when she discovers her, at first unwanted, duty, only to be persuaded and cajoled to pursue it, first by Merrick (*Buffy*, *Buffy: The Origin*) and later Giles ("Welcome to the Hellmouth," B1.1). Her role is, at times, brutally enforced by the Watchers Council (e.g., the rite of passage, the "Cruciamentum," in "Helpless," B3.12), who mirror their African counterparts that began it all. Much is forced upon Buffy, but she finally chooses to continue as the Slayer, battling evil and saving humanity. In rewriting Merrick's death, the importance of choice and self-sacrifice are emphasized—a generous act that helps form the origin tale. We find this in Superman's origin story, with his father on Krypton, Jor-El, launching the infant Kal-El (Clark Kent) into space before the destruction of the planet. Fittingly, Buffy acknowledges her own similarity to this type of hero, describing herself as "some kind of supergirl" ("Normal Again," B6.16), and reveals that her childhood was even shaped by these figures as she played at being Power Girl ("Killed by Death," B2.18). Both Power Girl and Supergirl have similar origin stories to Superman.[5] While arguably most superheroes give up much in the roles they assume (no matter their origin), others like Superman and Buffy are more fully defined by a will to self-sacrifice.

Merrick's rewritten death highlights this focus in *Buffy*, but also draws attention to a battle between the forces that birth the superhero in other *Buffy* characters. Merrick's appearance in the double episode "Becoming"

(B2.21 and 2.22), connects the Watcher to another "origin" point in Whedon's storytelling, and the importance of choice. The benevolent demon Whistler narrates "Becoming," and explains: "There's moments in your life that make you, that set the course of who you're going to be. Sometimes they're little subtle moments. Sometimes they're not" ("Becoming, Part One," B2.21). "Becoming" reveals many such moments. In flashbacks we see Darla's siring of Liam, creating the vampire Angelus in Ireland (1753); we see Angelus tormenting Drusilla before siring her in England (1860); and we witness Angelus's soul restored by the Roma in Romania (1898). We then see Whistler discovering Angel living off rats on the streets of New York in 1996; he challenges Angel to become something more: a hero. Upon seeing Buffy, newly called by Merrick, Angel is inspired to help, to become "someone to be counted" ("Becoming, Part One," B2.21). We witness the mythic creation of Angelus, then Angel. His power and soul are forced upon him; his mentor arrives, and then he makes a choice. His decision turns an immortal figure into a superhero, one, like Buffy, defined by his abnegation of the self for others.

The episode also reveals Drusilla's origin story (driven to madness) and reveals the origins of much future narrative and character development. Meanwhile, the death of the Slayer, Kendra, leads to the calling of Faith to be Slayer—Faith, now empowered, will lose her mentor, and later show how selfish choices turn a superhero into a villain. Joyce Summers finally discovers her daughter's secret identity (highlighting that aspect of the superhero—the episode, in a sense, reassembles the essential components that make a superhero). Finally, Spike works with the Slayer for the first time, in order to defeat Angelus. This event begins Spike's relationship with Buffy and the Scoobies, and eventually leads to the restoration of his soul, and finally to an act of self-sacrifice that defeats the First Evil ("Chosen," B7.22). Such "self-sacrifice" is not only, as *Buffy* critic Melanie Wilson argues, necessary for Spike's redemption (and Angel's), and part of a process that simply makes him more human (137), but rather it is a choice that confirms him as more than human, as (super)hero ("Chosen," B7.22): the apotheosis of humanity.

Buffy makes a similar offering in "Becoming, Part Two," killing her lover Angel, moments after he regains his soul, in order to save the world. Her journey with Spike, begun here, leads her to symbolically sacrifice alongside his death in "Chosen," when she shares her unique Slayer/Superhero identity among the many potential Slayers (B7.22).

The aptly named "Becoming" episodes establish a mythical origin point, re-examining the beginning/becoming of the Slayer, and the origin (siring) of vampire characters. From this episode protagonists set forth on their new journeys of becoming—a superheroes' journey, one of their choosing. Again, Whistler's narration of the episode illustrates this point:

> The bottom line is, even if you see them coming, you're not ready for the big moments. No one asks for their life to change. Not really. But it does.... The big moments are gonna come; you can't help that. It's what you do afterwards that counts. That's when you find out who you are ["Becoming, Part One," B2.21].

Thus acts of self-sacrifice birth the superheroes of the Buffyverse. The rewriting of Merrick's death in the comic now begins it all, aligns him with the "Becoming" episodes, and helps set in place a template for superheroes to come. He becomes the origin point of a mythical pattern that connects the show's superheroes—a mystical "in the beginning" that allows the quest for "perfection" to begin (George 12), the superhero to be born.

Notes

1. *Buffy* and *Angel* contain numerous references to comic book superheroes; many connect to Buffy herself. For extensive listings of these (and many other pop culture references in Whedon's work), see Valerie Estelle Frankel's *Pop Culture in the Whedonverse* (USA: LitCrit Press, 2014).

2. Examples of Spider-Man intertextuality include the Master's use of the famous lines, "With great power comes great responsibility" ("Angel," B1.7), and Ben asking Buffy if she has a "radioactive spider bite" ("No Place Like Home," B5.5) when he notes her super-strength. A more oblique reference in *Angel* sees Lilah's "Our friendly neighborhood vampire" ("Five by Five," A1.18) reflecting the often-used "friendly neighborhood Spider-Man" phrase of the comic.

3. We find inspiration for Superman in such mythic heroes as Hercules or Samson, or indeed Achilles, but similarities to the story of Moses have also been noted, with Superman's origin tale reminiscent of that of the leader of the Israelites, cast off in a basket (Superman in a rocket) to be amongst another people, where he will rise to be a hero (*The Mythology of Superman*). Moses gives up a life of privilege to lead his people to the Promised Land—a place he cannot enter himself. Sacrifice defines him. A number of essays discussing *Buffy* address the presence of mythic storytelling in the show, with a particular focus on the structured quest of the mythic hero, with reference to Joseph Campbell's discussion of the journey of the archetypal hero in *The Hero with a Thousand Faces*. Here, the hero's journey is also a rite of passage. Campbell writes, "A hero ventures forth from the world of common day into a region of supernatural wonder: fabulous forces are there encountered and a decisive victory is won: the hero comes back from this mysterious adventure with the power to bestow boons on his fellow man" (Campbell 30). In his discussion of superheroes, Lawrence Rubin references Campbell's study, suggesting that superhero storytelling takes over the older mythical tales' role of

offering, through the hero's story, meaning and structure—a way for society to understand itself (42). *Buffy* might be read as such a new mythology. On the subject of the hero's journey and *Buffy*, see Lynne Edwards, "Slaying in Black and White: Kendra as Tragic Mulatta in *Buffy*," in *Fighting the Forces* (85–97); Rhonda V. Wilcox, *Why Buffy Matters* (30–45); Janet K. Halfyard, "Hero's Journey, Heroine's Return: Buffy, Eurydice, and the Orpheus Myth," in *Reading Joss Whedon*.

4. References to Batman include Buffy's use of "Bat Signal," as a call to arms ("Some Assembly Required," B2.2), while Xander refers to Sunnydale school library as the "Batcave," and to Giles as "Alfred" ("The Yoko Factor," B4.20). In *Angel*, Doyle and Cordelia both joke that Angel has a Batcave hidden away somewhere ("City Of," A1.1; "Eternity," A1.17). *Buffy: The Origin* continues the Batman intertextuality, with Buffy referring to Merrick's hideout as the "Batcave."

5. Supergirl also originates from Krypton, sent to Earth by her father; Power Girl (the Earth Two version of Supergirl) is likewise saved by her parents' self-sacrifice, and sent to Earth.

Buffy Is in Bed with a Woman?

Problematic and Perfect Gay and Lesbian Representation

LISA GOMEZ

• • •

The first time I held a *Buffy the Vampire Slayer* comic in my hands was a magical moment I know I will not soon forget. I had just graduated from college, was a 21-year-old trying to navigate her way in this new, frightening and aimless world. I had just finished the heart-wrenchingly magnificent "Chosen" and couldn't stop feeling as if one of my best friends had just died, because the show was done (B7.22). This was it. The journey was most definitely over. That was when my best friend Josh let me borrow his impressive Buffy comics collection—in it was the very first trade paperback of *Buffy the Vampire Slayer, Season Eight*. I marveled at Georges Jeanty's beautiful and unique artwork; his style made the show characters appear while also expressing his own creativity. I grinned, reading Joss Whedon's usual snark and wit, laughing at the appropriate jokes and gasping at some surprises. Very quickly, it felt like I was home again with the Scooby gang. Just by one glance at the stack of trade paperbacks on my bed, I saw how much more of a journey I had to go and it made my heart swell. However, very early on, something happened. When my eyes first stumbled upon a certain panel, my heart stopped. My eyes narrowed in confusion. My fingers tightened their grip on the glossy paper and I didn't care that they left a smudge. An event occurred that split the entire fandom in half, more than any event in the Buffyverse before. Hundreds of fans showed their rage or incredible love on the subject, on message boards across the internet, including the most renowned Buffy fan websites: Whedonesque.com, SlayAlive.com and Buffyfest.blogspot.com.

Buffy Summers slept with a woman. A Slayer. And no, it wasn't Faith.

Why was Buffy sleeping with a woman such an outrage? First, one must look at what sexual orientation is and with which Buffy most likely identifies. "Sexual orientation is defined as an often enduring pattern of emotional, romantic and/or sexual attractions of men to women or women to men (heterosexual), of women to women or men to men (homosexual), or by men or women to both sexes (bisexual)" ("Lesbian, Gay, Bisexual, Transexual Orientation"). Of course, there are more sexual orientations, including but not limited to asexual and pansexual, but for the cause of examining the Buffy comics, these three will suffice. Never, in the entirety of the canon, has Buffy Summers ever hinted at being interested, sexually, in the same sex. Many would disagree and argue about Buffy's and Faith's relationship, but while Faith is very obviously interested in her, Buffy doesn't reciprocate. No matter how much they dance together ("Bad Girls," B3.14) or tease each other with suggestive language like "let's see who lands on top" ("This Year's Girl," B4.15), it's never officially confirmed that Buffy has sexual feelings towards Faith. Even when Buffy kisses Faith on the forehead after stabbing her, it isn't out of sexual desire but out of apology ("Graduation Day: Part Two," B3.22). Meanwhile, when Willow comes out to Buffy, Buffy is shocked ("New Moon Rising," B4.19). She takes the news respectfully, though a little stunned. It takes her half a season to be completely comfortable with Willow's lesbian relationship ("Family," B5.6), but not out of homophobia, but just the way any friend would react to a life-changing admission. Meanwhile, Willow herself seems less-than-comfortable with the label:

> **KENNEDY**: Let's start with the easy stuff. How long have you known ... that you were gay?
> **WILLOW**: Wait. That's easy? And what, you just assume that I'm gay. I mean, presume much?
> **KENNEDY**: Okay, sorry. How long have you enjoyed having sex with women? ["The Killer in Me," B6.13].

Problematically, Willow doesn't identify as bisexual or pansexual, especially when she has had sex and has been in love with members of the two sexes, but that's an entirely different essay.

In the course of the television show, Buffy has had romantic and sexual feelings towards Angel, Owen Thurman, Scott Hope, Parker Abrams, Riley Finn, Spike, and Robin Wood. According to a study done by Ball State University, "even if people do not have sexual experiences until they are adults, their sexual orientation is determined early in life" ("Gay, Lesbian and Bisexual Issues"). Based on the above evidence, the fact that Buffy has shown no sexual interest in a woman and only men from her adolescent years to her early adult years is substantial enough evidence to infer that Buffy Summers is a straight woman.

It's evident from the first few arcs in the *Season Eight* comics that Buffy's sexuality remains exactly the same in the comics as it was portrayed in the television show. As Helene Frohard-Dourlent agrees in her Buffy essay "Lez-faux Representation":

> The *Season Eight* comics unsurprisingly build on this heterosexualized identity that the audience has come to expect of Buffy: for example, she fantasizes about men (8.03 and 8.10), she dresses up to meet an ex-boyfriend (8.16) and she enthuses over a male actor's attractiveness (8.23). These images do not challenge Buffy's established heterosexuality. On the contrary, they bolster it by over-representing her (male) object of desire and making it plain her desire for these men in multifarious forms. Additionally, they undermine the idea that Buffy's heterosexuality is a default assumption ... [it's] representative of a (hetero) sexuality that Buffy has appropriated and embraced.

Central here is Buffy's relationship with the Slayer Satsu, who is introduced right at the start of Season Eight. She is seemingly a background character, another one of Buffy's slayers that is strong, accountable, and well put-together, with such cool hair that Buffy has to comment on it and ask Satsu to check in with her later for hair tips (*The Long Way Home*, #2). So far, so good.

The stakes change when Amy casts a "Sleeping Beauty" type spell on Buffy and only "the kiss of true love" can awaken her. Besides being an admittedly weak plot device, one can't help but wonder who on earth near Buffy could be in love with her. It can't be Willow, since she's the one to direct Buffy's admirer to come forward and break the spell. Could it be Xander? He's arguably more put together now than when he was doing construction work in Sunnydale (although he was sexy back then, too) and they have scenes in this issue with just the two of them, in which it's obvious that Xander is someone Buffy can trust. Although shippers are rooting for Spike or Angel, Xander is a worthy opponent. Or so we are led to believe. In an interview, Whedon smiles that he thought "it would be fun to have the kiss of true love, make people think it was Xander ... or Willow, and then say, oh no, it's neither of them" (Warn).

It isn't until the third arc of Season Eight, *Wolves at the Gate* written by Drew Goddard, that it's revealed that Buffy knows Satsu is the one that kissed her ... and that Satsu is in love with Buffy. From a writing and characterization viewpoint, this could have been an incredibly poignant unrequited love story across the gay/straight boundary. It's a storyline with which a lot of readers could relate or at least empathize, and would have been a worthy plot to add to Buffy's incredible journey. In true Whedon fashion, while Buffy and Satsu are discussing Satsu's feelings, they are also attempting to take down some vampires. When Satsu asks if she's kicking her out of the Slayer squad, Buffy replies: "You are so missing the point ... I think [your crush] it's the sweetest thing ever.... And honestly, I think it's kind of awesome. You're hot, you have great taste, you're a hell of a Slayer and you smell good."

"But you're not gay," Satsu points out.

"Not so you'd notice," Buffy retorts respectfully (*Wolves at the Gate*, #11).

Great. It's very clear in the text that Buffy does not feel romantic or sexual attraction to women. This scene is a wonderful scene for Satsu because it makes the audience feel sorry for her, the age-old tale of loving someone who can't return it. However, the very next issue completely contradicts this entire conversation. In the infamous issue 12, readers are engulfed by the developing relationship between Xander and Renee and even revel in Xander's telling piece of dialogue, "Who wants to be alone on a night like this?" (*Wolves at the Gate*, #12). Readers turn the page ... and there's Buffy. In bed. With Satsu. Although Georges' art work is stunningly beautiful, it's a very suggestive panel. Buffy's and Satsu's naked bodies are clearly outlined through the sheets, which appear to be stuck to them. Satsu is cuddling onto Buffy's shoulder and has her arms wrapped around the Chosen One. Buffy, face full of satisfaction, simply says, "Wow" (*Wolves at the Gate*, #12). For obvious reasons, it's an incredibly memorable panel due to Georges' stellar artwork but also ... wait a minute. Buffy is in bed with Satsu? Buffy is in bed with a woman? The same person that she rejected a few pages before?

A moment like this in the Buffyverse, especially such a huge character moment, should inspire feelings of exaltation, excitement and awe. It did nothing but conjure up dread. Buffy Summers is not bisexual and therefore acts completely out of character by going to bed with a female Slayer. One can argue that experimentation and exceptions can exist and that sexuality can be very fluid. In other words, someone that has been straight her entire life could in fact start becoming attracted to the same sex. Sexual fluidity can happen to anyone and at any time. It's not a choice. "Because even the most sexually fluid person can't wake up one morning and say, 'Eh, I think I'll dig guys now for the rest of my life,'" explains Jarune Uwujaren in "How Fluid Sexuality Fits into the LGBTQIA Spectrum." Uwujaren adds:

Think of being sexually fluid the way you would any other type of fluid. Fluid has no fixed shape, but it still has a fixed volume and consistency. So it may be with fluid sexuality—just because a person may prefer men right now doesn't mean that will hold true for the rest of their life or even the rest of the week.

Is Buffy experiencing some sort of flux in her sexual orientation or was this indeed a one night stand? In regards to the infamous night spent between Buffy and Satsu, Whedon believes that "it puts the reader in this 'Oh my God' moment, and it puts Buffy in an 'Oh my God, what did I just do?' moment" (Gustines). The readers are to assume that this tryst that Buffy has just had with Satsu, given the fact that Buffy has always been a straight woman, is a big deal and that this moment shouldn't be taken lightly. "Sexual fluidity is not about somehow choosing one's desires or identities, in the way that the antigay opposition has portrayed gayness," says Leila J. Rupp, a professor of feminist studies at the University of California, Santa Barbara. "Sexual desires and behaviors and identities may not always align and they may change over time, but they do not change lightly, in the same ways that religious identities are not something that change on a whim, although they do change" (Ring). Undoubtedly, this is a huge, groundbreaking moment in Buffy's life. Because Buffy has never experimented with a woman before, it should be assumed that she has considered this to be a very delicate and serious matter, one that she has either seriously thought about or, possibly, not at all. Instead, could this event be a one-time incident, an exception?

"So ... how do we handle tomorrow?" Satsu asks timidly, staring longingly at Buffy while they're in bed.

"What do you mean?" Buffy replies.

"I mean ... I know what this is. I know you didn't just ... turn gay all of the sudden...."

"Right."

Satsu asks again, "What do we do about tomorrow?"

"You mean the whole we slept together thing?" Buffy smiles, a wistful look on her face. "I don't know. I had a wonderful night. And ... it's been a while since I said that. So ... tomorrow, I'm gonna think about what we did. And I'm gonna blush. And then I'm gonna smile. But I'm not sure it goes any farther than that" (*Wolves at the Gate*, #12).

This prompts Satsu to immediately leave the bed, as if she understood the very clear message that Buffy thinks of this as a good time but nothing more than that. Buffy then attempts to stop Satsu from leaving and urges her to stay until the morning. Buffy is in no particular rush to get rid of

Satsu and yet says, "Do me a favor, though. Don't mention this to anyone.... It's not that I'm ashamed or anything. It's just ... you know, for now, it's better if we keep this between us." Why wasn't Buffy comfortable with telling her friends? Is she completely mortified? Or is it Drew Goddard telling us how out-of-character this all is? "We're not going to make her gay, nor are we going to take the next 50 issues explaining that she's not," explains Joss Whedon in defense of this controversial comic book issue. "She's young and experimenting, and did I mention open-minded?" (Gustines). This very statement is problematic at best; being young and open-minded does not necessarily lead to either experimenting or sleeping with a member of the same sex. Joss is almost implying that for someone with these traits, this sexual act is inevitable. "It's something that just made sense," says Whedon. "I was talking to Drew about it, and we were saying it'd be fun to play here with the idea of, 'Oh, here's this person who's really cool, and who digs me, and I'm lonely, and open-minded.' It's not that Buffy has changed her orientation" (Turnquist). Open-mindedness isn't everything—when one is straight and not attracted to the same sex, there is a very slim possibility that she will engage in homosexual activities and enjoy it so much. Further, as Malinda Lo, popular YA novelist and editor of the famous lesbian pop culture blog *After Ellen*, explains of the comic, "There *is* a loss here. The community of lesbians that was created because of identity politics will undoubtedly change if young women would rather be known as open-minded than as lesbians."

"She's alone, she's vulnerable. And she has the weight of the world on her slender shoulders. If that's not a recipe for an ill-conceived one night stand, I don't know my H.G.O.G.A cookbook," Willow explains to a sulking Satsu. This was a huge sigh of relief to the audience. It was a one-night stand. If this was the case, there would be no need to try and define Buffy's sexuality; it would never happen again. "She's not like us. She's the general. We're the army. And that's never gonna change. Also, she's not, you know...." Willow trails off.

"A dyke," Satsu points out (*Wolves at the Gate*, #13).

If Buffy didn't change her orientation, it certainly seems as if she did a few issues later. Buffy blushes, covers her mouth and thinks of Satsu, "I can't believe I find it sexy when she calls me ma'am" (*Wolves at the Gate*, #14). Certainly, that seems like typical thought behavior after being physically intimate with someone, but here Buffy is admitting that she finds Satsu "sexy." These are not typical thoughts for a straight woman.

As if all of this couldn't be more contradictory, in a later issue, Buffy and Satsu sit on a bed, dressed, and talk more about their relationship.

Satsu admits that she feels like she needs to not be around Buffy because the only way to get over her is to not be around her. They both agree that the best course of action is for Satsu to stay in Japan and help lead the Slayers are stationed there. Their conversation quickly swings back to their relationship.

"I just hope … I just hope I didn't hurt you," Buffy admits.

"Nah, I'm tough. And for what it's worth … it was one of the best nights of my life," Satsu smiles.

"Mine too" (*Wolves at the Gate*, #15).

Immediately, this rings false. The reader is brought back to Buffy's and Angel's first time and how both characters found perfect bliss, especially considering that Angel lost his soul because Buffy brought him "a moment of true happiness" ("Innocence," B2.14). The readers also revisit Spike holding and comforting Buffy on a bed and when Spike says it was the best night of his life, Buffy admits that she was "right there with him" ("End of Days," B7.21). Is Drew Goddard really insisting that a random night filled with passion, an "ill-conceived one night stand" with a female Slayer should rank up there with these two moments with the true loves of Buffy's life?

"What do we do now? Say goodbye? Go our separate ways and such?" Buffy inquires.

"Well, I suppose we could always save goodbye for tomorrow…." Satsu leans in suggestively and Buffy's eyes sparkle with desire.

Oh no. The reader turns the page and Buffy and Satsu are once again naked, in bed, kissing, with only the sheets to wrap around them. Because Buffy and Satsu have slept with each other more than once, the readers can now argue that Buffy is sexually attracted to Satsu and finds pleasure and comfort from sleeping with her. The first time they slept together is no longer a one-night stand or an "exceptional" night. Buffy has now slept with a woman twice—yet she still identifies as straight. This is not an accurate representation of a straight character.

Sexual experimentation, although having many variances, is believed by some to be a gateway into admitting or revealing one's own innate sexual orientation, one other than straight. Rupp, an author of the study "Queer Women in the Hookup Culture: Beyond the Closet?" found that "the college hookup culture, generally characterized as heterosexual, is, for some women, a setting "to explore and to later verify bisexual, lesbian, or queer sexual identities" (Ring). "I see bisexuality and fluidity as definitely linked," says Ellyn Ruthstrom, president of the Boston-based Bisexuality Resource Center. "Fluidity is easy for bisexuals to understand," she says, as "people are attracted to people, not just genders, and it can happen in different ways at different points in life" (Ring).

"I think that fluidity is simply a way to express the gray area that reality really is," says Denise Penn, a member of the board of directors for the American Institute of Bisexuality. "I think that fluidity is a way of talking about bisexuality" (Ring). Lo adds, "Buffy and Satsu may be a sign of things to come. Maybe in the near future, it really won't matter what your gender is when it comes to who you fall in love with," emphasizing her view that the relationship is one of love and also fluidity. What could have been a great example of a bisexual character, or even a character experiencing sexual fluidity, within pop culture turned into a conflicting, inaccurate portrayal of straight sexual orientation, considering that Buffy dismisses the incident with Satsu as a one-time incident and a "phase" (*Twilight*, #31).

On March 5, 2008, the all-important issue 12 was published. Across the internet, praise and criticism burst forth. Hundreds of fans posted their brutally honest thoughts all over message boards across the internet, ranging from positive and excited to disappointed and downright angry. Daniel Joslyn, an editor on *Popcults*, described the Buffy/Satsu incident as a "high point" of Season Eight, and argued that while "this [issue] could have been a disaster of a sales stunt ... instead was set up well and resolved well." In *After Ellen*, Sarah Warn excitedly proclaimed that because of it, this was the "Best. Lesbian. Week. Ever." "I'm so done," posted love4ba, "but hey, bonus, I know I won't be tuning in to *Dollhouse* now either. Thanks Joss" ("For the Discussion...." *Whedonesque*). WilliamtheB wrote "that Buffy may be (from some perspectives) disrespecting the gay community by jumping into bed with someone while, pretty much, straight" ("For the Discussion...." *Whedonesque*). Perhaps the most thought-provoking comment came from newcj, whom argued that this issue does nothing but reinforce the stereotype that

> lesbians are constantly portrayed as angry, vindictive bitches and ... [that] all strong females are portrayed as lesbians. I realize the comic does not say Buffy is now a lesbian, and I can see Joss making all kinds of points about labels, the fluidity of sexuality, yada yada yada. The thing is, all my life I have been dealing with the "all strong, competent women must be lesbians" cliché and, hey, here it is in BtVS. Willow is the strongest person there seems to be anywhere, Tara was the only one in the college group with any actual magical powers, Kennedy was the strongest potential, Satsu is the best of Buffy's group and now Buffy is going to bed with another woman and reacting with a "Wow." That does not make Buffy a lesbian or even bi-sexual, but from my end of the Kinsey scale, it does not make her straight either ["For the Discussion...." *Whedonesque*].

The criticism for the Buffy/Satsu arc seems infinite. It's one thing to inaccurately portray sexual orientation but it's another thing entirely to also write the lesbian character weakly with no significance to the plot aside from her orientation. Every scene with Satsu after she's revealed to be a lesbian emphasizes her orientation, as if that trait defines her entire character. "A by-product of the traditional heteroflexible narrative is that, because the straight character is always the primary character, the sexual minority character ends up reduced to a minor role or written out of the story altogether" (Frohard-Dourlent, "'Lez-faux' Representations").

This is especially highlighted in the conversation that Kennedy and Satsu have in the arc *Predators and Prey*. Despite the fact that Buffy has explained that she will not have a romantic relationship with Satsu, here she identifies herself and Buffy as having "true love" and adds that their tryst wasn't just a "skinny dip in that [lesbian] pool." Satsu reinforces that "it was a plunge. A big wet—." The fact that this conversation is still happening a few arcs after Buffy and Satsu slept together and that Satsu is clinging to the concept of their relationship is deeply upsetting and downright annoying. It's disappointing that Satsu, who could have been an interesting supporting character and new addition to the Scooby gang, is degraded into being nothing but a lesbian slayer who sleeps with Buffy.

In the first arc of *Twilight*, Buffy admits to Xander that she's in love with him. Xander argues and insists that she is only telling him this because Buffy saw Xander and Dawn kissing.

"Feelings develop. People change!" Buffy insists.

"Hey! That's a big deal. I'm a potential romantic interest! I'm on the list—right after being gay." Xander quips. "I rate almost as good as trying to change your sexual orientation. You went—through gay—to me."

"I was having a phase! I'm supposed to have that phase!" (*Twilight*, #31).

This scene would potentially come off as hilarious if it wasn't blatantly screaming with inaccuracies. Joss is essentially calling experimentation "a phase," a destructive way of describing sexual fluidity. This criticism, which many bisexual people must deal with on a daily basis, is simply painful. In trying to be progressive, Whedon set back the correct definitions of sexual orientations back a few decades.

Time of Your Life is also problematic, as Willow's and Kennedy's relationship is overtly sexualized. When they meet up again, they embrace and wrap their arms around each other suggestively, not romantically as they quip with come-hither eyes.

KENNEDY: Hey, Red
WILLOW: Didn't even think about you.

KENNEDY: Kinda forgot you.
WILLOW: And I would know you from…? [*Time of Your Life*, #16].

Despite boasting Joss Whedon's usual sharp dialogue and Karl Moline's always pleasing artwork, nothing could stop this next scene from feeling deprecating once again. Willow and Kennedy are researching and trying to figure out a way to retrieve Buffy from the future, but Willow soon reveals that the only way to solve the dilemma is to contact her advisor Saga Vasuki in a different dimension. Her path to this other dimension is, problematically, for Willow to have sex with Kennedy. Although the two women love each other, this is borderline objectifying and using Kennedy. Why? It's exceedingly clear that Willow is in love with Saga Vasuki. In the communication between them, Willow is completely naked. Vasuki is half naked, with her breasts exposed, albeit covered with her long white hair. Willow, tantalizingly, tells Vasuki, "You know how grateful I am for what we—what you taught me" (*Time of Your Life*, #18). At the end of their incredibly sexual exchange, Vasuki expresses disappointment that Willow's stay was so brief and she cups Willow's face with her hands, saying with heavy double meaning, "Do come again." Cut to Willow and Kennedy in bed, Willow bitterly putting her blouse back on and Kennedy naked and looking satisfied under the covers. Really? Could the authors not think of any other way for Willow to contact Vasuki? Whedon, clearly seeking media buzz, notes in an interview: "There is a scene—it has to do with a dream dimension and … mystical sexuality. And [Willow] happens to be naked in the scene, but you know, it's always tasteful." As he adds jokingly, "Damn it, it's always tasteful! I hate taste!" (Warn). In "Willow: Goddesses and Monsters," the cover of the issue—expertly drawn by Jo Chen—depicts a naked Vasuki and Willow embracing each other longingly. This all just seems like an attempt to get readers interested by objectifying the female body—with a cover too salacious to appear in the action-packed Buffy stories.

Despite all of this lesbianism in Season Eight, there is not a single panel that represents gay sexuality. In the comics, Andrew Wells grows to become one of the new Watchers. Where is his boyfriend? Shouldn't he, a gay male character, have relationships, much like Buffy and Willow have this season? Fans have long-believed his character is gay because of his undying devotion to Warren ("Two to Go," B6.21), his disinterest when he sees two women kissing ("Storyteller," B7.16) and his tear-filled devotion to Spike ("You're Like Gandalf the White, resurrected from the pit of the Balrog, more beautiful than ever") ("Damage," A5.11). And yet, neither in the show nor in Season Eight does Andrew Wells find a boyfriend or even come out. In a striking double standard, there is an overabundance of lesbianism and female nudity in Season Eight and yet absolutely no gay representation despite the obviously gay character. One could hope that when the season was all well and done, Joss and company could consider their impact and move forward. Thankfully, they did.

In Season Nine, Joss Whedon made the incredibly bold move to introduce a male Slayer named Billy Lane. Billy, a teenager, has come out and lives in Santa Rosita, California. After leaving his parents' house because of their rejection, he lives with his "hippy" grandmother. Constantly bullied for being gay, he trains to protect himself while dealing with his crush on "the coolest boy in school," Devon. What makes Billy an incredibly likable character from the start is that this is a realistic, honest and heartbreaking portrayal of a young gay man. Unfortunately, harassment, homelessness of gay teens, suicide because of shame of being gay and the need for self-defense, all topics explored in this issue, are very real problems that plague gay youth today. Not only does this paint an accurate picture of what some gay youth undergo, it's all swimming in metaphor by making Billy a Slayer. Some fans have always wished men could be Slayers. Now Billy proves that being a Slayer has nothing to do with gender or the bestowment of supernatural powers, but with the courage to battle for those he cares about—though Season Ten reveals that it was his own desperate wish to join the community and be a hero that made his choosing possible. No one implies he has feminine qualities—he's simply regarded as a male Slayer. Billy's and Devon's relationship is nothing short of adorable and by the end of Billy's second issue, they share a passionate kiss, albeit a bit briefly. No sexual objectification. No odd questioning of sexual orientations. It's a beautifully written story by Jane Espenson and Drew Greenberg, as the writers explore the perils of being gay in today's still-biased society, through delightful characters that belong in Buffy's world (*Guarded,* #14–15).

In Season Ten, they're arguably the only stable couple as other relationships on the team crumble. Devon gets the same endearingly fumbling quotes given to Buffy or Xander in the early seasons as he haltingly defines his Watcher duties as "I like to watch. Uh, I like to watch Billy. Slay" (*New Rules,* 10.1). Similarly, in a bold move, Andrew Wells finally realizes his sexuality in a touching moment written by the brilliant Christos Gage.

> **JULIE**: When you close your eyes and picture yourself kissing someone, who is it? What are they like?
> **ANDREW**: Clive. I picture myself kissing someone like Clive. I think … Julie, I think I'm gay ["Love Dares You," #11].

Season Eight had its unusual hiccups with Buffy's tryst with a female Slayer, Willow's overly sexualized relationships with Kennedy and Vasuki, and Andrew Wells' lack of a boyfriend but recovered strongly with the inspired character of Billy Lane and the long-awaited coming out of Andrew Wells. Accurate gay and lesbian representation does still need to move forward, not fall backwards, in the Buffy comics. There remains a lot of work to be done, but readers still have faith in Joss Whedon. After all, we must never forget the immortal words that a very smart man wrote once: "Let's go to work" ("Not Fade Away," A5.22).

Separate Worlds or One?
Canonicity, Medium and Authorship

David Kociemba and
Mary Ellen Iatropoulos

• • •

 How can the comics of the Whedonverses help fans and scholars understand and explore the relationship between medium, auteur, canon, and fandom? Although clearly successful in connecting with audiences hungry for more stories set in these universes, Whedonverse comics like *Buffy: Seasons Eight* and *Nine* and *Serenity: The Shepherd's Tale* illustrate how the marketing of auteurism obscures as much as clarifies complexities in authorship in different industries, the resulting differences in collaborative production, the different reading style demanded of audiences across different media, and the relative importance of dynamics between intention vs. reception and narrative continuity vs. formal dissimilarity. These issues have broader cultural and economic importance, with contemporary examples including Disney's proposed erasure of a great deal of the *Star Wars* Expanded Universe and J.J. Abrams' radical alterations of one of the most intricate and best-policed canons in media fandom, *Star Trek*. Meanwhile, the comics fandom's approval of the relative authenticity of Marvel's Cinematic Universe serves as an important form of grassroots marketing. Canonical authenticity is central to global media conglomerates, certainly, but in the context of the Whedonverses, in which fan input is highly valued, the creative process is highly collaborative, and stories are told, expanded, and enriched across media platforms, the question becomes more complicated. When both fans and creators are "creating" meaning out of these transmedia texts, what counts as canon—as the "real" character or story? By what criteria and to what critical end is such a judgment made, and to whom do we grant the right to make such judgments? If Joss Whedon declares the Whedonverse comics to be a part of the broader Buffyverse canon (and he has, in interviews and through their titles), are readers and scholars obliged to read these texts his way?

During the early issues of the *Buffy: Season Nine* comic books, a controversy unfolded in three parts that illustrates the ways in which the comics of the Whedonverse—highly collaborative, transmedia texts that encourage dialogue and exchange between audience, author, and artist—serve as a site through which the relationships between medium, auteur, canon, and fandom are constantly (re)negotiated. The scandalous storyline begins in "Slayer, Interrupted," the fifth issue of the season, when a bewildered and bereft Buffy—abandoned by Willow, whose sudden, mysterious departure has left Buffy alone with her guilt at destroying The Seed—returns to her apartment with a store-bought brown paper bag, ignores her roommates' concerned comments, and shuts herself up in the bathroom. As the successive panels frame Buffy in closer and closer angles, her thoughts appear as text over the imagery: "They're already scared of me. Because I'm a Slayer. But that's okay.... Because I'm scared too" ("Slayer, Interrupted," #5). The final panel features an extreme close up of a pregnancy test, revealing that it's positive; Buffy seems pregnant.

At this point, Buffy believes she got pregnant while black-out drunk at a party, and the reveal immediately prompted impassioned responses from fans on message boards making sense of the development. On Whedonesque, for example, some expressed excitement for a Buffy baby (one user, Slayin Days, comments, "I am beyond excited for this storyline!"), some happily speculated over the baby's gender, and still others debated, along typical shipper lines, who they'd most want the father to turn out to be, Angel or Spike ("Discuss *Buffy* Season 9 #5"). These enthusiastic utterances were echoed within the pages of the comic series itself, as the corresponding "Slay the Critics" letters-to-the-editor section featured several different fans expressing joy and gladness that Buffy would be having a baby. "Buffy is pregnant! That is great news!" writes one reader, while another phrases it more enthusiastically: "Aahhh! OMG, Buffy is pregnant!" ("Slay the Critics," B9.08). Other fans, however, viewed Buffy's potential conception during inebriation as offensively out of character. One Whedonesque user thinks, "Buffy being pregnant without fully making that choice for herself to become a parent is, IMO, the final degradation for the character" ("Discuss *Buffy* Season 9 #5"). User aphasia put it in more emotionally raw terms: "Loved the issue, hate the pregnancy. Ugh. I actually hate this so much that I feel kind of depressed about it" (Ibid.).

Whether they loved it or hated it, fans of the *Buffy* comic books understood the comic book as continuations of the same character and story they'd followed for years in televisual form.

While fan reactions to Buffy's pregnancy were complicated at best, they became outright polarized by the following issue, "Nikki the Vampire Slayer" (#6). The final pages show Buffy, emotionally exhausted from wrestling with the incompatibility between Slayerdom and motherhood, sitting with Spike by her apartment complex's pool, forlorn and despondent as she arrives at her decision: "I'm going to have an abortion." To say that this decision divided Whedon's comic-reading audience would be putting it mildly. Some fans supported Buffy's decision, seeing it as both a natural progression for the character as well as a valuable commentary on women's reproductive rights. "Buffy is going to terminate her pregnancy! Wow! That requires some courage, not only from Buffy … but also from you at Dark Horse" writes one fan, while another applauds the comics' creators for "tackling the sensitive and controversial subject with unflinching honesty and realism" (Slay the Critics, "Apart of Me Part 2" B9 #9). Still, others vocalized a starkly contrasting view, condemning both Buffy the character and the comic itself for featuring such a storyline. "I was very disappointed and disturbed," writes one fan, "by deciding on an abortion, Buffy puts the lie to her claim that she's a Slayer, not a killer" (Slay the Critics, "Apart of Me Part 2" B9 #9). Again, regardless of the opinion, such comments demonstrate that fans understood the characters of Season Nine as extensions of the characters from the *Buffy* television show.

As with the pregnancy's reveal, Buffy's abortion decision caused fans to reconsider the degree to which the comics present a faithful continuation of the television show's story and characters. For instance, the Whedonesque open thread on "Nikki the Vampire Slayer" (#6) features many comments voicing concern that the comics just aren't the same as the show. User Emmie, for one, writes, "I don't agree that this feels the most like the show … this story in the comics is very straightforward and tonally flat in comparison," and user Fred_Sonja surmises that "it just doesn't feel like Buffy. It doesn't even feel like the Buffy characters in a non–Buffy situation. Just not Buffy at all" ("Discuss Buffy Season 9 #6"). Upset with the translation from TV show to comic form, such fans used this moment to voice their disapproval, and some even sought for where to place the blame for what they perceived as a betrayal of Buffy's character. In the words of user Enisy, "I'm kinda disappointed. And I miss Joss" ("Discuss Buffy Season 9 #6"). Such comments demonstrate auteurist thinking permeating Whedon fandom, namely, the notion that if the key to the comics "feeling like Buffy" lies in Joss Whedon's direct involvement, the blame for their failure to do so lies in his absence.

Yet the controversial storyline proved to be short-lived, as in the very next issue, when a ravenous zompire tears off Buffy's arm, the wound erupts into a tumble of mechanical circuits and glowing green goo, revealing the pregnancy test to have been a false positive as she realizes aloud to Spike: "this means I'm not pregnant ... I'm a f$$@ing robot!" ("On Your Own Part Two," #7). The revelation that Buffy was never really pregnant brought further speculation as to what purpose, exactly, such a contentious red herring served in terms of the overall storyline. Once again, fans took to message boards such as Whedonesque to express bewilderment and to parse out the question of whether the comics really "count" as part of the same canon, or overall storyline, as the television show. User Moscow Watcher, for example, questioned the reasoning behind featuring the abortion scare at all: "What for? Only to present Joss with a chance to make a political statement? I will hope that it's a mislead to distract us from the real story. I don't believe Joss would defy all narrative logic for the message's sake" ("Some *Buffy* Season 9 Info from Dark Horse's Scott Allie"). Another commenter, Five Horizons, chimed in on the same page to say that the "storyline has taken such a turn for the pointless and ridiculous that I had completely refused to believe that Joss would allow it to go that way."

The *Buffy* abortion plot was not the first time controversial content had fans questioning whether the characters portrayed in the *Buffy* comics remained faithful to the TV show characters. As Helene Frohard-Dourlent notes in her study of fan responses to the Season Eight tryst between Buffy and fellow Slayer Satsu, "readers' incapacity (or unwillingness) to engage with the comics' complex take on heteroflexibility points to the limits of a liberal version of sexuality" ("Buffy/Satsu" 9). By looking at examples of fan responses to Whedon comics, Frohard-Dourlent draws larger conclusions about what such responses demonstrate in terms of larger trends in fan readership and interpretation. Along these lines, this chapter endeavors to use Whedonverse comics—and fan responses to them—to understand what's really happening when vocal and engaged fans of a cult television show follow their beloved auteur across media to continue the story in another format. What insights into the relationship between medium, fandom, canon, and auteur can be gleaned from examining the creation and reception of the content of Whedonverse comics? How integrated are the transmedia narratives of the Buffyverse and the *Firefly/Serenity* 'Verse?

Understanding Canon

The term "canon" identifies a privileged primary text, a center, while other texts are shunted to the periphery or excluded altogether. These practices define what belongs in the canonical fictional world as opposed to the maximal fictional world of all texts minimally related to the canonical one. Canon features a strong bias towards normativity, authority, and classical definitions of beauty based on harmony, coherence, and singularity in its construction of closed texts. With mass media texts, canon privileges the already privileged.

In his 2013 essay, Roy T. Cook provides a useful overview of canonicity practices in massive serialized collaborative fictions like the Whedonverses, identifying five relevant factors for how canon functions with these kinds of texts: interpretational relevance, medium, politics and commerce, ret-conning, and their participatory qualities (272–3). Even if a reader decides that the Whedonverse comics are semi-canonical or not part of the canons of the Buffyverse or Serenityverse, these texts may prove useful in understanding the core texts by negation or speculation; while a *Buffy* fan may not consider the comics canon, s/he may certainly reflect on their previous interpretations of the character in light of the debate. Canon distinctions are also sensitive to medium, audience size, and order, as is the case, for example, with the *Star Wars* films being privileged over novels, comics, and animated series. Jedi Knight Aayla Secura and Harley Quinn first appeared in the separate canons from the Star Wars and DC universes only to be incorporated later into the primary canons (Cook, "Canonicity and Normativity" 273). In *Angel: After the Fall*, Betta George's line "I've hung out with vampires" tries to compensate for this by mentioning his prior appearance in non-canonical comics *Spike: Asylum* and *Spike: Shadow Puppets*. Canons also shift in relation to popular politics, as for example racially insensitive works featuring Captain America, Bugs Bunny, and Superman, amongst many others, have quietly been relegated to non-canonical status. Finally, canon debates foster community within participatory and interpretative fandoms and between fandoms and industrial cultural producers. Cook writes, "In short: canonicity practices involve complex negotiations between producers and consumers aimed at identifying (but rarely *actually* settling on) something like an *ideal canon*, where an ideal canon is maximally coherent (where coherence involves far more than mere logical consistency) and maximally aesthetically, artistically, or socially valuable" ("Canonicity and Normativity" 273). Canonicity encourages textual coherence and streamlining, keeps characters

Buffy talks to Giant Dawn, using the comics medium to indicate movement. Joss Whedon (writer), and Georges Jeanty (penciller). *The Long Way Home*, Season 8, Vol. 1. Milwaukie, OR: Dark Horse, 2007.

current with social mores, and fosters brand loyalty, all without the producers of the fictions being forced to pass judgment on the legitimacy of their own or freelancers' contributions (274–5).

However, it also means that authors are not the sole source of canonical legitimacy: fans play a role. Personal canons and critical canons have long been a part of literary canon formation, for while "a canon is nominally made up of texts, it is actually made up not of texts in themselves, but of texts as read" (Harris 117). Who has the right to be the authority deciding the boundaries of texts is hotly debated among artists, corporations, scholars, and audiences. Scholars and audiences should not cede veto power over their intellectual labor to corporations and their authors just because the perception of a text's authenticity can be worth billions of dollars to a franchise (Daniels). It may be the license-holder's copyright, but the text and its readings are part of the cultural commons belonging to us all.

Comics vs. Television: Narrative Continuity vs. Formal Dissimilarity

To begin unpacking the factors justifying canonicity decisions, it's important to consider the ways in which comics are not television. The two present distinct, although certainly related, art forms: pictorial, narrative, sequential, the influence filmmaking and comics techniques have had on each other, etc. As Roy T. Cook explains, the debate over whether comics represent more rudimentary forms of films—what he calls The Filmstrip Argument—has been ongoing and hotly contested ("Why Comics Are Not Films" 184). However, comics are not static films on paper, however much they may resemble filmstrips and film's pre-production storyboards. Different media communicate meaning differently and are received differently by audiences.

Other Whedon studies scholars have concurred, even with tightly related media like television and film. Stacey Abbott, for example, investigates the effect of the medium shift in *Serenity* on the pre-established aesthetics of *Firefly* in "It (Re-)Started with a Girl." If the medium shift to comics is sufficiently central to the work's strategies and reception, then it could be considered part of a separate canon partially on those grounds. McCloud believes that comics narratives require notable reader participation in constructing the experience, through implication in the comics narratives and a much more fluid experience of time than the linear experiences of film and television narratives.

McCloud is one of many comics theorists who discuss the techniques of the comics medium. Like other texts, comics become complete only in the mind of the reader, but panels and gutters provide the cues to fill in senses other than sight and suggest time lapses and movement. Movement in a static medium is also represented through motion lines, zip ribbons, onomatopoeia, streaking and blurring effects, subjective action, and continuous backgrounds (McCloud 108–116). Lines, shapes, color, backgrounds, symbols, lettering, and narration make emotions visible and legible (McCloud 118–137). Because the reader plays such an active part in constructing the narrative and world, implication plays a more prominent role in this medium (McCloud 68–69). *The Long Way Home*, the first book of *Buffy the Vampire Slayer Season Eight*, showcases these techniques. The first image of Giant Dawn uses word balloons to guide the eye and shows time lapse within a single image. It presents Dawn as a constant background to show Buffy's movement (and thus visually narrates this scene from Buffy's perspective), with a thicker panel line in the center to create a pause and a splash page to allow viewers to take in the entire scene before offering dialogue to refocus readers on its linear development.

Space translates into time in this still image medium, with time lapsing even within a single panel, as the sound, words, word balloons, back and forth dialogue, reactions, and panel size and orientation all create the sense of time lapse. Gutter size and panel borders do the same (McCloud 94–103). Likewise, time is relative to the reader rather than embedded in the text. Whatever panel the reader views is the present; wherever in the panel the eyes rest is "now," and thus the reader, not the director or actor, determines the pacing of a scene, which in turn can influence how the text's tone is received (McCloud 104). Along these lines, the shift in medium becomes a give and take; the comics can't feature the chemistry between actors onscreen notable in Whedon's works, but the reader is free to superimpose intonations onto characters' dialogue.

There are several narrative advantages to the comics medium that Whedon and Jeanty make use of in *The Long Way Home*. Whedon has spoken about how the comics freed him from television's typical budget restrictions and CGI limitations (Vineyard). Buffy parachuting out of a helicopter on the opening splash page emphasizes how important that medium shift was for this narrative, and follows it up later in the arc with dream sequences, flying car chases, and Godzilla-sized monsters in multiple mass combats. The shift to the comics medium freed the story from the more restrictive sexuality representation regime of network television, beginning with Buffy's imagined threesome with Spike and Angel in *The*

Long Way Home and ending the season arc with Buffy and Angel's multiple-page, fully visible oral and penetrative sex scene. *The Long Way Home* also makes use of two reveals magnified by turning the page: Amy's failed attempted murder of the sleeping Buffy and Willow's sudden appearance to magically duel Amy. The last panel of "The Chain" at the end of *The Long Way Home* uses white space to represent death in a way much more effective on the printed page than on screen. The experience of these comics intentionally highlights the medium shift rather than presenting *The Long Way Home* as just another episode of *Buffy the Vampire Slayer*.

The white space quietly designates death for Buffy's stand-in. Joss Whedon (writer), and Paul Lee (penciller). "The Chain" *The Long Way Home,* **Season 8, Vol. 1. Milwaukie, OR: Dark Horse, 2007.**

In a sly nod to the world of comic book aesthetics, one Season Eight issue even features a dream sequence in which the comics' art shifts to a more stereotypical, cartoonish "comic book" visual aesthetic as part of the issue's metacommentary on the series' progression across media ("After These Messages ... We'll Be Right Back!" #20).

Despite the efforts towards narrative continuity in the Whedonverse comics, there are specific formal distinctions between television and comics that open up space for difference and deviation between stories told across media. The depiction of characters through visual art rather than through physical actors impacts readers' interaction with and interpretation of the text. Lauren Schumacher, for example, presents a fascinating overview of how radically Buffy's image changes by artist. Schumacher asks readers to question whether the Comic Book Buffys and Television Buffy(s) are the same person. If so, how can one reconcile the fact that they are so often visually dissimilar? Earlier noncanonical comics present a buffer Buffy, she observes, as the artist showcases Buffy's strength visually in ways Gellar's body doesn't allow. While the parameters of Gellar's physicality removed from the artistic equation (literally), all representations of Buffy's character have remained notably bustier than Gellar, calling attention to her bosom through the use of black lines, prominent position, and tight clothing. To see to what degree illustrators are auteurs in the Whedonverse comics, she looks closely at several artists' renditions of the Buffy character, noting how both Cliff Richards (*Viva Las Buffy, Slayer Interrupted, Anywhere But Here*) and Georges Jeanty (*Time of Your Life, No Future for You, Wolves at the Gate*) are influenced by Sarah Michelle Gellar. Richards showcases Gellar's large eyes with deeply curved lower lids and her multiple piercings, and Jeanty similarly struggles with how much the actor should influence the character in the comics: "I really sweat over [actor likenesses], but Joss Whedon told me something that really set me on the right path.... He said I don't want you to draw Sarah Michelle Gellar, I want you to draw Buffy. Which just clicked with me. I still struggle, but not as much" (Hellmouth Central). Jeanty's words imply that Buffy's character transcends the specific actors or artistic tools used to visually depict her in different media. Each artist strips down the image of Buffy to what they find iconic, Schumacher feels, to balance the qualities of their personal style, the specifics needed for depiction, and the stylized abstraction needed for identification and projection. Eliminating particulars makes images more universal icons, and it sparks more audience involvement, encouraging them to imagine and perceive the action. So abstraction leads to more identification and projection, while detailed environments build the complexity of the world and lend a sense of visual weight, otherness, and particularity (McCloud 24–45). Along these lines, the Buffy of the comic book is fluid and open to artistic interpretation, which again places different responsibilities on the reader from other media platforms, allowing readers to hold the many Buffys in creative tension in their minds rather than measure each rendering on television and in comics against an Ideal Buffy. Such individualized multiplicity of interpretation speaks to evidence that the complex collaborations of comics production processes result in audiences treating these texts as separate but related canons, rather than a single unified Buffyverse across comics and television.

So what does it matter if the comics and the TV show belong to separate canons? Well, for one thing, the question of how the separate canons interact with and influence each other comes into play. According to one school of thought, the comics may be transmedia like the official video games or tie-in novels that often accompany franchises. At the same time, Whedon has called Seasons Eight through Ten canon, along with the adaptation of his own script into *Buffy: The Origin*. However, he and his office barely supervised earlier *Buffy* tie-in comics and novels, leaving them officially "noncanon," even those written by Espenson, Petrie, and other *Buffy* staff writers. His own *Angel: Long Night's Journey*, problematically, appears among these.

These two sets of comics might be any of the following: a canonical part of the story, conditionally canonical depending on creator approval and yielding to future developments of the primary text, a separate but related canon, or not canon at all, like fan texts and parody. In *Complex TV*, television studies and paratexts scholar Jason Mittell argues that the canonical status of paratexts like tie-in novels, video games, and comics should be determined on a case-by-case basis. One criterion is the nature of the work. Treating transmedia stories like a new episode of a television series "makes sense for highly episodic shows, as the established characters and setting can easily host a new set of narrative events without much need for policing canonical boundaries" (Mittell). Staying true to the tone and characters is the appeal, with the plot being fairly irrelevant to the tie-in novels of shows like *Murder, She Wrote* or *CSI*. But for the expanded universes and complex narratives of cult television, continuity rises in importance. Fans "often have a love/hate relationship with the books, as they try to police boundaries of canon, seek tonal consistencies, and otherwise explore the borders of their favored fictional storyworlds" (Mittell). As we can see from the multiplicity of fan responses and how engaged they are with the question of the "real" Buffy and Joss Whedon's involvement, the *Buffy* comics present a vivid example of Mittel's theories playing out.

Henry Jenkins sheds valuable light on canon integration in the age of transmedia, describing the transmedia storytelling of this world as a common ground between communities, encouraging active interpretation and speculation of its audiences, and as a cult artifact whose completely furnished world provides resources for consumers to construct their own fantasies and participatory cultures. Coherence and single authorship are no longer central values; indeed, as Jenkins notes, the stylistic and formal differences between, for example, the *Matrix* film franchise and *The Animatrix* encourage heterogeneity (*Convergence Culture*, 93–113). He writes on his blog later about his current understanding of transmedia:

> Most discussions of transmedia place a high emphasis on continuity—assuming that transmedia requires a high level of coordination and creative control and that all of the pieces have to cohere into a consistent narrative or world.... They make the author or some designated agent an arbiter of what counts within the canon. On the other hand, there are forms of commercially produced transmedia which really celebrate the multiplicity which emerges from seeing the same characters and stories told in radically different ways. This focus on multiplicity leaves open a space for us to see fan-produced media as part of a larger transmedia process, even if we then want to try to sort through how different elements get marked as official canon or fan alternatives ["Transmedia 202: Further Reflections"].

Jenkins' "equal but different" model better fits the pleasures of the transmedia storytelling of the Whedonverse comics than a single, unifying official canon that elides the differences of various media in favor of privileging plot continuity.

We can see these issues playing out in *Serenity: The Shepherd's Tale*, the one-shot comic released in 2010, which, according to writer Zack Whedon in his introduction, endeavored to "take a beloved character from a beloved show, and ... tell his ultramysterious backstory." In order to make the story feel cohesive between TV show, film, and comic book, several formal elements make those overarching connections abundantly clear for readers, as does the plot. The comic begins, for example, at the Haven Mining Colony during the timeline of the film *Serenity*, depicting the moments just after Captain Mal and crew depart and just before the Alliance's utter decimation of the peaceful encampment. The comic enters the same setting and scene as the film, using similar imagery, but fills in the gaps left blank in the film and gives voice to Book's thinking process as he sacrifices himself to destroy their attacker. A series of flashbacks also provide this explicit narrative connectivity, as in the moments before he dies (a scene shown in the film), Book flashes back to the decisions that resulted in him meeting Kaylee and bartering passage aboard Serenity (a scene directly uprooted from the show's pilot). These elements all suggest narrative continuity is the intention and the goal in *The Shepherd's Tale*.

However, the degree to which these elements successfully tie together the disparate media platforms of TV, film, and comics into a continuous narrative remains wide open for debate. For example, one reviewer on Amazon points out that Book's disgraced dismissal from the Alliance officer ranks in *The Shepherd's Tale* doesn't gel with the immediate esteem and respect his Alliance Ident card earns him in "Safe" (F1.06). The Amazon reviews are one space for fan interpretation of discrepancies in characterization across media: some fans thought the comic fit perfectly, while others found it out of character and, to some, a discriminatory reiteration of racist stereotypes (as the Black character grows up in a poor and abusive household before turning to crime). Despite the canonical authenticity implied by the involvement of Joss Whedon in sketching out the story and the story's placement into the show's/film's specific timeline and imagery, consensus fails regarding how the Book revealed in *The Shepherd's Tale* reflects on or changes fans' interpretation of the character. This is, in layman's terms, a battle over the boundaries of the canon.

Participatory audiences, though they can destabilize canonical rigidity and auteur status in favor of playfully productive cultural work, in some ways still depend upon the textual organizing principle called an auteur, in order for them to be a community. This is where it all comes together: what it means to be part of an auteur-approved canon and whether that approval matters in terms of how fans receive and interpret new texts involving familiar characters while reading stories in the medium of comics.

Multiple Authors

Whedon Studies scholars need not regard Whedon as the sole auteur with the creative rights to declare the boundaries of the legitimate text. (Whedon does not have the legal right to do so, as he is not the copyright and trademark owner for *Buffy the Vampire Slayer*, *Angel*, or *Firefly/Serenity*—Fox is.) Scholars must acknowledge the many creators involved in each work. Despite its name, the field of Whedon Studies is actually fairly amenable to problematizing the auteurism theory of artistic creation. Many scholarly works showcase the complexity of how the television series, films, web series, and comics attributed to Whedon are created. In *Why Buffy Matters*, Rhonda Wilcox argues that some cases merit using a different model of authorship:

> For years now, when I have thought of the art of a television series, I have thought of the master builder of a cathedral and his workers: a cathedral is a creation which is certainly accepted as art, but which was worked on by many differing people over many years ... *Buffy* itself ... has taught me to envision the interaction in a much livelier and less one-way, top-down fashion [5–6].

She describes a School of Whedon, evoking the importance of writers like Marti Noxon and Jane Espenson, Directors of Photography Michael Gershman and Raymond Stella, production designer Carey Meyer, Emmy-winning makeup artists Todd McIntosh and John Vulich, composer Christophe Beck, costume designer Cynthia Bergstrom, and, of course, the actors. Stacey Abbott's excellent production history in *Angel* finds a similar "collective vision of Mutant Enemy." Many other scholars have traced the impact of other creators at Mutant Enemy.[1] Wilcox argues that "it is not just the talent of each individual that matters here, but the synergy invoked by the central figure—Joss Whedon. And one can imagine it growing—the more good people were working well, the more good people would want to join in" (7). Auteurism masks the feedback loops of collaborative creation. Nonetheless, *Buffy Season Eight* through *Ten* obviously bring a new staff of artists and use none of the show's production contributors. While original staff writers Jane Espenson, Andrew Chambliss, and Drew Goddard have written some of the comics, many new writers have joined as well, from the ranks of comics rather than television.

Thus, when the comics subtract virtually all of the original collaborators, scholars must consider whether the transmedia storytelling within them represents a separate but related body of work rather than the original author's continuation. Truly, would audiences just accept a wholesale recasting of *Firefly*, a third season of *Dollhouse* as an animated cartoon series, or *Dr. Horrible 2* as a silent film? After all, fan reaction to Warner Brothers' proposed film reboot of *Buffy the Vampire Slayer* starring Vanessa Hudgens of *High School Musical* fame was quite hostile. Still, these kinds of wholesale revisions (recasting, use of drawn figures, lack of sound, removal of key creators) are exactly what the comics do with the *Firefly/Serenity*, *Angel*, and *Buffy* texts. If comics readers do accept these works as part of a continuous canon with the television/film works, it may be because of the cultural power of Whedon, but it may also be due to the lack of other options. Indeed, one way to interpret the status of the comics is to regard them as fanfiction equivalents that extend narratives or fill in gaps, albeit with different production values and without the imprimatur of Whedon.

The Whedon Studies field does not give the same level of attention to the transmedia comics of the Whedonverses as it does to the primary screen texts. In the eight years since *Buffy: Season Eight* debuted, there's been very little scholarship on the Whedonverse comics.[2] Even more telling, scholars almost never include the comics in their writing on the narrative techniques or cultural implications of various representations. Stacey Abbott and Ensley Guffey are two exceptions.[3] Scholarly practices before this volume show a near-unanimity in treating the transmedia storytelling of the Whedonverses in the comics, video games, and other works as belonging to totally separate canons from their small screen counterparts.

Finally, there may be some question as to whether Joss Whedon counts as the auteur of the Whedonverse comics from a comics studies perspective, even though he serves as a creator, producer, and writer. Narrative alone is not enough to make comics; they require images, juxtaposition, sequence, and intention to create particular meanings and experiences (Uidhir 63). In her "Comics and Collective Authorship," Christy Mag Uidhir notes that comics audiences follow line artists (like Rags Morales and Lee Bermejo), inkers (Joe Sinnott, George Roussos), and colorists like Laura Martin and Lynn Varley (47). She argues that "technological innovations in certain production processes have created an environment in which the contributions of colorists, inkers, and even letterers can become just as significant as those of writers and line artists (e.g., Dave Stewart's coloring in *The Umbrella Academy*, John Severin's inking run on *Sgt. Fury and His Howling Commandos*, and Todd Klein's work as letterer in *Sandman*)" (48). One feels the presence of these comics visual artists more palpably than in other media. Their style signs each image, word, and panel.

Padmini Ray Murray notes that the case for a comics auteur works best for creators who write, illustrate, and ink their own work, even though it can be shaped by editorial and other influences (341). Alan Moore is the best model for a comics auteur who does not illustrate his own work. Moore does panel-by-panel breakdowns of contents and composition, as well as their layout on the page. There's no indication that Joss Whedon inks, letters, or illustrates his comics; nor has there been more than the barest suggestion that Whedon panels his work in writing the scripts. Given how few comics Whedon pens, a collaborative authorship model may be the better way to understand Whedonverse comics, with Whedon as an auteur by management and responsibility overall, an author-function created by the text in a Foucaldian sense when fans perceive the comics as Whedonesque, and an auteur by origination when he pens a comic (Mittell). Meanwhile, these comics artists serve as auteurs by origination through their creation of the visuals, rather than of the narratives.

The Whedonverse comics' plot and character continuity and Whedon's intention allow readers and scholars to regard them as canonical, yet these features also allow them to regard it as a strongly related but separate canon to the screen Whedonverses. If plot and character coherence are not the only standards that define Whedonverse canon, but also tone, aesthetics, modes of interaction, and usefulness for participatory cultures, then the radically different modes of interaction and aesthetics of *Buffy* on screen and on the page must be acknowledged. Much is different: production strategies, patterns of representation, theories of auteurism, reception, aesthetic techniques, storytelling tools, and the audience size for the comics as opposed to the series. Even if scholars and audiences decide to treat these texts as part of a single canon, that decision should be made in cultural conversations among audiences and scholars, not by the fiat of one entity, even if it is the author. Authors, audiences, and critics all contribute intellectual labor to canonicity debates, so all have the right to define the borders of important texts.[4]

Notes

1. Laura Kessenich, "'Wait Till You Have an Evil Twin': Jane Espenson's Contributions to Buffy the Vampire Slayer," *Watcher Junior: The Undergraduate Journal of Whedon Studies* 3.1 (September 2007); David Kociemba, "Understanding the Espensode," *Buffy Goes Dark: Essays on the Final Two Seasons of* Buffy the Vampire Slayer *on Television*, eds. Lynne Y. Edwards, Elizabeth L. Rambo and James B. South (Jefferson, NC: McFarland, 2009), 23–39; Kendra Preston Leonard, ed., *Buffy, Ballads, and Bad Guys Who Sing: Music in the Worlds of Joss Whedon* (Lanham, MD: Scarecrow Press, 2011); Cori Mathis, "Bringing the Pain: An Examination of Marti Noxon's Contributions to *Buffy the Vampire Slayer*," *Joss in June: Selected Essays*, eds. K. Dale Koontz and Ensley Guffey, Special Issue of *Slayage: The Journal of the Whedon Studies Association* 11.2/12.1 (Summer 2014); Gwyn Symonds, "'A Little More Soul than Is Written': James Marsters' Performance of Spike and the Ambiguity of Evil in Sunnydale," *Slayage: The Journal of the Whedon Studies Association* 4.4 (March 2005).

2. A few examples include Kevin Chiat, "Giant Dawn and Mutant Superheroes: Joss Whedon in Comics," Money 341–352; Hélène Frohard-Dourlent, "'Lez-faux' Representations: How *Buffy* Season Eight Navigates the Politics of Female Heteroflexibility," Waggoner 31–47; Roz Kaveney, *Superheroes! Capes and Crusaders in Comics and Films* (London: I. B. Tauris, 2008), 201–225; Elizabeth L. Rambo, "Banter, Battles, Betrayal, and 'Kissy th' face!': *Sugarshock!*'s Playful Whedonverse,"

Joss in June: Selected Essays, eds. K. Dale Koontz and Ensley Guffey, Special Issue of *Slayage: The Journal of the Whedon Studies Association* 11.2/12.1 (Summer 2014); Lauren Schumacher, "The Many Faces of Buffy: An Analysis of the Disharmonious Visual Representations of Buffy Summers in Primary and Secondary Texts." *Watcher Junior: The Undergraduate Journal of Whedon Studies* 4.2 (June 2010); Patrick Shand, "Much with the Moral Ambiguity: An Examination of the Fallen Heroes and Redeemed Villains in *Buffy the Vampire Slayer Season Eight* and *Angel: After the Fall*," Money 361–367.

3. Stacey Abbott, "It (Re-)Started with a Girl: The Creative Interplay Between TV and Comics in *Angel: After the Fall*," *The Literary* Angel*: Essays on Influences and Traditions Reflected in the Joss Whedon Series*, eds. AmiJo Comeford and Tamy L. Burnett (Jefferson, NC: McFarland, 2010). 221–232; Ensley Guffey, "'We Just Declared War': Buffy as General," *Watcher Junior: The Undergraduate Journal of Whedon Studies* 5.1 (July 2011).

4. Thanks for assistance on this essay go to the contributions of Ian Dawe, Hélène Frohard-Dourlent, Ensley Guffey, and Mary Ellen Iatropoulos, personal conversation, 18 July–28 July 2014.

Part Two
Angel and *Spike* Comics

• • •

Dark Horse published *Angel* comics from 2000 until 2002, and then IDW took over in 2005. (Whedon himself wrote a multi-part *Angel* comic for them called *Long Night's Journey*). IDW also produced a *Spike* series including *Spike vs. Dracula*, *Spike: Asylum* and *Spike: Shadow Puppets,* all reprinted in the *Spike* compendium.

IDW's 17-issue *Angel: After the Fall*, written by Brian Lynch and plotted by both Lynch and Joss Whedon with the story arc once planned for *Angel*'s Season Six as a comic book continuation, came out between 2007 and 2009. Los Angeles is literally plunged into hell, and Angel's friends, separated and lost in a new world, must discover how to save it. This series and *Buffy Season Eight* were confusingly separate, with Angel and Spike's appearances in the latter throwing continuity into confusion. A Spike comic by Lynch attempted to bridge some of the continuity. Thomas Johnson examines the closure of Wesley's new ending versus the original show's ending in his "Live in the Lie for a While" while Bryant Dillon explores Spike's growth (or reasons for its lack) through a myriad of Spike comics by different authors.

In 2011, Dark Horse reclaimed the rights to *Angel* and published the series *Angel and Faith* as a companion to *Buffy: Season Nine,* complete with crossover characters and plots, much like the early entwined stories of *Buffy* Season Four/*Angel* Season One. Angel quests to fix his terrible act in the Season Eight comics, a worried but loyal Faith at his side, as they battle through a transformed world without magic. *Spike: A Dark Place* and *Willow: Wonderland* in turn break off from this series as the characters embark on individual journeys. A second *Angel and Faith* series parallels *Buffy Season Ten.*

"Live in the lie for a while"
Closure in *Angel: After the Fall*

Thomas Johnson

• • •

Writing about a year after the initial airing of the *Angel* series finale "Not Fade Away" (A5.22) in May 2004, Roz Kaveney argues in her essay "A Sense of the Ending: Schrodinger's *Angel*" that, in the absence of any further canonical material within the Buffyverse, the episode's narrative identity remains ambiguous.

> How we assess "Not Fade Away" ... depends radically on whether this finale is in fact the end. Joss Whedon has stated, repeatedly, that this ending was in most respects what it would have been had the show been renewed for a sixth season. Further, Whedon—and also writers David Fury and Jeff Bell—have indicated, both generally and in detail, the theme and some of the plot arcs of a sixth season that would have followed this finale. With vague talk of some future project that would unite at least a few members of the *Angel* cast ... the status of "Not Fade Away" as definitive concluding statement is uncertain [58–59].

The very existence of *Angel: After the Fall* implies that the television finale was not a "definitive concluding statement." A seventeen-issue comic book series published monthly by IDW between November 2007 and February 2009, *ATF* is the result of collaboration between *Angel* co-creator Joss Whedon and Brian Lynch, a writer for IDW who had previously scripted the *Angel*-affiliated limited series *Spike: Asylum* (September 2006—January 2007) and *Spike: Shadow Puppets* (June—October 2007). Whedon describes the series in an online interview as "season six" of *Angel*, "the storyline we were planning to pursue—made much more epic and fleshed out quite a bit" (Ryall). In an introduction to the omnibus collection of the first five issues of *ATF*, Lynch celebrates how he is able to influence "what happened after Angel, Spike, Gunn and Illyria stood in that alleyway, ready to face down hordes of evil." Comments like these give the impression that *ATF* is meant to offer closure to the narrative of *Angel* that the television show was deficient in providing.

This notion runs contrary to statements like that made by Jeffery Bell in the DVD audio commentary to "Not Fade Away" that "the point" of the episode's ending "isn't whether [Angel and his companions] win or lose, but what the series has been ... about," which "is the fact that these guys will always be fighting. If they won this battle then another battle would come along." Bell is arguing that the final scene of the finale performs a purely thematic function, and should not be interpreted as an invitation to further narrative. Some fans of *Angel* object to the existence of *ATF* out of a belief that, by clarifying the narrative consequences of the fight it the alley, it retroactively undermines the thematic closure offered by the finale. In comments accompanying Noel Murray's May 2012 review of "Not Fade Away" for the *A.V. Club*, multiple readers pair their praise for "Not Fade Away" with expressions of dismissal or derision for *ATF*.

A commenter with the handle JMP declares that "Not Fade Away is the end of Angel's story" before adding sardonically, "I'm glad that no one followed any boneheaded idea to continue it in other media because that would be just stupid." Persia reaffirms this sentiment by saying that any continuation of *Angel* would "be resetting what made the ending so great." Cliffy is most emphatic in his/her disavowal of *ATF*'s canonical status, proclaiming, "THE COMICS DON'T COUNT!" A commenter with the handle natty, on the other hand, damns *ATF* with faint praise by characterizing it as an innocuously forgettable addition to the Buffyverse: "I'm not really clear on how [*ATF*] can retroactively taint anything about this perfect episode of television. The very fact that [the comics are] in a totally different medium allows me to disassociate them [from the television show] pretty easily.... The comics were briefly entertaining to read, but watching the show again, I don't think about them at all."

The scholarly attention that has been given to *ATF* since it concluded five years ago has been more appreciative of the series' aesthetic merits than the kind of passionate, protective fan reaction quoted above. Jason Mittell, in discussing the "resurrection" of serialized television shows, charitably attributes "the motivation" behind the creation of both *ATF* and the *Buffy Season Eight* comics as being "driven by having more stories left to tell, and the freedom to tell them differently in another medium." In her essay "It (Re-)Started with a Girl: The Creative Interplay between

TV and Comics in *Angel: After the Fall*," Stacey Abbott examines a variety of "stylistic, narrative, and generic conventions" in *ATF* that distinguish it from its televisual predecessor, towards the end of arguing that the comic series "is ... a reworking of *Angel*'s narrative that interrogates the relationship between television and comics." Among the comic-book conventions that Abbott explores are use of serialization, visual and narrative scope, and lack of sound. This essay aims to analyze how *ATF* makes use of the convention of closure in comparison to its televisual predecessor and to argue that the comics' use of closure actually reaffirms, rather than undermines, existential themes central to the television finale and series as a whole.

Closure, as defined by Scott McCloud in *Understanding Comics: The Invisible Art*, is the "phenomenon of observing the parts but perceiving the whole" (63A). In a television show like *Angel*, "closure takes place continuously—twenty-four times per second ... as our minds, aided by the persistence of vision, transform a series of still pictures into a story of continuous motion" (65B). Therefore, whether or not viewers of "Not Fade Away" find the ending narratively satisfying, they have experienced a sort of closure, because the quick juxtaposition of film frames forces them to perceive the episode as a single, cohesive unit. One could argue that a reason the final moments of the television series provoke such strong reactions from *Angel* fans is that the sudden cut from Angel proclaiming "let's go to work" in the alley to the end credits interrupts continuous motion at a point that viewers may not expect it. The disjunction of these two frames, and the necessity of reconciling this disjunction in order to make sense of the narrative, forces viewers to become aware that they are engaged in a process of closure that had previously been reflexive on their parts. To paraphrase Will Eisner, viewers of "Not Fade Away" are necessarily "imprisoned until the [episode] ends" (*Graphic* 71), in that they are powerless to influence the temporal flow of the narrative. In comparison, the Fang Gang's ability to defy the Senior Partners, however slightly, is an impressive example of agency.

In comics, closure is the prerogative of readers, not writers and/or artists. Because narrative is presented in this medium through successive panels that "fracture both time and space, offering a jagged, staccato rhythm of unconnected moments," the onus is on readers to consciously "construct a continuous, unified reality" (McCloud 67B). Readers of *ATF*, therefore, unlike viewers of "Not Fade Away," can choose whether or not to embrace the possibility of closure offered by the narrative, rather than having it foisted upon them. In making this choice, readers of *ATF* find themselves in a place similar to many of the characters, who often face the decision to either try to remain in an artificial stasis or to embrace the reality of impinging circumstances. Angel must choose whether to own up to his new, inconvenient humanity or to deceive others into believing that he is still a vampire. Gunn must choose whether to recognize that he is a soulless vampire who is a pawn of the Senior Partners or to try to fool himself into believing that he is an essentially human, heroic agent of the Powers That Be. Spike must decide whether to continue trying to prevent Illyria from reflexively taking on Fred's form or to admit that his fighting companion's identity crisis needs to be addressed head-on. Illyria must choose whether to cling to the hope that she retains some element of Fred's personality or to accept that Fred's "not part of [her]" (*ATF* #14).

The character who chooses to embrace closure most overtly in *ATF* is Wesley. He already experiences a form of closure in "Not Fade Away" through his tragic death, a plot twist that had not originally been part of the finale Whedon envisioned, but that was incorporated at the suggestion of "Jeff Bell and the *Angel* staff" (Ryall). Bringing Wesley back as an incorporeal servant of Wolfram and Hart in *ATF* was Whedon's idea, and Lynch's expressed wish was to avoid cheapening Wesley's "powerful and moving death on the show ... by bringing him back and giving him nothing to do" ("Questions"). However, far from invalidating Wesley's end on the television show, his presence in *ATF*, and his narrative arc in issue seven specifically, provides a medium-specific type of closure for the character that complements his final appearance onscreen.

Wesley self-identifies as a character who is determined to recognize the reality of his circumstances, no matter how dire they may be. In a conversation with Illyria during the second act of "Not Fade Away," he explains his reticence to ask her to take on the guise of Fred: "The first lesson a Watcher learns is to separate truth from illusion, 'cause in the world of magics it's the hardest thing to do. The truth is that Fred is gone. To pretend anything else would be a lie. And since I don't actually intend to die tonight, I won't accept a lie." Wesley recognizes that since finding genuine emotional closure without Fred is impossible for him, he will only accept a simulacrum of emotional closure with a faux–Fred when it is clear that his death, a physical closure, is approaching. Sure enough, it is when he is mortally wounded, and recognizes that his sudden death is inevitable, that Wesley allows Illyria to assume Fred's form.

One of the reasons Wesley's death scene is so "powerful and moving" (Lynch, "Questions") is because the temporal nature of the televisual medium helps viewers to empathize with the character's situation. Wesley's death scene is brief, running less than three minutes from the point at which he is stabbed by Cyrus Vail to that at which he expires in Illyria's arms. Illyria's assessment following Wesley's stabbing that he will "be dead within moments" is nearly as damning for viewers as it is for Wesley, because they have as little time left to watch Wesley as he has to live. Just as Wesley is powerless to extend his own life, viewers are powerless to extend or delay the automatic process of closure that is involved in the depiction of his demise. Viewers' "imprisoned" (Eisner, *Graphic* 71) perspectives are also analogous to Illyria's quandary in this scene. Once powerful enough to bend space and time to her will, Illyria is forced to recognize that she "can't help" (A5.22) Wesley cheat death—she too is condemned to watch. Illyria's offer "to lie to" Wesley by assuming Fred's form, and Wesley's willingness to be lied to in the moment of death, are rendered all the more poignant by viewers' direct experience of the time constraints the characters face.

Whereas the temporal nature of television is conducive to helping viewers relate to Wesley's experience of impending mortality, the atemporal nature of comics is conducive to helping readers relate to the character's entrance into eternity. Death is never the assured end of conscious existence in the Buffyverse (Spike's return as a ghost in Season 5 of *Angel* after being incinerated in "Chosen" is only one of myriad examples), and *ATF* #7 recontextualizes Wesley's death scene in "Not Fade Away" by showing his personified spirit entering an ethereal realm. The section of *ATF* #7 devoted to the character opens with a completely white panel, on which the title "Wesley" is embossed in large black letters, with Lynch, illustrator Nick Runge, and colorist John Rauch credited in smaller black letters underneath. In and of itself, the meaning of this monochromatic panel is unclear; it is only by viewing the second panel, directly below the first, in which Wesley is shown sitting in a chair floating in front of a cloudy white background, that readers can perform the process of closure and thereby draw tentative conclusions about the meaning of the first panel. Starting in the second panel, Runge draws Wesley as wearing the same clothes as in the character's final appearance in the "Not Fade Away," a choice of wardrobe that implies that this scene begins immediately following Wesley's death. In recognizing this narrative circumstance, readers perform an act of closure more complex than "bridg[ing] the gaps in action" (Eisner, *Comics* 39) between two panels. Readers are instead required to "bridge the gaps" between different types of media, and in production time. They must accept that the repercussions of a narrative event depicted on television are being related through the medium of comics, and that regardless of the roughly four-year gap between the initial airing of "Not Fade Away" and the publication of *ATF* #7, Wesley's death and Wesley's entrance into the afterlife occur consecutively.

Once readers have performed this impressive act of closure, they may interpret the first panel as either a rendering of Wesley's point-of-view passing from life to death, or as the empty ethereal void prior to Wesley's entrance into it. This latter interpretation seems especially likely, given that on the television series characters like Angel and Gunn interact with conduits of the Senior Partners in a white void (A3.17, 4.8, 4.22, 5.4, 5.15), and, though it is not immediately apparent, Wesley interacts with a conduit of the Senior Partners in this issue. The break between the first two panels—a convention that McCloud refers to as "the limbo of the gutter" (66D)—places the responsibility on readers to imagine the precise moment of Wesley's entrance into a literal limbo. That the passage of time is up to the interpretation of readers from the start of the "Wesley" section of *ATF* #7 is appropriate, given that the limbo in which Wesley finds himself seems to be literally outside of the flow of time.

If readers continue to proceed through *ATF* #7 beyond the opening panels, they find that Wesley is approached by a woman who appears to be Fred, who presents him with a vision of Heaven. The question for both Wesley and for readers is whether to accept this happy ending uncritically or to reject it as a deception of the Senior Partners. From an existentialist point of view, both Wesley and readers are faced with the temptation to "ignore [their] freedom of choice, essentially to pretend for as long as possible that a decision is not required, or even possible" (Richardson and Rabb 29). Lynch and Runge thus create a dramatic situation that inverts and parallels Wesley's final scene in "Not Fade Away." In the *Angel* finale, Wesley cannot ignore his power of choice—he only has a few seconds of life in which to accept or reject Illyria's offer to "lie to [him]" (A5.22). Viewers, on the other hand, because "[t]he closure of electronic media is continuous, largely involuntary and virtually imperceptible" (McCloud 68A), have no choice but to passively accept Wesley's.

Readers of *ATF* #7, contrastingly, can forestall Wesley's moment of decision, opting "to live in the lie" concocted by the Senior Partners "for a while" (Whedon), even though Wesley does not. Because the onus is on readers to move from panel to panel, they theoretically have all the time they want to "dwell ... and fantasize" (Eisner, *Graphic* 71) on Nick Runge's strikingly lifelike depictions of Wesley and faux–Fred. A rectangular panel dominating the middle of the third page of the section is particularly luscious, showing a long-shot of Wesley embracing faux–Fred underneath a

The idyllic sunset suggests an interlude outside of time. Joss Whedon, Brian Lynch, et al. (writers), Franco Urru (penciller). *Angel: After the Fall: First Night Volume 2.* San Diego: IDW, 2008.

tree, on top of a green hill looking down on a verdant valley, opposite a mountain on which the last rays of sunset are falling (*ATF* #7). The expansive width of the panel, and its prominence on the page, "make[s] a difference in" readers' "perception[s] of time," giving it a "feeling of greater length" (McCloud 101D) than the panels immediately preceding it. These qualities suggest that Runge is attempting to seduce readers into temporarily suspending the act of closure, into forgetting that they have the freedom to bring the narrative to its conclusion, just as faux–Fred is attempting to fool Wesley into ignoring his freedom to call out her bluff.

By forcing a confrontation with faux–Fred, Wesley shows that he is still an expert at "separat[ing] truth from illusion" (A5.22). While he was willing to be lied to by Illyria when he believed himself to be short on time, now that he knows that death has not provided him with ultimate closure, he would prefer to "get to it" (*ATF* #7), "it" being the reality of his afterlife. In his notes on *ATF* #7, Lynch argues that this commitment to truth is "why Wesley is a cool character. He gets a moment of perfect bliss. He's lying in bed with his true love ... he could very easily stay in this moment, but he doesn't want to. It's not real, and he won't accept it" ("Notes"). Readers, too, can "easily stay in this moment"; if they choose to continue the process of closure, they will actually end up having a greater power of action than Wesley, who is bound by snakes and rendered incorporeal moments after confronting faux–Fred. By performing closure,

58 PART TWO: *Angel* AND *Spike* COMICS

Wesley, dead, stands in the panel gutters of limbo. Joss Whedon, Brian Lynch, et al. (writers), Franco Urru (penciller). *Angel: After the Fall: First Night Volume 2*. San Diego: IDW, 2008.

readers are complicit, along with faux–Fred, Lynch, and Runge, in robbing Wesley of his ability to physically affect the world around him.

As McCloud writes, "Every act committed to paper by the comics artist is aided and abetted by a silent accomplice[, an] equal partner in crime known as *the reader*" (emphasis in original) (68C-D). Whereas in watching "Not Fade Away" viewers can only wait to see how Wesley will choose to spend his final moments as a living, corporeal being, here readers are active while Wesley is forced into a passive position. If readers sympathize with Wesley's plight, they may not be entirely comfortable holding this position of power over him, but it is one that brings Wesley full-circle in his development as a character. Faux-Fred demeans Wesley by reducing him "to his earlier foppish persona, replete with the all too familiar spectacles and three piece suit of his first appearance on *Buffy*" (Abbott, "It (Re-)Started with a Girl") as a naive, incompetent Watcher. Whatever similarity Wesley might bear to his younger self, however, his five years in Los Angeles over the course of *Angel* have changed him irrevocably: he is not only competent, but heroic. Readers who continue with *ATF* through issue 16 find that it is Wesley who finally recognizes the way in which Angel can force the Senior Partners to turn back time and restore Los Angeles to a non-hellish state—in other words, "to return to a world without" (*ATF* #16) Wesley. Wesley in *ATF* thus experiences a more active kind of closure than that which he experiences in "Not Fade Away," since he can choose the death that is originally out of his control.

Angel fans, likewise, in reading *ATF*, can experience a more active kind of closure than they experience in watching "Not Fade Away." Rather than being helplessly drawn, via the "closure of electronic media" (McCloud 68A), towards an ending-point, readers of *ATF* must choose alongside Lynch, the artists, and the characters, to bring the story to an end. Through performing the comics-specific kind of closure required by *ATF*, readers make decisions alongside characters like Wesley, and thereby reaffirm the existential principle of free will that is crucial to *Angel*. Just as Wesley's presence in *ATF* highlights both the ways in which he has remained constant and the great extent to which he has evolved as a character since his introduction to the Buffyverse, fans, by reading *ATF*, both demonstrate the constancy of their engagement with *Angel*, and evolve from spectators of the story to participants in it.

An earlier version of Thomas Johnson's "'Live in the Lie for a While': Closure in *Angel: After the Fall*" was previously presented at the Third Annual Conference of the Mythgard Institute. Linthicum, Maryland, Jan 10, 2015.

The Trouble with Spike

An Examination of William the Bloody's Problematic Progression

Bryant Dillon

• • •

Spike, the bleach-blond, ensouled vampire who captured the hearts and minds of Whedon fans on the small screen in *Buffy the Vampire Slayer* and *Angel*, underwent an impressive rollercoaster of character growth throughout the two series, from villainous rebel to lovelorn crusader; however, his leap to the sequential art medium vastly limited his progression as a player in the continuing *Buffy* saga, despite the efforts of the talented writers assigned to carry on the Slayer mythos. This is not to suggest that the character has been miswritten or that the comics and graphic novels focused solely on Spike are of anything less than stellar quality. Rather, this stunted character progression is the result of Spike's innate, problematic nature as a character and the unforeseen obstacles in the world of *Buffy* and *Angel*'s licensed comic publishing.

In the canonical *Buffy* and *Angel* comics books published by IDW Publishing and Dark Horse Comics, three inherent flaws within the character of Spike prevent him from advancing beyond the ever-pining, lovesick counterpart to the slayer. Given Spike's popularity between both the fans and the writers behind the television series, these problematic elements are often overlooked in an attempt to maintain his presence within the storyline; however, it becomes a significantly harder task for the writing team to advance the character than with the other core players, such as Buffy, Willow, and Xander.

The first problematic element inherent to Spike is the fact that he is a character that was not designed to be part of the grander plan of *Buffy* creator Joss Whedon. Spike was originally imagined by Whedon as a minor villain who would appear for only a few episodes before being dispatched by his opposing heroine. The main purpose of the character of Spike (and his undead soulmate Drusilla, played by Juliet Landau) was to help the show avoid a villain-of-the-week feel by providing entertaining and memorable baddies that could battle the Slayer over a number of episodes before ultimately meeting their demise. Spike was never intended to love anyone beyond his vampiric sire. James Marsters, the actor behind the British vampire, has often commented on just how adamantly Whedon expressed to him the lack of a future the character had on the show.

> I remember doing those first five episodes, and it must have been episode three, and Joss almost physically pushing me up against a wall and saying, "I don't care how popular you are; you are going to die, die, die." He made it very clear he did not want the show to be taken over by another romantic vampire. He was not enamored with vampires, and that's putting it mildly [Norton].

While Whedon made no secret of his disinterest with further exploring the concept of romanticized vampires in *Buffy*, that was not his only initial issue with Spike's unexpected fan love. As Marsters also realized, the character of Spike and the popularity surrounding him would present a problem, thematically, for the story Whedon intended to tell.

> When I was cast, Joss did not imagine me to be popular; Spike was supposed to be dirty and evil, punk rock, and then dead. Things started to turn out differently, and I think Joss was passionate that I would not corrupt his theme, which was basically trying to find a metaphor for all of the problems you encounter during adolescence. Vampires stood in for those problems, and I think I endangered that theme by being popular. He did not want people to like me at all [Norton].

While Whedon is notoriously known for this advance planning (i.e., his intentions to kill Buffy at the end of the fifth season of her series, the appearance of the Slayer's younger sister Dawn, and his long-term plans for Willow's homosexuality), it is safe to say that he never saw the popularity of Spike coming. Whedon eventually warmed to the character, as did his writing staff, but unlike the Scooby core of Buffy, Xander, Willow, and Giles, the character of Spike was a wildcard whose path was far less steady and cemented in Whedon's vision. In fact, Whedon admits that he and the writers played fast and loose with Spike as part of the cast, allowing the character to find his own footing when it came to finding his place among the other series regulars and what his future would hold. Whedon notes:

TV's like whitewater rafting: Without rocks, there wouldn't be rapids, and it wouldn't be as much fun.... [Rolling with it] gave us Spike falling in love with Buffy.... You plan your ideas and themes, and then you let the rest form naturally, and then it feels real. It doesn't feel like you're imposing something on everybody [Miller].

While the character's impact on the fans and the show is a testament to the talents of Whedon and his writing staff, as well as the amazingly charismatic performance by Marsters, the fact still remains that Spike's lack of a defined position in Whedon's plan, plot-wise and thematically, left the character without a solid direction for other writers to follow. Buffy is the slayer and meant to stand against the vampires, demons, and other forces of darkness. Her other ensouled vampiric counterpart, Angel, is on a mission of redemption for his evil acts and is charged by "The Powers That Be" with helping the helpless. The soul-infused Spike wants to be a hero, as well ... but just not in any way remotely similar to Angel. (That last statement is in jest, but the sentiment is sincere.) Spike's path is undefined, and while he is often included in the comic book storylines that followed the television series, he is also very often reduced to simply looking cool, being snarky, and kicking ass as necessary.

Given Spike's status as a fan-favorite character, his existence in the *Buffy* and *Angel* comics was a foregone conclusion; however, the second hurdle faced by the comics' writing teams existed in the simple fact that the romantic relationship between the Slayer and the bleach-blonde vampire had ... passed. While Spike's history and romantic feelings for the Slayer cannot be ignored in the Buffyverse comics without drawing the ire of fans and betraying the nature of the character, there's no denying that Spike and Buffy played out their love story to the extreme during the final seasons of the television series. From torrid sex, to true intimacy, to final admissions and fiery self-sacrifice, Buffy and Spike may still have heat together, but the flames almost certainly reached their pinnacle long ago on a television series not so far away. (Thank you, Netflix!) This isn't to say that the fire couldn't be brought back to a roar, but Whedon and the writers have always been cautious to avoid retreading the same path without a reason connected to the overarching plots and themes of the season. For example, during the final story arcs of *Buffy: Season Eight*, Angel and the Slayer do finally rekindle their physical passion and use their newly (and temporarily) adopted super powers to pull some naked aerial maneuvers that shake the world to its core (the fans lovingly dubbed this event the "space frak"), but, in true Whedon fashion, the momentary happiness between the two former lovers bring horrific and life-altering consequences for all and, as a result, drive the two of them even further apart than ever before.

At the time, Buffy fantasizes of a similar encounter with Spike and calls him her "dark place" in whom she can always confide, but makes no effort to take things further than memories (8.8). While Spike and Buffy have avoided falling back into each other's arms, the few times writer Andrew Chambliss flirted with the idea of Buffy and Spike spending their lives together in *Buffy: Season Nine* only further revealed Spike's stagnant state at the Slayer's side. He notes just after in *Spike: A Dark Place*, "There was a time when I thought Buffy was pregnant and I could take care of her and we'd maybe have a play at a normal life. Talk about *fooling* yourself." In Season Ten, Buffy notes ironically of her friendship with Spike, "It's all good now. This is exactly what I wanted. Yay for maturity" as she and Spike fight side by side then he gives her a platonic hug. Nonetheless, she makes no effort to change it. Simply put, at this time there does not seem to be an intent from the writers to reignite the romantic relationship between the two characters, and that means that Spike, like his grandsire Angel, must move on.

In all fairness, Spike does spend some of his time in the sequential art medium mooning over Buffy. His love and loyalty for the Slayer are some of the most beloved traits of the character—not acknowledging the flag Spike still carries for Buffy would have been a big mistake, perhaps even the biggest mistake the Buffyverse comic writers could make. Whedon himself credits Spike's love for Buffy as the "great motivating force that made him more than just the wacky vampire neighbor" (*Buffy the Vampire Slayer: The Complete Sixth Season*). If the concept is examined, even just briefly, it becomes clear how true Whedon's words are. Not only did the romance/redemption storyline with Buffy bring Spike front and center on the TV series, but it is also the compelling factor that caused Spike to resist killing, bond with members of the Scoobies (like Dawn), search out a way to regain his soul, and become a "champion" (a common term in the Buffyverse for a warrior who fights the forces of evil) himself. Spike's love, loyalty, and romanticism for Buffy are so closely intertwined with his definition of who he is as a character that trying to separate him from it is nearly unthinkable. The characters of Angel and Spike are similar in this way. We've seen that Angel, after two seasons of his own series and the (temporary) death of his beloved Buffy, was able to pursue other romantic relationships, but given the intensity of their love affair and personal intimacy, Buffy still continues to inform Angel's actions, whether the vampire is helping birth a new universe (*Buffy: Season 8*) or resurrecting a fallen Watcher (*Angel & Faith: Season 9*). Spike's romance and intimacy with Buffy are just as deep and intense, but those are not the only things he shares with Angel when it comes to Buffy. For both Spike and Angel, their romantic arcs with Buffy have already peaked.

One might assume that it is a fairly simply task to move Spike's storyline past one that involves the Slayer. His inclusion in the cast of *Angel: Season 5* demonstrated that the character could stand on his own, without the Slayer. Still, while Spike may be a champion now, his time on *Angel* also demonstrated that the character actively avoids mirroring his fellow ensouled vampire. The writers also have a vested interest in highlighting the differences between Angel's and Spike's paths. As previously stated, there is no use in covering the same ground twice. The fact that Dark Horse Comics and the writers decided to keep Spike committed to the *Buffy* comic series instead of a book of his own was the final nail in the coffin for the notion that Spike might follow in Angel's footsteps. In the end, most Whedon fans would surely agree that Spike would sooner give The Powers That Be the finger than start following their instructions.

The final problematic element with regard to Spike as a character is the fact that he is, very simply, still in love with Buffy Summers. While many canon comics have used the character aptly and tested the waters as to the reasons or partners who could potentially convince Spike to put down the torch he carries for the Slayer, the writers have failed to convince the fan base, and perhaps themselves, that William the Bloody is over Buffy. In "Spike and Faith," the twentieth issue of *Angel & Faith*, Spike flirts with Faith upon hearing she's broken up with Robin Wood, only to be told she's "nobody's rebound girl." Lavinia and Sophronia, Giles' aunts, seem interested, but ultimately decide that he looks like the type to "get attached" to women. He finally climbs into a shower with Harmony, but this too is short-lived. Faith comments wryly, "You won't get over Buffy by getting laid. But you'll probably get laid when you get over Buffy."

Writer Andrew Chambliss even let the words pour from the vampire's mouth during *Buffy: Season Nine*, right before Spike and his bug crew headed out on a solo miniseries titled *Spike: A Dark Place*, written by Victor Gischler. While Gischler's *Spike* was an entertaining romp that saw Spike cut ties with his bug crew, lose his spaceship, and be tempted by a sultry succubus, it did little to quell the vampire's feelings of true love for Buffy. The succubus Morgan tells him, "We could've been this century's power couple.... But there's no way to get to you without getting past her. I can't compete with a memory" (*Spike: A Dark Place*). Even while writer Christos Gage has Buffy describing her relationship with Spike as "all good now," full of maturity and "exactly what I wanted" in the current *Buffy: Season Ten* comics (*New Rules* 10.1), for Spike, all it takes is a few pints with Xander at the local pub to admit that "if you love someone, you do what's best for 'em, even if it's not what's best for you" (10.2). There's no mistaking that Spike still carries his torch and that it is still burning him; he has just learned to deal with the pain a bit better. Could Spike move on, if the right girl came along? There is no reason to believe that is not possible, but if Buffy asked him to spend the rest of his life with her, he would not hesitate for an instant.

While the facts that Spike was not designed to be part of Whedon's grander plan, that his romantic arc with Buffy has already peaked, and that he clearly is still in love with the Slayer cause Spike to be a more difficult character to write, these problematic qualities are not the only reasons that Spike's character growth has been slower than the others around him. One major factor has been completely outside the writers' control and concerns the separate intellectual property rights for the *Buffy* and *Angel* licensed comics. As always, it seems timing is everything.

While Dark Horse Comics originally held the licensing rights to produce *Angel* comics, they ended their non-canon run in 2002. As Dark Horse still maintained the rights to produce *Buffy* comics, IDW Publishing acquired the *Angel* comic rights in 2005, and given Spike's status as a regular in the final TV season, he was part of the package. Writer Brian Lynch gained praise for his writing of the characters (Spike especially) in early, non-canon IDW series like *Spike: Asylum*. Lynch's creative script for *Asylum* pits the British vampire with a soul against the Mosaic Wellness Center, a rehab facility for demons, vampires, and other things that go bump in the night (but still wish to be more acceptable members of civilized society). Attempting to uncover a lead on a missing former Mosaic patient, Spike checks himself into the demented hospital in an attempt to go "undercover" but quickly finds himself in over his head and pinned between his malicious caretakers and the other violent patients with whom he's locked. Lynch's creepy concepts, such as the forced surgical removal of the "vamp face" from Mosaic's blood-sucking patients, made the rehab center a worthy and original foe. This penchant for darker material paired with Lynch's talent for witty dialogue and pop cultural references helped win over the hypercritical fan base and set the stage for an even more impressive and impactful place for Lynch in *Angel* history.

While *Spike: Asylum* gained critical accolades from a number of devoted fans, it was the announcement of a Whedon-written *Buffy: Season Eight* in 2007 from Dark Horse Comics that really got the ball rolling for

IDW Publishing's *Angel* comics. Inspired by Dark Horse Comics' bold concept of a canon comic book season of "television," Lynch and IDW Publishing approached Whedon about the potential for a similar official *Angel: Season Six* series at IDW. Whedon agreed, impressed by Lynch's writing in *Spike: Asylum*, and the result was a 17-issue epic called *Angel: After the Fall*.

Angel: After the Fall and Lynch's two Spike-focused miniseries, *Spike: After the Fall* and *Spike*, marked a golden period for both licensed *Angel* comics and the character of Spike. While *Angel: After the Fall* continued the events of *Angel: Season Five,* as the original vampire with a soul (along with everyone in Los Angeles) is sent to a hell dimension as a result of Angel's transgressions against Wolfram & Hart at the end of *Angel: Season Five*, the companion piece, *Spike: After the Fall*, focused completely on the blond vampire and laid the groundwork for Spike's emancipation from the supporting character position. In Lynch's Spike-centric story, the blond vamp learns the price of leadership, meets a slightly demonic new love interest, and continues to develop a touching, yet bizarre, friendship with Illyria that was only hinted at in the fifth season of *Angel*. He forms his own crew of demons, plus Illyria and Connor, while Illyria jealously fights the demon women, protesting when Spike has "intercourse with a lesser." After a fierce kiss, Spike assures Illyria she will always be his top priority.

In IDW Publishing's eight-issue *Spike* miniseries, Lynch's tale features the vampire hero making a special trip to Sin City itself, Las Vegas, in order to thwart Wolfram & Hart once more as it attempts to reestablish itself after their massive defeat in Los Angeles. Spike explains that on Angel's team "I'm just along for the ride. Sick of riding the coaster. Wanna steer.... I keep the team small, I keep it with people I can control, keep it simple. No back-stabbing, no dying, no picking up and leaving, and no aerial sex" (this last being a reference to *Buffy: Season Eight*). Lynch described the miniseries as "what would happen if Spike headlined his own TV show," and the plot certainly matches that description, moving the vampire into a starring role, mining the character's rich history and connection to other characters in the Buffyverse (such as Drusilla, Willow, and Groo).

Spike actually gives up his soul then reacquires it and reunites with Drusilla, who tries to marry him. These seem like game-changing moments. He also has his own team from his earlier Lynch adventures, with the pyrokinetic woman Beck, telepathic fish Betta George, and fanboy Jeremy Johns. As Willow observes, Spike is evidencing notable character growth. She cries happily: "You blossomed on your own. Having team-ups, observing traffic signals, reaching out to Team Scooby! And Spike, you hugged!"

The book also provides an origin to match Spike's sudden appearance in *Buffy: Season Eight* with a spaceship manned by a crew of human-sized bugs (Manning). (IDW Publishing and Dark Horse Comics worked together to make the miniseries mesh with the events of *Buffy: Season Eight* as much as possible.) After Beck confides her love, Spike kisses her and comes close to saying he loves her, suggesting a trajectory towards his own storyline. However, he leaves her, as he comes to a resolution that makes him abandon Beck, Jeremy, and Betta George behind for their own safety. He explains:

> No one is in control of anything. Innocents become dangerous. Heroes can turn on a dime. Sometimes, evil can do an about-face and want to help. People come into your life. People leave. Everything's changing. Everything's always changing. Bottom line, the only thing any one of us is in charge of ... is ourselves.

In 2010 it was announced that the *Angel* rights would be reverting back to Dark Horse Comics in 2011, so that all of the Buffyverse characters and comics could be published under one roof. While there were many benefits to this move, including the brilliant *Angel & Faith* run by Christos Gage and Rebekah Issacs, one casualty seems to have been the majority of character development and advancement made by Lynch and the IDW *Angel* and *Spike* comics. The Dark Horse Comics acknowledge that the events in *Angel: After the Fall* are canon, but only in the vaguest of ways. While the volumes of the IDW series are still available for purchase and can be enjoyed by fans everywhere, the inevitable effect they should have had (specifically regarding the character development of Spike) was nullified. Instead of building upon progress made by Lynch, the writers at Dark Horse ignored the IDW plot lines and covered ground previously explored by Lynch's miniseries. While the absence of various confusing continuity threads with another publisher's books may have been advantageous in regards to the creative freedom of the writers employed by Dark Horse Comics (as well as a smart business decision), it left Spike (and some other choice characters) with a fractured "history," where past events in the IDW books are supposedly canon, but are very rarely acknowledged by the characters or writers. Hence, despite the major strides the snarky, ensouled vampire made in IDW's *Angel: After the Fall, Spike: After the Fall,* and Lynch's *Spike* miniseries, his first miniseries under Dark Horse's watch, *Spike: A Dark Place,* has the character, once again, admitting that he's lost: "What have I become? Not the same villain. Nobody's idea of a hero. Drifting somewhere in no man's land." He's stuck "figuring things out" and trying to "define who he is and what he wants." His new writer Victor Gischler explains:

His soul is still a new thing for him. It's like when I got my first smart phone: I had no idea what all the buttons did, but I instinctively sensed all the potential. "Hero" and "villain" are terms too limiting for a character like Spike, but these are the issues Spike must ponder [Glendening].

While Gischler's writing talents are not to be denied and *Spike: A Dark Place* has plenty of other merits, the writer was clearly starting out "fresh" with the character, unhindered or unaware of the advancements previously made during IDW's time with Spike. Creative choices like this one made it near impossible for Dark Horse to avoid retreading a number of plot points and character moments in regards to the blond vampire.

While time and progress may have been lost and Spike may be a problematic character to write in the ensemble cast of the current *Buffy* and *Angel & Faith* comic series, there is no need to give up hope or look down on the progress that has been made. The popularity of Spike continues to endure, and the latest writer entrusted with him, Christos Gage, has already tapped into meaty territory in the current *Buffy: Season Ten* by forcing Spike to room, once more, with his old pal, Xander Harris, by diving deep into Spike's messy past with Buffy (i.e., whether he ever truly loved her when he lacked a soul), and by examining why he does not have a split personality similar to the Angel/Angelus dynamic.

In addition to the standard *Buffy: Season Ten* comics, actor James Marsters has written a solo Spike graphic novel, *Spike: Into the Light*. The graphic novel was recently released by Dark Horse Comics and explores the character's time shortly after his soul was restored at the end of Season 6. Spike explains, "Once ... a long time ago, I was a very bad man. I thought I was protecting myself, but I was only hurting people. Now I've ... woken up, and I'm trying to help people." Still reeling from his recent ensoulment, the vampire is forced to devise a way to replace his deteriorating boots without adding more killing or stealing onto his conscience. The plotline also features a potential love interest named Dylan whose looks are based on Marsters' actual wife Patricia Rahman. While *Spike: Into the Light* suggests that potential to "reinsert" character development and moments into the already established timeline, it remains to be seen how this tool will be used by Dark Horse Comics and its writers. Given Dylan's brief reappearance in the seventh issue of *Buffy: Season Ten*, it feels as if Marsters' one-shot will end up functioning as more a setup for a yet-to-be-revealed Season Ten story arc. Will William the Bloody finally meet a girl that can get him beyond the Buffster? Only time shall tell...

In the end, Spike is a fascinating character that writers love to write for and fans love to read about. While passionate, die-hard fans of the rebellious vamp with a soul (this author included) may feel frustration regarding the paths not taken during Spike's time in the sequential art form, the problematic nature of the character and the unpredictable roadblocks encountered regarding the shifting ownership of the property licenses must be taken in stride. Many fans will surely remember not only the floundering state of the character and those writing him during Buffy: Season Four, but also the brilliant story arcs given to Spike from Season Five through the end of the TV series, once the writers found their footing with the character. Despite the setbacks, Spike continues to interest fans and writers alike, and each additional season in Dark Horse's *Buffy* canon comics brings a new opportunity to advance the character and his development. As long as *Buffy* and *Angel* continue in sequential art form, there will surely be a place for William the Bloody among the pages of comic books and graphic novels, and fans will surely follow.

Part Three

Tales of the Slayers

• • •

In 2001, Whedon edited a collection called *Tales of the Slayers,* as his favorite writers explored different slayers through history. Jane Espenson's "Presumption" is a Jane Austen-style adventure drawn by P. Craig Russell. Doug Petrie and Gene Colan tackle Nikki Wood, while Amber Benson's slayer (with art by Ted Naifeh) struggles through the French Revolution. David Fury and Steve Lieber's "The Glittering World," ties into the Navaho legends of the hero Monster Slayer, and Rebecca Rand Kirshner and Mira Friedman's slayer struggles to define evil in a world of Nazism. Whedon's own "Righteous" follows a medieval slayer accused of witchcraft after saving her town, with art by Tim Sale. His frame story begins with the First Slayer imagining those who will follow and ends with his futuristic slayer Fray reading about the lives of all the slayers in the collection.

Tales of the Slayer was a popular topic for this collection, with so many perspectives offered on the Chosen Ones through history. Traci J. Cohen examines hybrid gender in just three stories: "Righteous," "Presumption," and "Nikki Goes Down," with a close examination of art and text. Kristi Pope Key tackles Otherness in every story of the collection, comparing them to the larger theme. Delving into the slayer mythos allows these critics to reveal the symbolism and weight of the slayer tradition for Buffy and her friends.

The sequel and companion, *Tales of the Vampires,* followed in 2004 with stories of Spike and Dru, Angel, Jack the Ripper and many new vampires through history. Whedon's framing tale, featuring Rupert Giles's future grandmother, has many Whedon tropes with a savage vampire, hapless Watchers, and several little girls who are more than they seem.

"So I wear pearls"

Exploring Gender in Tales of the Slayers

Traci J. Cohen

• • •

Simone de Beauvoir once wrote: "An existent *is* nothing other than what he does; the possible does not extend beyond the real, essence does not precede existence: in pure subjectivity, the human being *is not anything*. He is to be measured by his acts" (272). Basically, de Beauvoir is saying that a man is defined by what he does—what he is capable of doing and what he dreams of doing do not account for his identity. It is only the actions he engages in that are part of what defines him. It is important to note that this formula really only works for men, because as de Beauvoir continues, "if one considers a woman in her immanent presence ... one can say absolutely nothing about her, she falls short of having any qualifications" (272). According to de Beauvoir a woman does not do anything. She possesses potential, but this potential is never realized. Women therefore lack definition and any definition they do have is based on a patriarchal system that puts restrictions on what women are allowed to do and in turn how they are defined. In the *Buffy* series, and more specifically the graphic novel *Tales of the Slayers*, slayers usurp traditionally masculine roles and try to define themselves as heroes; nonetheless, these women refuse to completely remove themselves from more feminine identifiers.

Three tales in particular follow the slayers' struggle with gender and their attempts to find definition through their roles as Slayers. The first, "Righteous," focuses on a medieval slayer. In this story the young girl initially refuses to claim her role, saying that God would not punish her so severely.

Eventually, the nameless girl comes around and trains hard to fulfill her destiny. She is shown studying and physically training for the battles ahead. In one panel the narrator states:

> Young men, on hunt to find a wife
> Surprised, looked oft her way
> But like a nun, she'd none of love
> She could not be seduced [18–19].

In these lines the slayer is shown as being above the men who hunt her, trying to catch and hold her. The imagery of the hunter and hunted is reversed in the training panel. The first set of images show the young girl studying and practicing both melee and sword fighting. After this panel, the men of the village are shown in the act of "hunting," but taking no action towards winning the affections of the young Slayer. As the art reveals, in actuality the slayer is the hunter, but she shows no interest in hunting for a husband, preferring the actual beast, the vampire. Unlike the men who run the village, her prey is more difficult to kill, and she will actually succeed in destroying it.

Men and women are juxtaposed in a crisscross as the slayer gains strength. Joss Whedon (writer), and Tim Sale (penciller). "Righteous." *Tales of the Slayers* (Buffy the Vampire Slayer). Milwaukie, OR: Dark Horse, 2002.

Later in the story, the narrator speaks of a vampire who attacks the village:

> "To arms!" the men were called, but none
> was man enough to fight
> In St. Just's way there stood but one
> One maiden, dressed in white [21].

In the first panel of the battle, the slayer is shown standing in a white dress, holding a sword and a stake. This image mixes both masculine and feminine imagery: The sword and stake in each hand are associated with physicality and war, from the world of men. A stake resembles a dagger, a weapon typically wielded by men. However, the wood's connection to mother earth makes it slightly more feminine. The mixture of masculine and feminine connections mirrors the slayer's association with both genders. While the stake acts as a quick visual representation for the slayer's more masculine side, the flowing dress symbolizes the slayer's femininity, together with the white of purity and chastity.

This image shows the gender duality of not only this slayer, but all slayers that have become before or will come after. Although her appearance is feminine, her actions are considered traditionally masculine and through this she finds a place of identity. The Slayer fights alone, as the men in the village, though "called," are unwilling. This goes against the general belief laid out by de Beauvoir that men are defined by action and women lack definition because they are considered inactive. In this moment the slayer has become defined under the masculine form, though in her dress she boldly proclaims her femininity.

After she slays their leader, St. Just, the vampires (all male), claim that they will "break [her] ... and see [her] cowed!" (24). The word "cow" implies using fear and intimidation to make someone submit. Their vow does not scare the slayer and she boldly replies, "Please try" (24). In telling them to try to break her, the slayer is undermining their authority, quipping defiantly as Buffy so often does. The vampires are not the only beings who wish to see the slayer cowed. After the vampire attack, a panel shows a young girl dressed similarly to the slayer who is battling a bully. A priest looks down upon this scene with a disapproving scowl. The next panel shows that the preacher is inciting the town to believe the slayer is actually a witch and telling them:

> She walks with Darkness, Satan's whore
> She's here to damn us all!
> There's but one way to save this town

And please our heav'nly sire
To bring that wanton woman down
And purge her soul with fire! [25–26].

The priest sees the young girl imitating the slayer, so he launches a crusade against the feminine strength. Like so many slayers, beginning with the first, she poses a threat to the patriarchal order. The preacher makes sure that his words specifically reference her womanhood. Because she does not act the way a woman should act, she is labeled a whore and must be executed. The story ends with the Slayer being burned at the stake and her Watcher despairingly setting the vampires loose on the town that killed her.

One of the other slayers in the collection attempts to avoid this issue altogether. In the tale "Presumption," a reworking of Jane Austen's *Pride and Prejudice*, the young Catherine attends a ball thrown by a gentleman, Edward, who is new to town. The narrator hints that as they come together, a vampire and slayer are meeting at last. He wears black, white, and grey, repressed colors that echo all the other gentlemen in their restrictive social uniform, while she wears pink, flaunting her femininity.

During the ball, Catherine makes a few rude comments about the young man and when he comments on this she retorts, "Our society affords women few freedoms except the ability to learn all she can and speak all she can get away with. I'd be foolish to neglect such small options" (42). The young woman is lamenting the fact that women in the nineteenth century have few opportunities for self-expression. This moment is one of the most obvious examples of de Beauvoir's criticism. Catherine, and nineteenth century women in general, lack definition because they cannot take action. After this assertion Edward offers a "challenge" that they both go out on the balcony, a scandalous breach of the social contract, as they are both young and unmarried. When out on the balcony, Catherine suddenly reveals herself to be the vampire and turns on the young man. Edward stakes her, and his Watcher comes out to check on him, calling him "Miss Elizabeth." Edward/Elizabeth has avoided the issue of the restrictions put on women by society by passing as a man. As such, she is given more freedom and can more openly function as a slayer. While the Slayer of "Righteous" is punished for trying to be a warrior and a woman, Elizabeth more realistically abandons her gender in order to fulfill her mission and still operate within society.

Despite her attempts at hiding her femininity Elizabeth still seems to long for what she is missing. Though Edward/Elizabeth walks away with her watcher, the last few panels reveal a couple dancing and the ashes of the vampire Catherine being scattered in the breeze. The text above these says, "But while she lived, the assumptions of others protected her, as a coat thicker than cloth. Dreams and regrets dwell far beneath. And really ... who are we to guess at those?" (44). Here appears Elizabeth's regret at her inability to live as a woman. The image of a happy young blonde woman (Elizabeth is blonde) dancing with a handsome young man shows the reader the glimmer of a life that Elizabeth cannot have—not only because she is passing as a man, but because as the slayer she could never be a normal woman.

One of the final stories, "Nikki Goes Down!" takes place in the 1970s. The slayer, Nikki Wood, is a black woman in Harlem; she is on the margins of society but self-satisfied. The story opens with a "Harlem sunrise. Beautiful" (69). The first panel shows the slayer in bed with her boyfriend, Li. She lies in the bed, her hands clasped behind her head with her arms spread. Her posture gives a sense of ownership of the bed, the room and even the man that lies next to her. Li, on the other hand, is lying with the blankets tucked up to his neck and taking up as little space as possible. Li's position is typically associated with females; whereas, Nikki's posture is typically displayed by males in the media. Despite Nikki's masculine image, her femininity is still prominent. A string of pearls adorns her neck and the blanket barely covers her breasts, both small reminders that she is still a woman and is feminine.

Although the story opens on a joyous note, things quickly take a turn for the worst. Li is a cop and goes on a stakeout to bust a possible drug cartel led by a man named Le Banc. The slayer follows him because she knows that Le Banc is not smuggling drugs; instead, he is transporting monsters. She jumps into the fray, but she is unable to save Li. Craving revenge, she tracks down Le Banc and finds that "Le Banc's having a party" (76). In a witty quip worthy of the best superheroes she states, "So I wear pearls" (77). She intends to challenge a man who smuggles monsters, but in saying that she will dress up for his party, she is facing him on her terms. The image of her arriving is reminiscent of the image of the slayer in the first tale. Instead of a soft gown with masculine weapons, Nikki has her famous coat, tight jeans, and a low-cut, pastel tank top. Her large white earrings and exaggerated pearl necklace stand as unavoidable reminders of her brazen femininity. The centerpiece of this outfit, however, is the two stakes she wields in each black-gloved hand, an image of double-strong visual power.

The pearls in particular are a recurring image in the story. She wears them in bed, then while following Li on his stakeout, like a talisman of

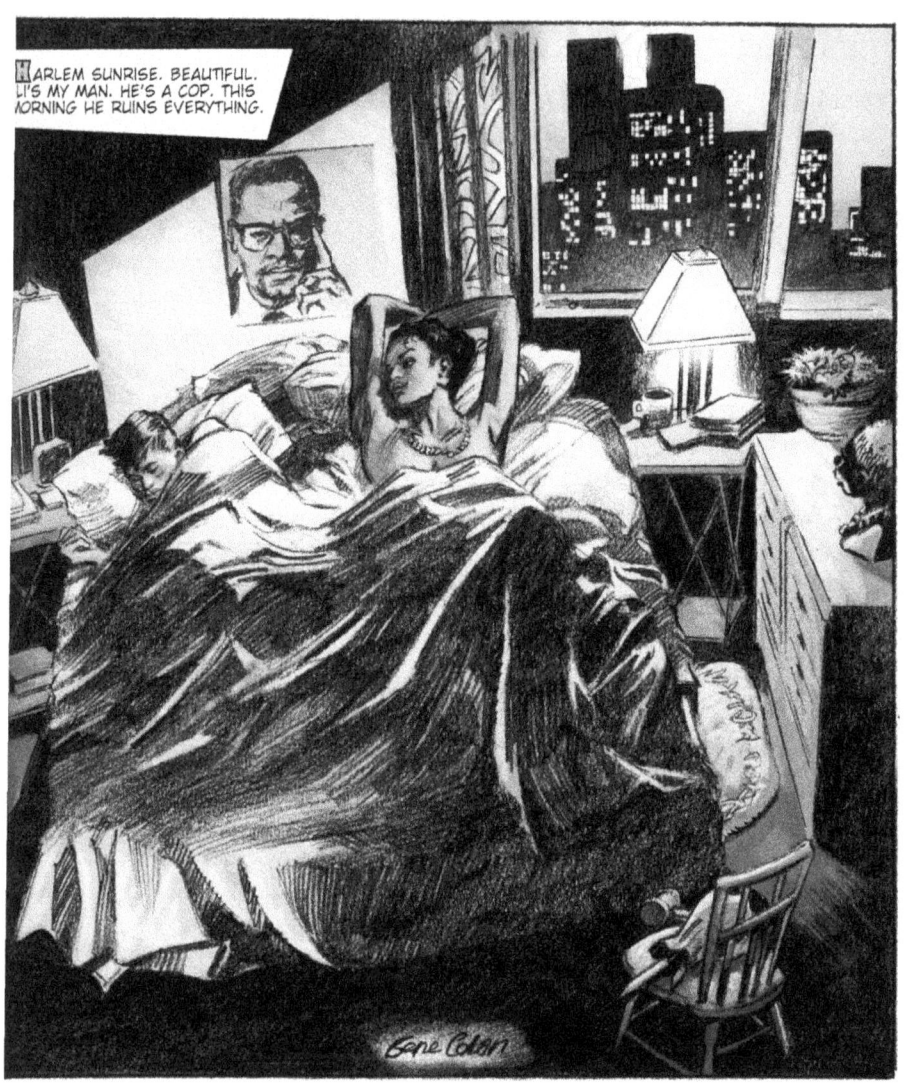

Nikki Wood lounges in bed with audacious, dominant posture. Doug Petrie (writer) and Gene Colan (penciller). "Nikki Goes Down" *Tales of the Slayers* (Buffy the Vampire Slayer). Milwaukie, OR: Dark Horse, 2002.

womanhood. "The pearl signifies humility, purity, innocence, and a retiring spirit," Jones notes in *History and Mystery of Precious Stones* as he describes the "modest splendor and purity of the jewel" (94, 113). Though this may not seem an appropriate description of Nikki, it does represent a trait from which most slayers are removed. Slayers are connected with creatures of the dark. Though slayers fight against evil, they cannot separate from it and, ultimately it becomes part of their identity. Slayers kill hundreds of vampires in their short lives and despite these creatures being considered unclean or impure the slayers seem to lose a bit of themselves through the act of slaying. Thus Slayers must give up their purity to act as saviors. The pearls' connection to purity and femininity is a way for slayers like Nikki to reclaim this lost trait. Furthermore, "pearls have for ages been significant for tears," making them especially significant for slayers (Jones 119). The life of a slayer is one saturated with loneliness and tragedy. Slayers die young and lose everyone they love along the way. In wearing these pearls Nikki is able to express her femininity and the sorrow of the life of a slayer.

Ultimately, it is these small talismans that save her. As she falls out of a window while fighting a giant bat, she uses the pearls as a form of weaponry. She fashions them into makeshift reins for the beast and triumphantly rides it. Because she is able to use this feminine necklace to harness the beast's power, a masculine action, she is not only able to survive but also defeat the creature.

Both the comics and the series emphasize that most slayers had lives before they were chosen to fulfill their destiny and step into the role of slayer. That being said, these women would have been shaped to have feminine characteristics appropriate to the societal norm before they were forced to take on masculine characteristics. Because of this, slayers for the most part do not forsake their femininity. Even Elizabeth, who passes as a man, still harbors desires that are considered feminine.

This theme is not just found in the comics, but is also prominent in the television series. Buffy consistently craves feminine activities. In the opening scene to the episode "Witch" (B1.3), Giles scolds Buffy for trying out for the cheerleading squad. Buffy is attempting to regain the girlish normalcy she had before becoming the slayer. In Season Two, she sneaks off to a frat party, then dresses as a noblewoman for Halloween. In Season Three, she tries out for Homecoming Queen, nostalgically recalling her triumphs as Prom Princess and Fiesta Queen before being chosen.

While Giles often scolds Buffy for attempting to live a life outside her position as the Slayer, Buffy also feels pressure from her friends. In "Helpless" Buffy explains that she will be meeting her dad for an ice-skating show. She feels the need to justify herself and tells her friends, "Look, I know you guys think it's just a big dumb girly thing, but it's not.... Okay, it's a big dumb girly thing, but I love it" (B3.12). It is not so much that Buffy states this is a girly thing, but the fact that she revels in it. Clearly, Buffy revels in her slayer power but also wishes to be able to partake in traditionally feminine activities.

Nikki Wood slays in a jumble of images, pearls flashing her feminine power. Doug Petrie (writer) and Gene Colan (penciller). "Nikki Goes Down" *Tales of the Slayers* (Buffy the Vampire Slayer). Milwaukie, OR: Dark Horse, 2002.

In the film and the first season ender "Prophecy Girl" (B1.12), Buffy's outfit mirrors that of the young slayer in "Righteous" but Buffy's outfit incorporates masculine elements. Both wear a flowing white dress and both hold their weapons at the ready, prepared for the fight ahead. Buffy, like Nikki, also dons a leather jacket; both the jacket and the stake are symbols of her masculinity that she carries with her as well as her femininity. Their combination represents "beautiful fragility wrapped in toughness" (Frankel 56). She knows masculinity will be respected and expected from her, but even while offering the appearance of strength, she will not remove herself from her femininity.

Through the slayers Whedon and his fellow writers are able to deconstruct the gender binary. Their slayers refuse to be either wholly masculine or wholly feminine, showing the fluidity of gender and allowing the reader/viewer to see how gender is constructed in society and how this construction does not work for everyone. The societal issues Buffy and the other slayers face are not all that different from those that women face today. Thus they show the reader how these issues impact women and allow them an opportunity to reflect how to remake the world, like Buffy and her friends do.

An earlier version of Traci J. Cohen's "'So I Wear Pearls': Exploring Gender in *Tales of the Slayers*" was previously presented at SC6: The Annual Slayage Conference on the Whedonverses. California State University-Sacramento. Sacramento, CA, June 19–22, 2014.

"There will be Others...Like me"
The Legacy of Otherness in Tales of the Slayers

Kristi Pope Key

• • •

Published by Dark Horse Comics in February 2002, the graphic novel *Tales of the Slayers* presented devotees of Joss Whedon's *Buffy the Vampire Slayer* with an additional insight into the mythology and history of the Slayer line. Produced by Whedon himself, *Tales of the Slayers* offers readers an opportunity to better understand the common experiences of the Slayers—the shared consciousness and powers to be sure—but also the social constraints under which these powerful young women labor.

For the purposes of this project, we may think about Otherness in terms of both W.E.B. DuBois' theory of "double consciousness," in which the subject always sees herself through the eyes of the majority, measuring herself against a cultural standard that doesn't fully recognize her, and in terms of the contemporary gender-based theories of de Beauvoir, Friedan, and Kristeva, among others, which suggests that patriarchal traditions default women to the status of Other in order to rationalize, justify and maintain the powers inherent in cultural dominance.

The idea of Otherness, as it relates to cultural commentary and literary textual analysis, allows for an exploration of the ways in which a member understands herself through the gaze of a culture that does not fully recognize her experiences as valid and worthwhile. Several of the chapters in *Tales of the Slayers* reflect the "Othered" experiences of the Slayer, ways in which society constrains her abilities, limits her options, and abuses her powers for its own, often nefarious, needs. The Slayer mythology in this collection serves as a series of confrontations with Otherness and Otherhood. Since the primary conceit of Whedon's Slayerverse is centered on female power, on women (and sometimes men) fighting the social demons of contemporary society, as has been indicated by Whedon himself, and any number of scholars and fans,[1] then it becomes clear that the Slayers in this narrative have been Othered because of their power. Additional tension in this book, and at times in the television series, derives from the Slayer's struggle with her alienation and her legacy at once. She, the Slayer, is both unique and a part of millennia of struggle. She is something radically different from her everyday world, and therefore Othered, and also something altogether expected and generic within her line.

The graphic novel in question, *Tales of the Slayers*, features eight "Tales," written by Joss Whedon, Amber Benson, Jane Espenson, David Fury, Rebecca Rand Kirshner, and Doug Petrie, names familiar to us all. Organized in chronological order of Tale—the stories begin with the First Slayer and work forward

The First Slayer learns she will always be alone. Joss Whedon (writer), Leinil Francis Yu and Dexter Vines (pencillers). "Prologue." *Tales of the Slayers* (Buffy the Vampire Slayer). Milwaukie, OR: Dark Horse, 2002.

through time, to end with Fray, Whedon's futuristic Slayer, first introduced in the 2001 Dark Horse comic book of the same name.

The opening tale, "Prologue" by Joss Whedon, begins with the words "I am alone." These words represent the thoughts of the First Slayer, Sineya. Fans of Buffyverse will likely recognize this phrase as indicative of a theme throughout the seven season run of the television series—the isolation and loneliness inherent to the life of the Slayer. In the opening pages, as the First Slayer, reflecting her name, slays the demon she's battling, she is interrupted by the presence of a girl from her village, sent by the elders to bring food, supplies, and the request that the Slayer leave. The village girl brings additional information about the Slayer's creation, including knowledge from the elders that the "Shadowmen made [Sineya] born with a demon inside" her that enables her to defeat the vampires, and that this is why the elders fear *her* and why they made only one Slayer. Finally the girl shares the last of her information: The news that when the First Slayer dies, then another girl will be chosen. As the First Slayer

Imitating her hero, a little girl turns warrior while disapproving elders look on. Joss Whedon (writer), and Tim Sale (penciller). "Righteous." *Tales of the Slayers* **(Buffy the Vampire Slayer). Milwaukie, OR: Dark Horse, 2002.**

walks away from the village of her origin, as she walks away from the girl who came with the gift of insight, Sineya's reaction is telling: "Others. The thought fills me with feelings I have to struggle to name. Confusion. Pity. Comfort. There will be Others ... Like me."

In the "Prologue" we see Sineya experience both social rejection from the patriarchy and empowerment in this meeting with the girl. Sineya is literally rejected by her community, in that the villagers, and most likely the male elders, fear her more than they do the vampires, yet she receives this valuable knowledge (the "Confusion. Pity. Comfort"), in this encounter with the gift-bearing girl. This, in essence, sets the stage for this edition of the slayer mythology: the slayer recognizes her isolation, must cope with communal, often patriarchal, rejection of her power and her presence, and may choose to mourn as well as take comfort in her legacy.

While none of the following stories are quite as overt in their use of the notion of Otherness, they nearly all follow a similar pattern. The next tale, also written by Whedon, entitled "Righteous," features a medieval setting and a young woman who slays an ancient vampire and saves her town from his scourge. However, when the young girl's actions begin to influence other, still younger girls in the town, the Church, a traditional symbol of patriarchal power—especially in the time frame in which this tale is set—turns on the Slayer. The village priest is clearly threatened by the Slayer's power: "A vampire is a heinous beast / But worse yet is a witch! / That girl has power like none before / Tis evil, by St. Paul / She walks with Darkness, Satan's whore / She's here to damn us all." (Yes, Whedon writes in rhymes.) She is accused of witchcraft, condemned, and burned at the stake. Part of the legacy suggested in both of these pieces is that while vampires and demons threaten society and social order, a larger threat is found in the woman who can not only battle but also defeat these supernatural forces. While Sineya is expelled from her village, the Slayer in "Righteous" pays a still higher price for her Slayer legacy.

Claudine, the Slayer featured in Amber Benson's tale "The Innocent," is exploited by her Watcher, Jean, for his own monstrous purposes. As Jean uses Claudine to kill nondemonic human aristocrats, set against the backdrop of the French Revolution, the Slayer is forced to recognize her manipulation at the hands of the man who is both her lover and her Watcher. When Claudine confronts Jean, he refers to her as his "angel of death." The character of Jean, the Watcher, functions as a twofold patriarchal representation of power. As an arm of the Watcher's Council, he represents the traditional patriarchy attempting to control the Slayer legacy—as was explored repeatedly in the television series and by many Whedon scholars.[2] Secondly, Jean functions as a governmental agent, one who would exploit the Slayer for political purposes, to ensure his ability to stay in power. While Claudine is neither banished nor murdered as a remnant of her Slayer legacy, she does articulate a crisis point in her fight against evil that balances on questions of whether she can believe in her own identity. Benson writes, "Evil just doesn't want to die. No matter how many times you try and kill it. The more you try, the more you see it all around you. In the faces of everyone—the people you love, the people you trust ... in your own reflection.... How do you fight that?" Benson leaves the Slayer washing her bloody hands in the river, effectively crushed beneath the weight of her own actions. Claudine is still alive, but she is Watcher-less, and lover-less, and alone.

The next tale, "Presumption," by Jane Espenson is a Jane Austen inspired parlor trick of verbal irony and social expectations. The story turns on our trust of Espenson's narrator who leads us into our own "presumptions" about gender and monstrosity. Espenson's characters dance about a formal party and verbally thrust and parry at one another about the lives of ladies and gentlemen. The reader presumes that the male figure, Edward, is the predator; however, Espenson turns that expectation on its head, when the female Catherine transforms into the monstrous vampire on the terrace. As Edward slays the creature and flees the scene, the tale's narrator explains:

> The life of a lady offers many limitations ... those limitations were why the Slayer had given up the life of a woman years before. To live as a free woman Miss Elizabeth Weston has to live as a man. I will not say she lived forever nor even long, but while she lived, the assumptions of others protected her as a coat thicker than cloth.

This tale offers commentary on gender assumptions, questions about the social gaze, and the ways in which women adjust their own exterior selves in order to be successful in the world—and it does so all in the context of a slayer/vampire relationship.

At this point the reader has encountered Slayers Othered by their society in the first three stories—one banished, one murdered, and one turned murderer. Espenson's creation centers on Othering by choice; because her world does not readily accept the Slayer legacy, Edward/Elizabeth takes on the guise of a gentleman in order to gain entry to the monstrosities in the society. In the form of Edward, the Slayer points out, "I don't like being the object of scrutiny. It is uncomfortable." In true Austenian form, Espenson ironically situates her female male Slayer under the gaze of the community and allows her/him to verbalize her dislike of that gaze. What Espenson also offers is an intact Watcher relationship at the end of the tale—the first we've seen in the collection. So we may Presume, to play with Espenson's own language, that when the Slayer chooses to gender bend in order for her protection and in order to complete her task, then the patriarchal Watcher system approves or is at least complicit in this act. Becoming a male action hero rather than a female one is blessed by the men in power.

The next tale, David Fury's "The Glittering World," offers a fascinating look into the Slayer legacy as akin to the experiences of a biracial Otherness. Set in the American West, the story features a Navaho Slayer, whose legend created the actual Navaho origin myth of Monster Slayer (notably a male). As the Slayer pursues and then battles a particularly troubling vampire—another native girl who has killed the Slayer's Watcher—the reader is invited to connect the experience of being the Slayer to that of being Othered by one's race. The vampire explains that her father was a white cavalry officer who dammed her "to never feel a part of either world … never belonging … but then you, of all, know how that feels, don't you, little slayer?" As the Slayer and the vampire fight, both are blooded, and as the Slayer stakes the vampire with her broken bow, she cradles the vampire in her arms until she catches fire from the sunrise. These panels reflect a connection between monster and Slayer, between the Otherness of the figures—not just as enemies, but as those for whom society holds no home, no place of comfort. The vampire indicates that she's become a monster specifically because she has no belonging, no place in the glittering world. It's worth noting that this Slayer rides off into the sunrise, not the sunset, with what appears to be a mortal wound from her battle with the Navaho vampire. Metaphorically and literally, the other mixed-blood woman's plight has struck her to the core. Additionally, Fury presents this chapter through a frame narrative which is only revealed in the final three frames. This Slayer's story is being related through the voice of a Catholic priest who is explaining local lore to an interested white man, the future mayor of Sunnydale, Richard Wilkins. As has been noted earlier, the story of the Slayer is often conflated by the narratives of the Church and the State, both symbols of traditional patriarchy and both wary of female power or legacy as represented in the form of the Slayer.

Rebecca Rand Kirshner's "Sonnenblume," set in Nazi Germany, continues to build upon ideas about social expectations for young girls and social responsibilities for the Slayer. The protagonist, young Sonnenblume (German for sunflower), is a member of the Nazi Youth Party and confronts in her own family the changing attitudes towards the Jewish community in her neighborhood. Sonnenblume explains, "Being alone can be scary. And sometimes I want to be just like everyone else. But I'm not like everyone else." As Kirshner's narrative unfolds, once again the Slayer makes observations about her society's expectations for her, her Watcher's expectations for her, and her responsibility for her own powers. She attempts to conform, but as a slayer and independent thinker, she cannot. The final panels of the tale center on Sonnenblume declaring her understanding of her duty to fight evil, she says, "because I can't be like everyone else." The Othered aspects of this narrative are built on the Slayer coming to understand her own difference in the face of a society that requires uniformity. In a connected conclusion, Sonnenblume embraces the fact that responsibility for her community is an aspect of her Slayer legacy, as may be seen in her willingness to physically strike out against the patriarchal Nazi officials while moving to protect her Othered Jewish neighbors.

"Nikki Goes Down," the next to last narrative in the collection, offers the least amount of social and cultural commentary of all the *Tales*. Written by Doug Petrie, this is Nikki Wood's story. Nikki Wood, the African American Slayer, mother to Robin Wood of Seasons Seven and Eight, was murdered by Spike in a New York subway as seen in "Fool for Love" (B5.7). While the pacing and artwork of this tale are compelling, what is, perhaps, most interesting here is the thematic break with the previous six tales. There's no clear reference to the burden of the Slayer legacy or to sexual/gender politics on either a personal or larger social scale. The reader is, generally, unable to extract any conditions of the Othering or Othered impulse that is found in the remainder of the book. This lack must be considered significant. Nikki, as an African American character, already represents the Other and the experiences of the Othered figure in American society. It's not that that her Slayer legacy doesn't also come with burdens and responses to social expectations, but rather that these aspects are doubled in the face of her racial experiences. Perhaps Nikki bears the weight of the Slayer legacy with greater efficiency than the previous Slayers because of her racial status as minority in majority-controlled society. Perhaps she's already reconciled herself to her Othered status, long before she became a Slayer.

The final narrative is authored, once again, by Whedon. "Tales" is the futuristic bookend to the ancient "Prologue" which opens the collection. In it, Melaka Fray discovers of a library containing Watcher's diaries. As she pores over the books, the Slayer connects to the legacy of her situation for the first time. As can be seen in issues #1–8 of *Fray*, Melaka was born with the physical abilities of the Slayer but with none of the memories and instinctual knowledge of the line. As such, she has a gaping separation not only from those around her but from the Slayer line itself. The library offers her a refuge, and by the events of *Time of Your Life* (B8.4) a home. The final words of the book echo the themes introduced in "Prologue": "I am the only one in the world ... but I am not alone."

We can understand the Slayer mythology in this collection as a series of confrontations with Otherness and Otherhood. The Slayers in this narrative have been Othered because of their power—fighting the social and cultural demons faced most often by young women—emphasizing that that struggle is an Othering Act. To pick up an earlier thread, part of the legacy suggested in this narrative is that while vampires are a threat to humanity, a larger threat is found in the woman who can address that. In this narrative, society (read: patriarchal society) is more comfortable with the vampire than with the Slayer, a theme also explored by the television series in which the police attempt to arrest Buffy, assist the demonic Mayor, and lock Faith away for decades. Because any textual conversation about mythology is invited to feature Joseph Campbell—at least a little bit—I'd like to offer this from him. Campbell suggests, "It is not the society that is to guide and save the creative hero, but precisely the reverse. And so every one of us shares the supreme ordeal ... not in the tribe's great victories, but in the silences of his personal despair" (337). In reviewing the Slayer legacy in this text, Whedon and his colleagues have offered us a great deal more of the "personal despair" mentioned by Campbell, than they have of the "great victories." Rather than celebrating the physical accomplishments of these Slayers, these tales have regularly explored issues of isolation, manipulation, and social condemnation as a result of our heroines' actions in battling elemental monstrosities and evils. The reader is reminded that the Slayer legacy offers more burden than celebration and that choosing to do "good" in the face of ongoing evil is neither an easy nor a safe choice. Our Slayers battle not just demons and monsters, but also patriarchy and social mores which privilege traditional notions of power and strength.

The additional tension in this book, and at times in the television series, is the Slayer's struggle with Alone-ness and the Legacy at once. She, the Slayer, is both unique and a part of a centuries-old legacy. In order to understand this tension, in order to balance this mindset, the characters must balance their own altered states and abjection. In "Choices" (B3.19), Wesley says to Buffy, "But you're a Slayer!" when she's discussing leaving town for college—essentially changing identities. Buffy replies, "Yeah, I'm also a person. You can't just define me by my Slayerness. That's—something-ism." Certainly, there's no way to know whether or not Whedon had that bit of dialogue in mind when he edited this comic book, but it seems appropriate to consider that the *Tales of the Slayers* center just as much on their personhood as on their Slayerness ... and that is a something-ism.

Notes

1. See Gerard Jones, "Vampire Slayers," *Killing Monsters: Why Children Need Fantasy, Super Heroes, and Make-Believe Violence (*New York: Basic, 2002), 149–164; Tracy Little, "High School Is Hell: Metaphor Made Literal," *Buffy the Vampire Slayer and Philosophy: Fear and Trembling in Sunnydale,* James B. South, ed (La Salle, IL: Open Court, 2003). 282–293; Rhonda V. Wilcox, "'There Will Never Be a 'Very Special' Buffy': Symbol and Language," *Why Buffy Matters: The Art of Buffy the Vampire Slayer* (London: I. B. Tauris, 2005), 17–29.

2. Holly Chandler, "Slaying the Patriarchy: Transfusions of the Vampire Metaphor in BtVS," *Slayage: The Online International Journal of Buffy Studies* 3.1 (August 2003); Kevin K. Durand, "The Battle Against the Patriarchal Forces of Darkness," *Buffy Meets the Academy: Essays on the Episodes and Scripts as Texts*, ed. Kevin K. Durand (Jefferson, NC: McFarland, 2009), 176–184.

An earlier version of Kristi Pope Key's "'There Will Be Others Like Me': The Legacy of Otherness in *Tales of the Slayers*" was previously presented at the Popular Culture Association in the South/American Culture Association in the South Conference. Jacksonville, Florida, September 2007.

Part Four

Firefly

• • •

Whedon's beloved scifi-western *Firefly* follows the misfit crew of the Firefly class ship Serenity as they take on semi-legal jobs on the ragged frontier of terraformed space. It boasts a large crew of misfits—Captain Malcolm Reynolds, once a soldier for the Browncoat rebellion against the alliance. His tough lieutenant Zoe and her goofy husband Wash, the pilot. Sweet lovable Kaylee Frye, and irreverent powerhouse Jayne Cobb. Beautiful Inara Serra, a high-status sex worker. In the first episode, the mysterious preacher Shepherd Book joins, along with Doctor Simon Tam and his genetically altered sister River, on the run from the Alliance.

Firefly lasted a single season, followed by the film *Serenity*, then several short comic runs. Both film and comics continue to question and subvert concepts like gender roles and individualism. *Those Left Behind* by Joss Whedon and Brett Matthews bridges between show and film, while *Better Days and Other Stories* is an anthology of short misadventures. Finally, *The Shepherd's Tale* by Joss and Zack Whedon offers a flashback of Book's life, told in reverse order. Following his Free Comic Book Day release "It's Never Easy," Zack Whedon took over production on a multi-part sequel to the film called *Serenity: Leaves on the Wind* (2014). On the run from the Alliance, Mal and his crew make new friends and are invited to lead the revolution even as they struggle to protect their own.

Thalia M. Mulvihill and Christina L. Blanch tackle *Firefly* for this collection, in "Do *Serenity* Comics Forecast Our Pedagogies of Identity Construction?" It shows off how themes of identity in each book—marginalization, religion, and gender construction—can be used to teach vital analysis of identity construction in the college environment. In the *X-Men* section, Melissa C. Johnson explores River Tam's origin in "River is Wolverine: Whedon Performs a Sex-Change," with some examination of *Leaves on the Wind*.

Do *Serenity* Comics Forecast Our Pedagogies of Identity Construction?

THALIA M. MULVIHILL and
CHRISTINA L. BLANCH

• • •

> If you look at your life as a chain of events, each responsible for the next and caused by the last, where does any story begin?—Shepherd Book, *Serenity: The Shepherd's Tale*

Teaching college students about identity construction from an intersectionality theoretical vantage point is aided by popular culture treatments portraying characters encountering the complexity of identity in the midst of human variety. Characters such as those presented in Joss Whedon's *Serenity* Trilogy (2007, 2008, 2010) and most recently *Leaves on the Wind* (2014) provide fertile ground from which professors in many disciplines can engage students in higher order cognitive thinking about human diversity. For example, when college students grapple with the inherent contradictions of the human condition juxtaposed with the characters presented theoretically or mythically within Whedon's work, new questions can be brought forward for examination.

Bloom's Taxonomy of Educational Objectives and the revised version can serve as an effective tool to help classify and arrange the types of learning desired. An interactive graphic developed by the University of Iowa provides a wonderful introduction to the integrated concepts comprising the taxonomy.[1] Tools such as those related to Bloom's Taxonomy can assist educators as they make a case for the innovative pedagogies that involve the use of comics in general, and the use of Whedon's work in particular, to help focus learning experiences around examining the cultural construction of identity.

To understand and apply new learning, one can imagine him- or herself being or knowing the fictional characters. When readers experience the created universe in *Serenity*, for example, they are confronted with making sense of their own social realities as they interpret the social realities presented to them by Whedon and his creative team of writers and illustrators.

The universe of *Serenity* was created for a short-lived television series followed with a movie, both created by Joss Whedon. While his work is often touted for its gender messages, his stories are also full of social issues that reveal the intersectionality of identity constructions. Through an analysis of his trilogy of *Serenity* graphic novels, *Those Left Behind, Better Days*, and *The Shepherd's Tale*, as well as *Leaves on the Wind* from 2014, this chapter examines how his treatment of current social issues as futuristic resonate with readers here in the present and offer educators unique possibilities for theorizing identity issues within university settings.

The universe in *Firefly*, or as they call it, the 'Verse, is all about humans, no aliens per se, and how they are expanding and exploring the rest of the galaxy. It also explores how those humans interact, what ethics they bring with them, modify, and create, and how much chaos they fabricate in the farthest reaches of space (Battis, "Captain Tightpants").

The comic books, which followed the television series and movie, continued the adventures of the crew. The first was *Serenity: Those Left Behind* in 2007. The story is by Joss Whedon and Brett Matthews, with Brett Matthews writing the actual script. The art is by Will Conrad with colors by Laura Martin and lettering by Michael Heisler. In this story, the team continues their quest for work and continues to bond as family.

Those Left Behind was followed in 2008 with *Serenity: Better Days and Other Stories*. This is a collection by different authors, including "Better Days" written by Joss Whedon and Brett Matthews (art by Will Conrad, colors by Michelle Madsen, and lettering by Michael Heisler). Other stories include "The Other Half" written by Jim Krueger, "Downtime" written by Zack Whedon, and "Float Out" by Patton Oswalt, though only the Joss Whedon story, "Better Days," will be analyzed here.

The final book in the series was *Serenity: The Shepherd's Tale* in 2010. Penned by Joss and Zack Whedon, with art by Chris Samnee, colors by Dave Stewart, and lettering by Michael Heisler, it reveals the backstory of Shepherd Book, a much loved character of the television series whose past was shrouded in mystery.

Afterward, Zack Whedon took over the comics, beginning with the one-shot "Serenity: Firefly Class 03-K64—It's Never Easy" drawn by Fábio Moon and released by Dark Horse Comics on May 5, 2012 for Free Comic Book Day. Through 2014, he wrote a six-part miniseries continuation comic called *Leaves on the Wind,* drawn by Georges Jeanty, which follows the start of the New Rebellion after the events of the *Serenity* film.

Marginalization

Encouraging students to engage in deeper discussions about social issues requires an advanced set of facilitation skills by faculty who are willing and able to artfully weave together the narratives under investigation with the lived experiences of the students in the classroom.

For example, some questions or prompts educators can use to help facilitate discussions of this nature that will lead to more nuanced understandings of the intersectional dimensions of identity development and identity display follow: How can students from different classes, religions, or ethnicities relate to each other? Are there similarities with which they can interact when they believe nothing in common exists between them? Can becoming aware of intersectionalities create a sense of camaraderie even though they are different? Can establishing difference yet understanding each other put them on the same side?

Whedon's work is especially intriguing because it prompts the students to not only contain their discussions in the present but to also imagine a series of future possibilities. Using popular culture to teach about identity allows for more dynamic discussions regarding the cultural codes embedded within comics and provides a space to investigate the interplay of masculine dominance and female subjugation (O'Brien and Sizeman 91). For example, students can try to understand from where the parameters come of what constitutes masculine and feminine or how marginalization contributes to character formation. Using the characters to discuss possibilities opens the conversations and lets students talk about others, then slowly realize they are discussing themselves.

While there are many more social issues considered in the television episodes and movie, such as medical testing on the Reavers and River, drug smuggling, and different forms of government involvement, a few unique concerns emerge specifically within the comic books, particularly inequality, religion and gender.

In the 'Verse, the Core planets represent comfort and safety. The people there are privileged, with money and power. The Rim planets, by contrast, represent adaptation and freedom (Buckman, "Wheel Never Stops Turning" 174). However, that freedom carries a price, which is continual change and fighting, and a struggle to survive. As mentioned in *Those Left Behind*, resources are strained on the outer planets and people are much poorer. The prologue explains:

> After the War, many of the Independents who had fought and lost drifted to the edges of the system, far from Alliance control. Out here, people struggled to get by with the most basic technologies; a ship would bring you work, a gun would help you keep it. A captain's goal was simple: find a crew, find a job, keep flying.

The comic opens with the Serenity crew trapped in a standoff with another gang of thieves. Ott demands the cash, and Mal agrees to protect his crew. However, when Ott demands Mal's gun as well, he flatly refuses. On the frontier, Mal's gun is almost his only possession. As Mal notes, his gun was one of two things that got him through the war, and stuck with him afterward (the other being Zoe). Mal drops it, but only to kick it into Ott's face and start a brawl. Ott and his team get away with the money, only after notifying the entire town of the heist. The townspeople give chase, labeling Mal and his friends as villains though they have technically done nothing. In this scene, the Serenity crew are closer to the margins of life than usual—considered the robbers of the town, not the Robin Hoods.

When Mal points out to Book that he has become an untrustworthy criminal as well, as he provided the distraction, "borrowed" a getaway vehicle, and did "what needs to be done to survive," Book punches Mal in the face. They later find an uneasy truce on the subject:

> **MAL**: Look, Shepherd, I'll make this plain... it don't matter to me that you hit me.
> **BOOK**: Which is exactly why I need to be away from you. Because sooner or later, it won't matter to me, either.

Book is increasingly uncomfortable with the criminal life, as this single punch reveals to himself. He feels marginalized as a criminal but also if he goes straight. Finally, Book and Inara each leave the ship, emphasizing that they have had enough of the ragtag life. Sometimes knowing how badly one fits in certain places can lead him or her to a true home.

Other ostracized characters include Badger, who sends them on a risky job, and Dobson, waiting to entrap the team. Dobson, now a cyborg, quips sarcastically, "The pound of metal grafted to my face is purely cosmetic ... you made me a freak." Mal retorts that he was one already (*Those Left*

Behind). It is River, the biggest misfit of all, who saves them by sensing the danger. The team escapes, heading off to new adventures on the fringes of society.

> Since 9/11 Western law has become particularly aware of the outlaw who feels justified in breaking the law. They are terrorists, and there is a tidy sub-story to the "Better Days" comic that has an Alliance special ops officer hunting down Mal as a "Dust Devil," the colloquial name for Independent military personnel who kept fighting after the end of the war [Tranter 287].

The Alliance soldiers set out after Dust Devils, insisting, "Remember that the war is not over until every last one is hunted down and executed" ("Better Days"). In fact, it's not Mal who's the Dust Devil. Respectable, straight-arrow Zoe is hunted, and her criminal status is revealed. The Serenity crew are no longer threats to the Alliance and the Dust Devil past is "ancient history" as Zoe calls it. Nonetheless, she's suddenly a feared criminal.

The Shepherd's Tale follows Book as an abused child, resistance member, and Alliance commander, as he transforms from outsider to insider on a "meteoric" rise. Nonetheless, he stays distant, as he volunteers for a lifelong undercover mission, leaving his allies to live among the enemy. Finally thrown out of the military, he travels from world to world, drunk and alone, lost on the fringes of society. At last, he finds a home among the Shepherds, then other homes on Serenity then Haven.

"Serenity: Firefly Class 03-K64—It's Never Easy" begins with Zoe, heavily pregnant, emphasizing that Mal shouldn't call her advanced pregnancy a "delicate state" or leave her out of missions. In fact, he's leaving himself out, since his last trip to town involved "shooting the locals." She and the crew leave, and Mal is left alone with the ship.

An elderly prospector named Frosty arrives and comments that he used to own a similar ship to Serenity, suggesting he's fallen on hard times. When he pulls a gun on Mal, demanding the ship, Mal retorts as he did with his gun in *Those Left Behind*: "Serenity here is all that's mine…If you want her as yours you'll have to kill me first." The ship is his only means of livelihood but also nearly his only possession.

The criminal life that has left Mal struggling on society's edge has also equipped him to handle the situation, as he adds, "I been on the wrong end of violence many times and always came out standing." Frosty declines to change his mind and shoots, but River, forgotten back on the ship, once more saves the day, plunging from the sky to throttle the enemy. Her reward? Having Simon run up and demand whether she shot the captain.

Like *Those Left Behind*, "It's Never Easy" emphasizes Mal and his crew's barely managing to subsist, as both times they fall into competition with fellow thieves on the outskirts of society. Though they lose the payout, Mal manages to keep his gun, his ship, and his crew—the bare minimum to survive.

Leaves on the Wind introduces our heroes on the run from the Alliance, now branded as terrorists. As they drift "not anywhere," their physical position reflects their ostracization. They are indeed "leaves on the wind," pushed about by outside forces. Meanwhile, they are censured on all the news channels for broadcasting the truth of Miranda. One inflammatory political commentator insists:

> You've got every whimpering Browncoat with access to the cortex claiming responsibility, but you take one look at those deadbeats and you know it can't be true.... Whoever caused this unrest needs to answer for the actions. These people need to stand before us. But do they? No. They're nowhere to be found [#1].

At the same time, the New Rebellion is beginning, as its champion, Bea, determines to track down Mal to be their new leader. The commentators describe the rebels varyingly as "activists," "terrorists," "rioters" and "criminals"—all but the first terms of blistering condemnation by those in authority. Mal resists Bea's entreaties, preferring a life in the shadows to one leading a war. However, with Zoe's future at stake, he's compelled to take the first steps.

A third group of outcasts appears as River discovers that there are many young women like her, all trapped and desperate for rescue. When they save one, called Iris, River reveals that her modifications have been completed, to the point at which "she doesn't know she used to be a person" (#6). Though River feels unwanted on the ship at times as well as disassociated ("Objects in Space," F1.14), she has never been reduced to this state. When Iris has recovered a bit, she proclaims a desire to go out into the 'Verse and "make them pay for what they did to me." Bea, who lost her father in Serenity Valley, feels the same. Thus the misfits will someday remake the world.

Religion in *The Shepherd's Tale*

It is mentioned in *Those Left Behind* that the religion of Buddhism prevails, there is 94% literacy, the average life span is 120 years, and social mores have evolved, so religion is still a very important social issue. However, Book defines the frontier as a world untouched by *His* hand (*The Shepherd's Tale*), emphasizing his religious journey into the wilderness.

Here, we learn the backstory of Shepherd Book. He tells how he found faith along with family in odd places (5). He tries to spread his faith to his Serenity family as seen in his encounter with Jayne. When he mentions to Jayne that God is putting him on the list of hell bound, this takes Jayne by surprise. Throughout the stories in *Serenity*, Jayne robs, steals, murders, and as he says lies "down with whore from time to time ... and that's not near as often as I'd like" (6). Jayne asks him to pray for him, to which Book replies he already has indicating that religion is always on his mind and motivating him to think of others. In this story, having religion even makes water taste better, as Kaylee points out, seeing the Shepherd reverently enjoy a glass and call it "life's foundation and its fuel" (8).

The book reveals that Shepherd was not always good but he found his calling in a bowl of chicken soup (16). Staring into it, Book reflects on the sacrifice of the animal, the simplicity of its existence, the design of the bowl, the physics of the planet and the purity of the universe in which all these things exist. "The universe. Existence. All of creation supports this bowl. Which supports the soup. Which supports me. It gives me life." While wondering at the way he's chosen to use his gifts, he rises from the table a religious man and devotes his life to aiding others. The reader finds that Shepherd is quite lost when he enters the church. As he feels it's time to rejoin the world, leaving the church where he could feel the presence of God, he says the prayer of Saint Francis and leaves it in His hands as to where he goes (11–12). That leads him to the ship, Serenity.

Once he boards the ship in the pilot, he and Mal find themselves constantly at odds. Mal is the atheist, noting, "If I'm your mission, Shepherd, best give it up. You're welcome on my boat. God ain't" ("The Train Job," F1.2). Book, however, remains open to compromise, noting for instance that God is vague about the morality of shooting people's kneecaps. Dying in the film, he tells Mal that faith is important, but not faith in God, adding, "It doesn't matter what you believe in. As long as you believe." The rigid true believer, the Operative, is the one discredited. As it turns out, organized religion is proved corrupt in the film: "Whedon changes the traditional terms of the myth: In *Serenity*, a world without sin is shown to be a world of death" (Wilcox, "I Don't Hold to That" 159).

The religious discourse on Serenity is fervent and opinionated, yet respectful. As such, it provides an opportunity for educators to explore the possibilities and the limitations of the concept of pluralism and what impact a pluralistic society may have on individual identity development. The Shepherd's complex journey reminds readers that religious leaders are, above all, human, all questing to discover the true path.

Gender Contrasts in "Better Days"

Gender is not about male and female but about the characteristics of masculinity, femininity, and androgyny (Udry). This can include the state of being male, female, or intersex and the ideas in a culture of what it means to be masculine or feminine. Exploring the paradigms onboard Serenity offers a study of archetypes such as Second Wave and Third Wave feminism, as well as the chance to engage in meaningful dialogue about how people with different gender patterns are treated. While iconic masculinity involves power, strength, and protective abilities, femininity usually concerns itself with appearance, nurture, and subservience. Most students do not realize the different attributes that can be assigned to both masculinity and femininity, so Whedon's work provides a clear example of various conventional, exaggerated, and nonconformist gender dynamics.

Joss Whedon has been praised for his representations of women from Buffy to the Black Widow (Amy-Chinn 1). In the 'Verse of *Serenity*, this is no different, with a spectrum of radically contrasting archetypes. What is neglected in scholarship is that he also writes masculinity from this perspective: The men on board Serenity vary widely within the spectrum of what is considered masculine. The male members of the Serenity family consist of Captain Mal, whom most people would consider the epitome of masculinity with a touch of sensitivity; Jayne, who could be classified as a "man's man"—very gruff, muscular, with a gun fetish and a yearning to be in power; Doctor Simon Tam, the least masculine of the group; Shepherd Book, the mysterious preacher; and finally Wash, Zoe's husband, who is portrayed as very childlike with his dinosaur figures. As the crew strike it rich and describe their deep fantasies of success while relaxing at a luxury hotel, the comic "Better Days" exaggerates their gender roles.

The entire concept of book-smart not being masculine is shown with Simon Tam. He is generally dismissed as a participant in their gun-toting heists, until his identification of the fine art they're stealing comes in handy ("Better Days" 11). Following this, the thuggish Jayne asks the doctor for advice on how to engage a companion through being refined and charming. He adds, "I know that if there was whores on this rock I wouldn't be wasting my time learning sissy talk from you!" (44), indicating that he does not really respect the doctor or women with power. Simon's great fantasy, revealed in the comic, is of returning to Osiris and practicing medicine with River beside him, though he admits he also enjoys traveling. He's still a civilized rich kid at heart, still part of the luxurious inner worlds rather than the rugged frontier.

Jayne of course is portrayed as very masculine, with muscles flexing, chewing on a cigar while he fires two machines guns out of the back of a truck (15). In a fantasy sequence, he is the captain of the "Radiant Cobb" and is even referred to as "his manliness" by the crew (33). His only visible crew member is young and female, and apparently afterward, Kaylee shows up in the fantasy, along with a shower scene. Throughout the stories he is seen as a womanizer, only wanting women for sex and to command. He is also portrayed as dumb—while stealing the fine art, he admires an ashtray, declaring how rich he will be, while the others laugh at him (10–11). His fantasy only provokes more humor.

Captain Mal is very masculine like Jayne, but with compassion and smarts. Nonetheless, he cross-dresses in "Our Mrs. Reynolds" (F1.6) and as a "very graceful" companion in the *Serenity* movie.

> **JAYNE**: I married me a powerful ugly creature.
> **MAL**: [dressed as Jayne's wife to lure bandits] How can you say that? How can you shame me in front of new people? [F1.6].

Like a child on a playground who is mean to the girl he likes, he calls Inara a whore, but is in love with her. She in turn may know Mal better than anyone, and she tells him when he seems selfish, he is really doing things for other people, which is sweet (79). His gruffness is little more than façade. In fact, he doesn't dream of a different life, but of the one he's living.

Wash, Zoe's husband, is the only married man on Serenity. Childlike, he is usually bossed around by his wife. He is a little jealous of Zoe and Captain Mal's relationship, seen in the episode "War Stories" (F1.10) and in "Better Days" when Zoe offers herself up as bait to save the Captain (63). In the end, he just wants to be her partner. His fantasy is very telling as it's quite domesticated: He, Zoe, and their children fly on their own luxury cruiser "you could land a *planet* on" as a little family unit. She also appears in very feminine clothing complete with sky blue floor-length skirt when presenting their child to him. While Zoe sees herself in utilitarian clothes, her husband dreams of her being feminine and playing the dutiful wife and mother, a view prevalent in our society.

The final male on the ship is Shepherd Book. He is a man of God and so is seen as not quite as masculine as someone like Mal or Jayne. However, he is seen lifting weights in *The Shepherd's Tale* (6) and saves the whole crew from sure death in *Those Left Behind* (12). His "Better Days" fantasy is shockingly, intensely masculine, with gambling, hookers, alcohol, a gun, and a cigar, but he subverts this by revealing to the shocked crew that he was "kidding." As revealed in *The Shepherd's Tale,* he was once a thug, a rebel, and an Alliance commander. Though he behaves mores subtly while on Serenity, his fantasy emphasizes a harder edge below the surface.

Western values would judge the female crew of the Serenity in different ways. Zoe is a tough-as-nails fighter and usually the voice of reason on most of the crew's missions. She appears throughout the comics dressed as the men are, usually in a shirt, pants, boots, and her gun. Kaylee is the ship's mechanical genius, yet she is still a gullible and sweet girl. She dresses as one would picture a mechanic but wants to be more girly. River, feminine, sensitive, and volatile, appears in different clothes in every story—generally simple short dresses of innocent green or blue. In one full-length scene, she wears a slouchy pink sweater and long patterned skirt, indicating she dresses for herself and not for others. By contrast, Inara, who views life as performance, always appears in beautifully exotic draping skirts and tight tops with perfect makeup. Nonetheless, her skills include the less feminine fencing, archery, and incendiary devices, as seen through the show.

In her own dream sequence, Kaylee describes opening a "little shop for my daddy and me" (*Better Days* 47). However, the pictures tell a more subversive story. The shop itself is an enormous factory. Then, through her innocuous language about getting machines to work properly and "really get 'em hummin,'" Simon appears, bringing her flowers and then engaging in a steamy sex scene. This shows many times women say what they think they should, but crave something beyond the boundaries of politeness. Kaylee has a crush on the doctor but thinks she is not feminine enough to have him as her beau.

River is arguably the most androgynous of the entire group as she appears too childlike for a relationship. While the other women luxuriate in an enormous tub, bosoms only concealed by steam, she's submerged nearly up to her nostrils. She dresses however she likes, but when she dreams of what she wants she wears a fancy purple ballgown surrounding by fanciful creatures from a giant fish in a tuxedo to a frog in a band hat, flower fairies, a dragon, and a distant castle (48). Hers is a safe fantasy—romantic but nonsexual, in a world of talking animal friends.

After hearing this, the tough Zoe quips that now her own dream is taken, suggesting she, like Kaylee, may crave something softer and more romantic than her exterior suggests or more likely, she is being sarcastic. However, as Wash is the one to imagine their future together, she is cast as the mystery figure of the story, adding a further touch of femininity to her character.

Inara has no fantasy to offer. Amy-Chinn notes that "the excessive performance of femininity is often seen as a trope of post-feminism ... performed purely for the benefit of the performer." Thus, alone with the crew, Inara offers no sexy enticing stories but merely exists, happy to be on the ship among friends. Like Mal, she doesn't dream of wealth but adventure and a surrogate family.

On the ship, the two females with the most masculine traits seem to have equal power relationships with the male crew members, especially Zoe who draws from second wave feminist discourse while Kaylee draws from the third wave. But, as McRobbie states, most women must renounce their femininity to be seen as equal (166). River is discounted as crazy yet in reality is the most powerful of all. Finally, due to her job as a companion, Inara has less power on the ship itself, but more power in society.

Masculine and feminine are not static categories but change not only through time, but also space. Power is not always masculine and caring is not always feminine. What students will realize through the *Serenity* comic books is that identity has nothing to do with ascribed gender descriptions. Women can be what is termed masculine and vice versa. Meanwhile, even the tough Jayne and Mal have soft sides.

Inara and Prostitution

Gender roles and their subversion is a major theme in the *Serenity* comic books as Inara is a companion. As Simon reminds Jayne, a companion is different from the common sex workers in brothels on the outer rim planets: "Engaging a companion isn't about sex for money. There's no shortage of men willing to offer that, and so the process is more formal and selective. They're not whores" ("Better Days" 44).

Inara is in charge of whom she engages as a companion, yet is still seen as subservient and providing a service. In "Better Days" (22–23) she is portrayed making love to a client, all with beautiful clothes, perfect hair, perfect makeup, perfect manners, etc. She also fixes a nerve cluster in her client's back. As on the show, everything she does is for his pleasure.

Is prostitution by companions then seen as empowering or as patriarchal? Kesler calls prostitution the "absolute embodiment of male patriarchal privilege" (219). However, Inara is the most respectable passenger or crewmember on the ship. That noted, it does not stop Captain Mal from calling her a whore on many different occasions and even calls her time on a nice planet a "working vacation" ("Better Days" 37). Some may describe Inara as a powerful, postfeminist prostitute as she chooses her clients, while others may argue the opposite (Amy-Chinn). In the world of *Serenity*, the companions are the epitome of femininity. At the same time, Inara has power which is considered a masculine trait by most people, as she has position, choice, and agency.

Nonetheless, she abandons her power and status. In *Leaves on the Wind*, Inara is no longer a companion, but grouped with the hunted members of the Serenity crew after the events of the film. Unlike River and the others, she likely has extensive options, from solo companion jobs to wealthy retirement to proclaiming her defense on airwaves across the 'Verse thanks to her respectability. In the end she chooses not to work and vanishes into oblivion beside Mal because she is in love. That does not make her any less powerful. She is choosing. That is power. Throughout *Leaves on the Wind*, Inara has abandoned her elaborate gowns to wear a simple buckled corset and cargo pants much as Zoe does. Stripped of her companion identity, she is much the same character, though now more united with the rest of the crew. She parallels Kaylee as well: each has a stable sexual relationship with her man now.

Whereas before she was the highest-status person on the ship, a passenger only dependent on the captain for transport, she's now the same status as the rest of the crew as she tells Mal he must take a job, however risky, to get food for all of them. It is also unclear what her current role is without companion status. Aside from being Mal's confidante, advisor, and romantic partner, she is not seen using her connections (presumably ended) or any ship's skills to help out. Thus she is left in limbo. Amy-Chinn notes that "as the series makes clear she has a choice: to renounce her professional identity and financial independence or leave. There is no third way." However, now that she has renounced it, she's revealed as having little besides a pair of comforting arms to offer the team.

Her new status emphasizes women's conflict between success and romance, between beating men in the corporate world or accepting a lesser, more socially acceptable position. As Inara shifts identities and leaves behind her role as ultra-feminine sexual attendant for an equally problematic one as captain's girlfriend, students can discover and debate the compromises required for power and accommodation.

Conclusion

We can view the ship Serenity like a campus. Just as students on a campus are trying to balance their needs with one another to create community, the members of Serenity are all trying to find their place and fit in. People in both arenas come from different lives and experiences and have different social statuses assigned to them. For both groups this may be the first time that they have come in contact with such a variety of clashing perspectives (Kaufman and Feldman). Students are looking for identity, to figure out who they are in this big world. Using this type of comparison in these comic books to help students identify with themselves and the many individuals around them can be invaluable (Blanch and Mulvihill).

Research and theory on identity change as time passes but one thing remains clear. One's identity is more than just masculine or feminine, religious or secular, welcomed or marginalized. It is malleable and changes along with the surrounding environment. Just as college changes students, being aboard the Serenity has changed the people it carries. However, as much as we want to define ourselves as our ideal, we are still constricted by the social issues that surround us.

Note

1. See http://www.celt.iastate.edu/teaching-resources/effective-practice/revised-blooms-taxonomy.

Part Five

Dollhouse

• • •

Dollhouse (2009–2010) is the least well-known of Whedon's five television shows. In contemporary L.A., the Rossum Corporation invents the technology to imprint a new personality onto a mindwiped human body, called a "doll." Then they sell these services, which range from creating a perfect date to virtual immortality. The show evokes questions of ethics, personhood, and the soul as the doll Echo's alleged "blank slate" personality evolves into heroism. The two seasons end with the episodes "Epitaph" and "Epitaph 2," which jump to a dystopia ten years in the future, revealing how the body-switching technology has destroyed the world.

Andrew Chambliss, a staff writer, joined showrunners Zack Whedon and his wife on the *Dollhouse* comics short run and trade paperback collection *Epitaphs*. He notes:

> The Epitaph timeline is so much fun to write because A) it's apocalyptic, and who doesn't like the apocalypse? (The fictional apocalypse, that is.); and B) anything really goes in the Epitaph timeline…. The Dollhouse tech is pushed to its logical extreme, people are switching bodies to stay young, Freakshows can swap out skills on USB drives and anyone can become a villain by answering the phone. It's a heightened reality, and there really are no bounds to the kind of things that can happen. That makes for fun storytelling.

The comics focus on the multi-personalitied villain Alpha's conquering his inner psychopath much like Angel does, even as multiple imprints of the Dollhouse assistant Ivy heighten the soul debate. S. Evan Kreider analyzes this philosophical issue of the mind-body split, showing the deep thought behind Whedon's world.

Mind-Body Dualism vs. Materialism

Personal Identity in Dollhouse: Epitaphs

S. Evan Kreider

• • •

Joss Whedon once made the comment of *Dollhouse*: "We're trying to create something that's more than the sum of its parts. And not just in an 'Oooh, we're heavy with mythology' way. Dare I say we're reaching for something more philosophical?" (Martin). Perhaps the most obvious issue raised by *Dollhouse*, an issue central to the history of philosophy, is that of personal identity. Who am I? What makes me *me?* Is it my body? Is it an immaterial soul? Is it my thoughts, my memories, my character? The comic book miniseries *Dollhouse: Epitaphs* is no exception. Two characters in particular, Ivy and Alpha, serve as fascinating case studies in personal identity, especially given the events of *Epitaphs*. It is during these events that Ivy comes to grips with her own transformation from Rossum Corporation lackey to freedom fighter after she sends her single personality into multiple bodies and that Alpha evolves from psycho killer to hero as he struggles with the multiple personalities inhabiting his single body.

Who Am I: Mind or Body?

In order to make sense of the issues raised about personal identity in *Dollhouse: Epitaphs*, it helps to have a basic theoretical framework in place. There are a wide variety of views about personal identity represented in the history of philosophy; however, the vast majority of them can be divided into two broad camps: dualism and materialism. These two categories do not exhaust the range of possibilities, but they will serve well enough as a basis to analyze the text.

Dualist views of personal identity are typically housed within a broader metaphysical dualism, which posits that reality is composed of two fundamental and distinct substances: material substance and immaterial substance. These two substances are distinct in the sense that one can exist without the other, though they may exist together in some instances, especially that of human nature. Such dualism is clearly present in the works of one of the earliest and most important philosophers in the western tradition, the ancient Greek Plato. Plato believed that the material world around us, the world of physical objects that we can perceive with the senses, is just one part of reality, and an inferior one at that. In addition to material reality, there also exist immaterial "Forms," perfect ideals such as the Good and the Beautiful, which are not mere descriptors of material objects, but things in themselves, things that exist perfectly, eternally, and independently of the physical world. In the case of human nature, Plato believed that it is twofold: each of us is a combination of a material body and an immaterial *psuche*, a Greek word typically translated as "soul" or "mind" (and from which English derives such words as "psyche" and "psychology"). Plato argues that the soul is of the same nature as the Forms, and therefore capable of existing separately from the body; moreover, he argues that the soul is immortal, that it survives the death of the body, and can be reincarnated into new bodies: "Our souls also existed apart from the body before they took on human form" (Plato 67). Plato's views on the soul were influential on medieval Christian philosophers, who held a similarly dualist view of human nature, including the orthodox Christian view of the immortality of the soul (minus the reincarnation), but Plato also influenced the so-called Father of Modern Philosophy, Rene Descartes, who held similar views, though he attempted to separate them from explicit theology, preferring to give the secular argument that our ability to conceive of the mind as existing separately from the body shows their logical (and therefore metaphysical) independence. "So that this I, that is to say, the soul by which I am what I am, is entirely distinct from the body, and is even easier to know than the body, and even if the body had never been, the soul would not fail to be everything that it is" (Descartes 135).

There is something intuitive about dualism for many people. For some, it is simply part of their religious beliefs, among which dualism is fairly popular. For others, it may be more a "common-sense" view that one's mind is something different from one's body, perhaps thinking along the same lines as Descartes. As for Joss and the rest of the *Dollhouse* creative crew, we might be tempted to place them in the dualist camp—if we were speaking of *Buffy* or *Angel*. A basic tenant of the mythology of these shows is that a vampire is a person who has died, whose soul has left his or her body, and whose body is now inhabited by a demon; this is something explained to Buffy (and the audience) very explicitly in the opening episodes. There are, of course, additional details added as those series progress that complicate the issues (not the least of which is Spike, who seems to retain some of his original personality and humanity even after losing his soul), but the starting assumption is clearly dualistic.

However, we see little such talk in *Dollhouse*. Instead, a straightforward reading of *Dollhouse* seems to involve a materialistic view. Materialism posits that reality is entirely composed of material substance of some kind, a physical nature the existence of which is empirically verifiable. On a materialist view, this includes human nature: we human beings are entirely material, and there is no distinct immaterial soul or mind that can exist independently of physical substance. This sort of view has historical roots as far back as ancient Greek philosophers such as the atomists Democritus and Luecippus, as well as finding expression in early modern philosophers such as Thomas Hobbes: "To men that understand the signification of these words, *Substance,* and *Incorporeall*; as *Incorporeall* is taken not for subtle body, but for *not Body,* they imply a contradiction: insomuch as to say, an Angel, or Spirit is (in that sense) an Incorporeall Substance, is to say in effect, there is no Angel nor Spirit at all" (Hobbes 439). *Dollhouse* certainly seems to endorse some kind of materialism. Even when minds are removed from or inserted into various bodies, there is still the suggestion that this all happens on a physical level. As Topher, Dr. Saunders, and Adele explain on more than one occasion, each Doll's original personality is wiped and stored, and various other personalities are implanted into his or her body, all with the use of computer technology, which treats the mind as though it were computer software, and the brain as though it were the computer hardware on which any particular mind is installed. However, as one can imagine, the issues are far more complicated than that. *Dollhouse* itself plays with these possibilities, inviting us to ask deeper questions about personal identity, and nowhere does it do this more than in *Epitaphs*, through Ivy and Alpha.

Ivy: One Mind, Many Bodies

Ivy is an arguably underutilized character on the television series, written as little more than an assistant and sidekick working under Topher at the L.A. branch of the Dollhouse, but she very much comes into her own in *Epitaphs*. At the beginning of the first issue, Rossum Corporation enacts the first stage of its diabolical plan to take over the world by launching a large-scale memory wipe of the population *via* telephone, turning the average citizen into a killing machine designed to cause chaos and to create a power void that the Corporation can presumably fill. In several instances shown, co-workers, friends, and lovers answer their phones, and a moment later, violently turn on those around them. In one scene, a young boy named Trevor is working in the garage on a carpentry project with his Uncle Wendall, who picks up the phone and hears the now familiar screech of the Rossum signal. He turns to Trevor, and we believe we are about to see yet another (and an especially cruel) example of violence, but then the former Uncle Wendall says, "Listen to me carefully. I'm here to help you.... My name is Ivy. And something terrible has happened" (*Epitaphs* 15).

The Uncle Wendall body imprinted with Ivy's mind comes to an unfortunate end, but we soon discover that Ivy has imprinted herself into other bodies as well. Alpha, former psycho killer and not-yet-full-fledged hero (analyzed in the next section), is holed up in Dodger Stadium, working on the technology that will allow him to upload information into people without wiping them, while still giving them the knowledge and skills to combat Rossum more effectively. Working alongside Alpha we find not one, but two Ivys, imprinted into the bodies of a man and a woman whose former identities remain hidden, both of whom are very attractive (the relevance of which will become clear shortly). Despite inhabiting two separate physical bodies with many differing characteristics, they appear to think and to act the same as Ivy would, initially responding to Alpha's questions with identical words. "One of you is redundant right now," says Alpha, to which the Ivys both respond simultaneously, "I want to be here when you activate the interface" (*Epitaphs* 37). At this point, the text suggests a sharp distinction between the mind and the external body (the face, arms, legs, etc.), but rather than positing a kind of dualism, in which the mind is metaphysically distinct from the body, the implication is that the mind is reducible to the brain, or more specifically, the various electrochemical brain states which it undergoes, a kind of "identity theory" associated with 20th century philosophers such as U.T. Place: "[A]n acceptance of inner processes does not entail dualism and ... the thesis that consciousness is a process in the brain cannot be dismissed on logical grounds" (44). This coheres with the aforementioned mythology of the television series, in which the brain is treated like computer hardware, and the mind as its software.

However, things are not quite this simple. Later, we are introduced to another Ivy, another woman, but this one less attractive than the other two. When Alpha first takes her to meet the others, they come upon the pair in a compromising position. "I'm hooking up with myself," says the new Ivy upon witnessing this, a situation to which Alpha responds: "I'm uncomfortable, and most of my personalities were designed to fulfill the sexual perversions of the extremely rich" (*Epitaphs* 49). Later on, the attractive woman Ivy is reprogrammed by Rossum *via* radio, and is shortly thereafter killed by Alpha. Notably, the remaining male and female Ivys do not engage in a sexual relationship. The male Ivy misses the attractive female Ivy, but does not have any interest in resuming the relationship with the less attractive Ivy. The conversation on is philosophically fascinating:

> **FEMALE IVY**: Were you in love with Ivy or her body?
> **MALE IVY**: Her body was hot, yeah. But her personality totally rocked.
> [Female Ivy suddenly kisses Male Ivy, who does not react well.]
> **FEMALE IVY**: So why won't you kiss me? I have the same exact personality she had. Oh, boy. It's because you're superficial.
> **MALE IVY**: I am not....
> **FEMALE IVY**: I know you're superficial because I'm superficial. I get it. I'd much rather kiss me in a supermodel's body, too.
> **MALE IVY**: So why are you mad at me?
> **FEMALE IVY**: We have the same brain. You figure it out. [Walks away.]
> **MALE IVY**: Girls [89–90].

It would be simple enough to take Male Ivy's claim of superficiality at face value, but his parting "Girls" comment implies something deeper. Ivy's mind has been in a male body long enough that she is starting to identify as a "he," in contrast to the "girls" with whom he speaks. More of this appears later when the two Ivys have a moment to discuss the previous incident.

> **MALE IVY**: I always thought I'd be different if I were a guy.... You don't know what it's like having all these male hormones running through my body.
> **FEMALE IVY**: What's [sex] like? On your end, I mean?
> **MALE IVY**: Different [96–97].

The philosophical implication is that his physical nature, whether that of his hormones or of his sexual organs, has started to become part of who he is, over and above any simple pattern of brainwave activity. This shows that the Dollhouse's theory that one's identity is nothing more than software programmed onto a brain, though perhaps essentially correct, is still a bit simplistic, as the Ivys hypothesize:

Male Ivy: Do you think our brains are still the same as [the original Ivy's]?
Female Ivy: Probably not. Our neural patterns diverge every day we're apart from her.
Male Ivy: So how long until our brains change enough to really make us different people?
Female Ivy: Alpha and Trevor are missing, and you want to have a philosophical debate about identify right now? [107].

That is, in fact, exactly what the authors want us to do. Here we are invited to explore the complexities of the Dollhouse's materialism. Perhaps the software analogy is flawed, as the hardware of the brain, while controlling the body, is in turn affected by it, making personal identity more than just a collection of brain states, but a complex feedback system between the internal states of mind and the external makeup and responses of the physical body. This is similar to "functionalist" views of personal identity found in the writings of 20th century philosophers such as Jerry Fodor: "Functionalism ... recognizes the possibility that systems as diverse as human beings ... could all have mental states. In the functionalist view the psychology of a system depends not on the stuff it is made of ... but on how the stuff is put together" (124).

The case of the many Ivys also suggests, but does not fully develop, the ethical dimension of personhood: who one is and what one does says a great deal about one's moral character, a core component of one's identity. These issues, and the manner in which they reflect back on the metaphysical issues, are explored more deeply and explicitly though the character of Alpha.

Alpha: One Body, Many Minds

Alpha's personal identity arguably undergoes more numerous and radical changes than any other character in the *Dollhouse* universe. In *Epitaphs*, one of the Ivys summarizes Alpha's backstory succinctly: "Alpha's a rogue active who escaped the Dollhouse with a serial killer in his head. Along with forty-nine other mostly crazy personalities"; however, as the two other Ivys point out, "He's changed" (50). As the television series reveals, Alpha's original personality was that of Karl William Kraft, a convict who traded the life sentence he earned for kidnapping, torture, and attempted murder in exchange for the typical five-year stint at the Dollhouse, during which he was programmed with a wide variety of personalities, many of whom were geared toward violent or sexually deviant missions. During his time there, Alpha began to emerge as a simple but independent personality, much like Echo did for Caroline. After this new Alpha personality attacked another Doll as a twisted sign of affection for Echo, he was slated to be wiped and placed in the attic, but an accidental "composite event" caused all of his previous personalities to resurface, and he became a vicious and brilliant mastermind and psychotic killer bent on taking down the Dollhouse and winning Echo's affections ("Omega," D1.12).

During the events of *Epitaph*, however, a great deal has changed. The Alpha meta-personality is largely in control of his other personalities, able to draw from their knowledge and skills, but also control their behavior, at least at first. He has developed a conscience and wants to help Echo and the rest bring down Rossum Corporation. He attributes this turn to having uploaded FBI agent (and generally heroic character) Paul Ballard's personality before almost killing him ("A Love Supreme," D2.8). In *Epitaphs*, Ballard catches up with Alpha and threatens to kill him. Alpha explains: "You won't do it…. Because your personality is the only thing that's kept me from killing. Without it, I wouldn't have gained control of the chaos in here. I wouldn't have decided to bring Rossum down" (110–111). Ballard's personality operates as a moral core amidst the storm of evil inside Alpha's head, allowing him to reflect on his past deeds. "Aren't there things you wish you could take out of your head?" Trevor asks, to which Alpha replies, "Lots of things" (52). As one of the Ivys points out to Trevor later, "Why do you think he's trying to save the world? Along with all those personalities, there's an awful lot of guilt in that head" (61). Alpha elaborates in a later discussion: "My original personality wasn't worth saving. Even before I had all those personalities dumped in my head … he did things you wouldn't like. He was a killer…. He killed because he enjoyed it. I don't want to go back to being him. I've changed. I've evolved. I have a purpose now" (95).

Things become more complicated after Alpha is subjected to one of Rossum's mind-wiping signals. His special constitution, like Echo's, along with his experience in dealing with multiple personalities, allows him to resist the signal. However, it weakens his control over his original self, and Kraft manages to compete with Alpha for dominance, occasionally forcing Alpha to relinquish control to allow Kraft to murder innocent people. "I had everything under control until I got zapped by a trigger-happy welder. Then it all toppled" (*Epitaphs* 113), explains Alpha to the group after his killings are discovered. Alpha rationalizes that he had to allow Kraft autonomy so that, in exchange, Kraft and the rest of the more violent personalities would allow Alpha's continued dominance the rest of the time and not interfere with his plan to bring down Rossum. As Kraft reminds Alpha, "We made a deal. You want to save the world, you let me have fun" (85), and as Alpha explains to the rest of the group, "It's the only way I could get everyone in my head to cooperate, to keep our mission on track" (102).

Near the end of *Epitaphs*, in a particularly violent episode, Alpha allows Kraft to kill a group of "butchers" (people turned into mindless killers by Rossum's mind-wiping signal) in order to save the team, including Echo, Ballard, Trevor, and two Ivys, so that they can continue the fight to bring down Rossum. "Ready to come out and play?" asks Alpha, to which Kraft replies, "Always" (*Epitaphs* 143). Immediately after, Alpha leaves. "He's gone," says Echo. "After what happened, he knows he's too dangerous to be around right now" (145). Similarly, in the very last episode of the television series ("Epitaph 2," D2.13) Alpha minimizes his contact with the core group, preferring to stay out in the field, presumably at least in part out of continued concern for their safety. He ends the series outside the safety of the Dollhouse as he fears Kraft's return. This shows Alpha regaining control, even if not completely, and still attempting to act morally and to atone for his past misdeeds, much like Angel's constant struggle with Angelus. What started as an artifact of Ballard's personality now seems to have become an enduring part of Alpha's own moral character. Alpha's explicit goal may be the downfall of Rossum, but his personal quest of transformation from killer to hero is largely complete.

Conclusion: "Did I Fall Asleep?"

There is a subtle irony to the Dolls' question "Did I fall asleep?" By the Dollhouse's design, there should be no real "I" at all in that state: the original personality has been removed and tucked away for safe keeping, any mission-related personalities have been wiped clean, and all that ought to remain is a blank slate, with little to no autonomy, barely even comparable to a child. "Think of them as pets," says Chief Security Officer Laurence Dominic at one point ("Needs," D1.8). The irony is, of course, that they are not wholly without personhood, even in that state, though the degree of personhood varies from Doll to Doll. This irony, presented in each episode, is an implicit challenge to the viewer to consider the philosophical issues of personal identity, issues developed throughout the television series, and most explicitly dealt with in *Epitaphs*.

There is never any hint of a traditional dualism of the kind in *Buffy* and *Angel*; instead we are invited to consider the subtle variations of the materialist account of personhood. In the case of Ivy, we are initially tempted to read a simple identity theory materialism in which personhood is reducible to quantifiable electro-chemical brain states, like software programmed into a computer. However, as *Epitaphs* progresses, we begin to see that the rest of one's physical being—one's external body, as well as one's internal biological and chemical makeup not merely limited to the brain—plays a significant role in how one identifies oneself (for example, with regard to gender), as well as how one thinks of others (for example, as an object of romantic interest or not).

In the case of Alpha, things are even more complex, as we begin to question the adequacy of even that kind of functionalist account. In particular, Alpha's case requires us to ask some difficult questions about the supposed distinction of one's original and "true" identity versus the supposedly "artificial" identities programmed into the brain *via* the Dollhouse's technology, and even suggests the possibility of something new arising from that mix, a sense of personal identity not merely reducible to either one's original self nor one's new personalities, but something emerging from out of them, something that seeks to form its own identity, with its own goals and values. On the show, Echo undergoes a similar transformation.

This sort of view perhaps comes closest to the view endorsed in the *Dollhouse* mythology, wherein the mind "supervenes" on the physical, as it was put by recent philosophers such as Donald Davidson: "Mental characteristics are in some sense dependent, or supervenient, on physical characteristics.... Dependence or supervenience of this kind does not entail reducibility through law or definition" (214). Admittedly, neither Joss nor the rest of the writers are professional philosophers, and so we may not find a single explicit statement of position on the philosophical issue of personal identity; but as with all good literature, *Dollhouse: Epitaphs* invites us to consider the possibilities, and perhaps to decide for ourselves the answer to the question, "Who am I?"

Part Six

Dr. Horrible's Sing-Along Blog

• • •

Dr. Horrible's Sing-Along Blog, co-written by Joss Whedon, his brothers Zack Whedon and Jed Whedon, and actress Maurissa Tancharoen, was filmed at Joss Whedon's home during the 2007–2008 Writers Guild of America strike and released online. It delightfully parodies both musicals and superhero stories as Dr. Horrible (Neil Patrick Harris) schemes to become a true supervillain and join the Evil League of Evil but is constantly thwarted by the macho, blustering Captain Hammer (Nathan Fillion). Felicia Day as Penny, the girl they both love, completes the main character roster, with a nod from henchman Moist (Simon Helberg). Many comic tropes appear as Dr. Horrible (unrecognized by Penny in civilian clothes) builds a freeze ray that fails at all the wrong moments. Captain Hammer, meanwhile, has "the command center, Hammer-cycle, [and] Ham-Jet," much like Batman or the X-Men. There's a trope of self-awareness throughout, as Dr. Horrible trains and consciously prepares to be a supervillain.

There's also a collection of prequel shorts in comic form—*Dr. Horrible and Other Horrible Stories*, written by Zack Whedon with art by Eric Canete, Farel Dalrymple, Jim Rugg, Joelle Jones, and Scott Hepburn. The five shorts include "Captain Hammer: Be Like Me," from his egotistical perspective, as he encourages the readers to become superheroes. "Moist: Humidity Rising" is an origin story, as is "Dr. Horrible." "Penny: Keep Your Head Up" takes a closer look at her sad, yet hopeful life, while "The Evil League of Evil" provides a gleeful look into their operations.

For this collection, Tracy S. Morris looks at the comics and at the show *as* a comic, comparing both to the celebrated comic *Watchmen* by Alan Moore. She focuses on ending, lasting impact, and the Women in Refrigerators trope as well as the dystopian setting and hybrid characters in both eminent works.

Joss Whedon, Alan Moore and the Whole Horrible Future

TRACY S. MORRIS

• • •

Remember the old song from Sesame Street: "One of These Things Is Not like the Other?" At first glance, *Dr. Horrible's Sing Along Blog* (hereafter called *Dr. Horrible*) and *Watchmen* fit this description, with seemingly very little in common. They exist as different media: Joss Whedon released *Dr. Horrible* as a live action video while DC comics printed *Watchmen* as a comic book, and later released it as a trade paperback (at least for the scope of this paper).

With its "supervillain blog" format, humor and musical numbers, the creators of *Dr. Horrible* infused it with a light, whimsical feel. By contrast, *Watchmen* mirrors the anxieties of its late 1980's publication time period including the threat of nuclear war. This serves to give it a much grimmer tone.

Even the creators couldn't be more different. Although both Joss Whedon and Alan Moore both stand out for their work in the superhero comics genre, Moore voices his opposition of movie adaptations whenever fans ask him. Whedon instead worked in television and movies most of his life and manages the creative direction of *Marvel's Avengers, Agents of S.H.I.E.L.D.,* and, to a lesser extent, other works in the Marvel cinematic universe. (Although Whedon collaborates with others, most notably his brothers Jed and Zack Whedon and his sister-in-law Maurissa Tancharoen, Joss produced *Dr. Horrible,* thus this essay will treat the work as his singular vision).

Looking deeper at *Watchmen* and *Dr. Horrible* reveals surprising similarities. Both Whedon and Moore used a self-referential storytelling method to create the works as superhero deconstructions. Deconstruction is a theory of literary criticism in which meaning depends on the reader.

Derrida, its inventor, insists that the insertion of texts into new contexts continually produces new meanings, creating a nested opposition between them. He adds:

> We can call "context" the entire "real-history-of-the-world," if you like, in which this value of objectivity and, even more broadly, that of truth (etc.) have taken on meaning and imposed themselves. That does not in the slightest discredit them. In the name of what, of which other "truth," moreover, would it? One of the definitions of what is called deconstruction would be the effort to take this context into account, to pay the sharpest and broadest attention possible to context, and thus to an incessant movement of recontextualization [136].

Meanings, based on reader interpretation, are arbitrary and contradictory—the act of examining them reveals their inadequacy. In other words, both *Dr. Horrible* and *Watchmen* criticize aspects of the superhero genre by examining the tropes of the genre and taking them to their logical conclusion. *Dr. Horrible's Sing-along Blog* and *Watchmen* offer numerous similarities and differences in how each focuses on the tropes of the superhero genre as well as how each criticizes and unravels these tropes through deconstruction.

The Setting

No one can argue that *Watchmen* isn't set in a modern-day dystopia (or at least modern at the point of publication). Although the United States has won the arms race thanks to Dr. Manhattan's aid, the world teeters on the brink of nuclear war as the Soviet Union races to catch up to America and surpass it in global supremacy (Moore, "Watchmen: Chapter II: Absent Friends" 11).

Additionally, the rights of various superheroes are vanishing in the name of politics, after a police strike over costumed vigilantes and the subsequent riots lead to the Keene Act, a form of superhero registration. Subsequent to its passage, superheroes must choose between finding government sponsorship and breaking the law by continuing their vigilante activities (17).

The plot of *Watchmen* picks up immediately with self-referential content. Matthew Levy points out that the story begins with the murder of a hero known as The Comedian. As another word for "comedian" is comic, Moore seems to be saying that comics as we know them (bright, shiny and without cynicism) are dead in this book.

Dr. Horrible also contains self-referential storytelling and moments that imply a dystopian setting. In the very first scene of the work, Billy (Dr. Horrible's true identity) looks at and addresses the audience directly as he details his efforts at getting into the Evil League of Evil through a blog format. (Zack Whedon wrote *Commentary: The Musical* as a separate self-referential musical, a dystopic one in its own way.)

Our first glimpse of *Dr. Horrible's* dystopian setting in action comes through Captain Hammer, a man who embodies (in Billy's own words) the concept "corporate tool." Captain Hammer fights for the status quo. In the process common people get hurt. In the prequel comic collection *Dr. Horrible and Other Horrible Stories*, he calls himself "the embodiment of good ... the definition of civic virtue" and his long line of fans seem to agree (Z. Whedon). Although Captain Hammer exhibits abhorrent behavior, everyone idolizes him right up until the first time he ends up on the losing side of a confrontation with Dr. Horrible/Billy ("Act III," *DH*). After this, the rather amoral groupies transfer their affection to Dr. Horrible. Clearly most people in this dystopic world don't care about right or wrong. They seem more concerned with following the person covered in glory at the moment. Worse yet, the fawning groupies who wear Hammer t-shirts and collect memorabilia down to his dry cleaning bill clearly echo comic book fans today, emphasizing a fandom that ignores role models' bad behavior. The comic even implies that society treats smart people like Billy as potential villain masterminds. In a society ruled by the media and people like Captain Hammer, the clever may have no other recourse. Shattering the fourth wall, Hammer directly addresses the reader, saying that to discover evil wherever it lurks he needs the reader's help keeping watch. Thus he recruits the readers to become bullies like himself, preying on anyone clever or nonconformist.

Although Billy plays the part of the villain, various signs suggest that he's really not that bad. The mayor of the city even writes him a condemnation letter so that he can get into the Evil League of Evil ("Act I," *DH*), an act that implies some sort of cordial relationship must exist. Perhaps the mayor and Dr. Horrible have a frenemies relationship, or the mayor wants to attract the evil vote when election time rolls around.

While the Evil League of Evil has an unspecified amount of power, their opposing "Council of Champions," mentioned in the comic, apparently goes out of town on retreats, leaving the city under the thumb of a crime syndicate rather than trapped between the dichotomy of heroes and villains. In fact, no member of the League is seen being punished by the law. Moreover, the story implies that dystopic elements drove Billy to a life of evil. He tells his viewers he's devoted to "destroying the status quo because the status is *not* quo. The world is a mess and I just need to rule it" ("Act I," *DH*). As such, his ultimate goal could even be considered altruistic, considering his society's condition.

Even worse, only Billy seems to value the one decent character in the series, Penny. Captain Hammer first pushes her into the trash to save her from a speeding van (that stops on its own) ("Act I," *DH*) and then starts a relationship with her just to hurt Billy ("Act II," *DH*). Her efforts for the homeless appear idealistic and ineffective until Captain Hammer gets her petition passed with only his celebrity power. Before this, everyone ignores her on the street as she begs for others to care about the unfortunate. Even Billy, who wants to impress her, must tell her she's naïve for wanting a new shelter, saying: "It's a symptom. You're treating a symptom, and the disease rages on, consumes the human race.... I'm talking about an overhaul of the system. Putting the power in different hands" ("Act I," *DH*). The groupies "have a problem with her" despite the fact that she helps the homeless, and when she dies, she's eulogized in the headlines as "what's-her-name" ("Act III," *DH*).

Both of these stories sit in contrast to the popular image of golden age comic books in which officials often welcome the vigilante activity of the superhero as helpful and necessary when the police can't do the job themselves—the Gotham Police use a bat signal to call Batman and the Metopolis Police work with Superman (Ellsworth et al., "Detective Comics #60"). In these worlds, rule of law continues, and many supervillains end the story in prison.

As an interesting side note, the popular golden age image of the superhero as Boy Scout is most deconstructed here. However, research indicates that our favorite comic book heroes didn't start out as paragons of virtue. Prior to the 1940s, superhero stories evolved from a subgenre of pulp fiction alongside detective stories such as *The Shadow*, *The Lone Ranger*, *The Phantom*, *Tarzan* and the *John Carter of Mars* stories. Thus, when a hero such as Batman was introduced in *Detective Comics*, he was originally intended to be an urban adventurer in the tradition of *The Phantom*: a gun-toting detective with a bat-theme (Sims), and Superman appears a palate swap of *John Carter of Mars*. Rather than an Earthling who travels to another planet where he develops super powers thanks to the difference in gravity, he is an alien who comes to our planet and develops superpowers thanks to the difference in sunlight (Andrae).

As children embraced comics as a storytelling medium throughout the 1940s, the once-pulpy stories begin to take on a lighter, more fun tone (Wright 17). *Dr. Horrible* and *Watchmen* rebel against the upbeat, family-friendly comics to offer a world of violence and despair, in which good people have no choice but to tear down the damaged system.

The Heroes

Moore modeled The Heroes of *Watchmen* after already existing Charlton Comics characters. DC Comics had recently purchased Charlton, and Moore planned to use the already existing characters. But DC vetoed this idea when they realized that they wouldn't be able to introduce the characters into future DC storylines once Moore had finished. Instead Moore created new characters loosely based on the ones before. Thus Nite Owl's counterpart in the DC universe is the Blue Beetle, and Rorschach's similarities to DC's The Question are intentional. However Moore created his new characters so that readers would see aspects of them in more well-known comics characters.

Moore portrayed the heroes of *Watchmen* as deeply flawed human beings who just happen to have unusual jobs. With the notable exception of Dr. Manhattan, most of them don't possess super powers. Still, if having issues counted as a super power, they would have that in bucket loads, truckloads and whole warehouses.

Take Sally Jupiter A.K.A. Silk Spectre I, the femme fatale of the series. Moore implies that she takes to crime fighting from low self-esteem and to fulfill a need for attention. When she's no longer able to continue a career as a crime fighter, she assumes the role of stage mother and pushes her daughter into the crime fighting life (Moore, "Watchmen: Chapter I: At Midnight, All the Agents..." 25). Later it's revealed that her daughter originates from a liaison with The Comedian, a man who assaulted her earlier at an earlier point in the book ("Watchmen: Chapter IX: The Darkness of Mere Being" 24).

Another character, Rorschach, acts like a detective in the mode of The Shadow—one driven by moral absolutism. Since he has no room in his life for shades of moral gray, he commits a form of suicide-by-cop rather than compromise his ideals, even if that compromise would lead to world peace ("Watchmen: Chapter XII: A Stronger Loving World" 24).

Thus Alan Moore presents characters' particular personality quirks to establish that psychological scarring is required to become a costumed vigilante.

Dr. Horrible contrasts with *Watchmen* in that Billy drives the plot of the entire story. Because of this, it's never entirely clear who wears the mantle of hero. From Dr. Horrible's viewpoint, Captain Hammer feeds his ego and seeks attention through heroics. The prequel comic implies that his treatment of Billy may be what drove him to become Dr. Horrible in the first place: Horrible shows off his invention of a weakening serum to Captain Hammer, who responds with the brutal public put-down "I see you tried it on yourself" and an unearned punch to the face.

Whedon casts the traditional paragon, Captain Hammer, in the mold of Batman and Superman, the entitled icon. Although the writers don't explicitly spell out Captain Hammer's powers, presumably they include some kind of super strength, because he attempts to stop a speeding van with his bare hands, and near-invulnerability (to everything but death ray shrapnel) due to the fact that he has never felt pain prior to the end of the series. It's also possible that a lifetime of bullying weaker characters has left him unharmed because he never engaged in a fair fight. In the comic, he describes himself as "born with a full head of hair and the ability to bench press five hundred pounds."

Dr. Horrible/Billy parallels a number of different superheroes or villains. In the hero mode are Reed Richards, Peter Parker, and Tony Stark: Geniuses who fell into the hero mold when they decided to use their intellect to make the world a better place. Billy does genuinely feel he would improve the world if he could. He's just trying to go about it differently. However, he also mirrors a number of evil scientists such as Lex Luthor, Dr. Octopus and Dr. Doom. (That each of these three have a backstory in which their villainy leads to physical scarring may indicate that the sequel to *Dr. Horrible* may not end happily for Billy either).

The duality in Billy's character gets to the heart of what Joss is trying to say with *Dr. Horrible*: That no man thinks of himself as a bad guy, and that every villain is the hero of another story. Dr. Horrible's actions make him the villain (with a little V) of the story. On one hand, he's stealing gold (rather ineptly) from the local bank, while on the other, he refuses to fight another local villain because innocent bystanders might get hurt ("Act I," *DH*). It's not until the end of the story that he becomes a Villain (with a big V) complete with a menacing costume change ("Act III," *DH*). Still, even after getting (almost) everything he ever wanted, Dr. Horrible isn't really happy. In this, Joss also seems to be saying (much like Moore with *Watchmen*) that one must be a really screwed up individual to fight (or commit) crime in a costume.

The Endings

Watchmen and *Dr. Horrible* both end on a bittersweet note as well. In *Watchmen*, the world achieves peace due to trickery on the part of Ozymandias (in which he swears there really are space squids. Really. He's not joking). Although the characters leave the stage on an up note, with Nite Owl II and Silk Spectre II going off to adventure together and the world at peace, Moore implies that the peace won't last, as Rorschach sent evidence of Ozymandias's deceit to a newspaper ("Watchmen: Chapter XII: A Stronger Loving World" 32). Moore even foreshadowed this by the character's name, directly referencing Percy Bysshe Shelly's sonnet in which a long-forgotten king's single remaining work is an inscription on a broken pedestal in which he entreats the reader to "look on my works, ye mighty, and despair" as the title of the penultimate chapter of the series (1).

For the most part, fans didn't see the downer ending to *Dr. Horrible* (Penny's death) coming, though there were clues. While the first episode began with a blog in which Dr. Horrible/Billy practiced his evil laugh and showed off his stolen gold bullion/bouillon, each episode grew darker and darker as Billy slowly morphed into Dr. Horrible. Given the unfortunate history of the Women in Refrigerators trope in comics and Whedon's tendency to suddenly and fatally impale much-beloved second-tier characters, Penny may as well have had a big glittery sign on her head that said, "I'll be shish-kabob by the end of this series."

This deconstruction on the part of both *Watchmen* and *Dr. Horrible* plays with the nature of comic books in general. Because of their episodic storytelling, ongoing storylines and rotating roster of writers, major changes in comic books rarely occur. One writer may make titanic changes in the status quo only for another writer to come along and undo those changes because he or she wants to tell a different story.

For example, the most recent reboot of DC comics, dubbed the "new 52," reset many storylines that had been changed in the last few decades. Among these changes, the original Batgirl, Barbara Gordon (who had been paralyzed after another Alan Moore story "The Killing Joke") suddenly regained the use of her legs and resumed the Batgirl identity (Simone).

In the comics industry, death rarely lasts. Superman, Batman, Captain America, Mr. Fantastic, Jean Grey (multiple times) and a host of other characters all died and then came back from the grave. When Marvel comics killed off the Human Torch in a recent storyline of the *Fantastic Four*, they practically announced at the same time that he'd be returning within a few months (M. Moore). As of this writing, the much-hyped death of Wolverine storyline has left fans speculating as to how long it will be before the iconic Marvel character returns from the dead (Law).

Even Joss isn't above retconning and revisiting relationship changes when he writes a comic book. During his run on *Astonishing X-Men*, Whedon revisited plotlines from the 80's introduction of Kitty Pryde, including the relationship between Kitty and Piotr Rasputin (Colossus). Though the two were briefly a couple in the second run of *Uncanny X-Men* in the 80's, Marvel's editorial staff mandated an end to the relationship due to their age difference in the book. While the *Age of Apocalypse* crossover referenced their relationship, Kitty outright rejected Piotr in favor of Peter Wisdom during their tenure in *Excalibur*. With Joss at the helm of *Astonishing X-Men*, Kitty and Peter rekindled their relationship with no mention of their decision to remain just friends in *Excalibur* ("Colossus and Kitty Pryde: The Rocky Road of Love").

Although *Dr. Horrible* ended just after the death of Penny, there are already hints that she'll be back from the dead in some form in the sequel to *Dr. Horrible* ("Will Dr. Horrible 2 Resurrect Penny? She Talks!"). Likewise, despite Alan Moore's not being happy with the fact, DC's plans include a follow up to *Watchmen*. However, since the project is a prequel, it's unlikely that DC will undo any of the comic's plot (Tantimedh).

Treatment of Women

As in comics in general, women aren't treated very well by Moore or Whedon in these two series. However, in Whedon's case, it may be a deliberate, self-aware choice.

Comic book fans, including now-creator Gail Simone, write about the fact that women fare badly in comics. In 1999 a group of comic book fans (including Simone) created a website titled *Women In Refrigerators* to catalog the number of times that a female character had been killed, maimed or depowered in a comic book. Simone and others took the title of the website from *Green Lantern* # 54, in which a villain killed the then-current Green Lantern Kyle Raynor's girlfriend Alex DeWitt and left her in Raynor's refrigerator for him to find (Martz). The specific trope emphasizes the woman's role as advancing the *man's* story through her trauma, rather than growing or changing herself. Since the term's inception, fans refer to any death of a female in comic books as "a fridging" ("Stuffed Into the Fridge"). There's a nod to this in the *Dr. Horrible* comic, when one superhero complains about his abundant strength, adding, "Do you know how many refrigerator doors I've torn off?"

Moore's treatment of women in comics isn't without controversy. As previously mentioned, under his pen, the Joker crippled Barbara Gordon (the first and current Batgirl) in "The Killing Joke" (Moore et al., "The Killing Joke"). As a part of the backstory of *Watchmen*, Moore does indeed "fridge" two female characters. A minor villain kills the openly lesbian character Ursula Zandt, A.K.A. The Silhouette, along with her lover. He then leaves them to be found in a compromising position ("Watchmen: Chapter II: Absent Friends" 32).

Critics of Moore also maintain that he fixates on rape as a plot point for many of his works, such as in the tale of Sally Jupiter. Moore dismissed criticisms that he focused too much on violence, particularly sexual violence, toward women in an interview with *The Guardian* (Flood). In the real world, according to Moore, rape occurs more often than murder, yet writers portray murder to be far worse than rape. He further defended himself in the article by saying that he portrays more violence of non-sexual nature in his work and more sexual encounters of a nonviolent nature.

In contrast to Moore, Whedon is a feminist ally known for producing a body of work with empowered women characters, such as *Buffy the Vampire Slayer* and *Firefly* as well as early drafts of scripts including *Alien: Resurrection, Wonder Woman* and *X-Men*.

Despite his propensity for writing strong females, Whedon writes Penny as just the opposite in *Dr. Horrible*. The classic hero's girlfriend, she helps the homeless, possesses endless optimism, sees the good in everyone, accidentally wanders into danger and dies at the end. Whedon hints that she might have eventually rejected Captain Hammer, but that scenario never gets to play out due to her death ("Act III," *DH*).

Because of Penny's lack of assertiveness, she stands out in stark contrast to Whedon's other female characters. One wonders if this contrast is the point: If in making us aware of the awfulness of a universe in which everyone but Billy forgets about Penny in the war between Dr. Horrible and Captain Hammer, Whedon shows us the disturbing nature of the Women in Refrigerators trope in comics.

Legacy

In analyzing *Watchmen* and *Dr. Horrible*, one should not overlook the impact that each makes on its respective storytelling medium.

Watchmen garnered a Hugo and an Eisner award. *Time Magazine* included it on its "100 best novels" list. Many cite the publication of *Watchmen* as a turning point in comics storytelling. Subsequent to *Watchmen*'s publication, comic books took on more complex storylines with an overall darker tone to them. One *New York Times* reviewer noted that in *Watchmen*, Moore's imitators were interested in exploring the inherent brutality of the comics world, but not the consequences that come from that brutality (Itzkoff, "Behind the Mask"). Since *Dr. Horrible* deconstructs the comics that grew out of that grim and dark tradition, one could argue that the former had some influence on the latter.

"*Dr. Horrible* was an instant hit: the original distribution site crashed because of heavy traffic, and the soundtrack was number 2 at iTunes USA on the day of its release, later making it to number 39 on the Billboard 200" (Leonard 275). *Time Magazine* named it #15 in "*Time*'s Top 50 Inventions of 2008." It won the People's Choice Award for "Favorite Online Sensation," the 2009 Hugo Award for Best Dramatic Presentation, Short Form and a 2009 Creative Arts Emmy Award for Outstanding Special Class. *Dr. Horrible* also dominated the inaugural 2009 Streamy Awards for web television with seven awards.

Because of the newer nature of *Dr. Horrible*, its long-term legacy remains unestablished. Thus far its biggest impact does not seem to be in comics, but instead in introducing consumers to the idea that quality entertainment can be found on the internet and can exist independently of a major studio. Following its success, Whedon released his own studio's *Much Ado About Nothing* in independent theaters, then his *In Your Eyes* directly through the web. More projects are surely forthcoming.

Clearly, *Watchmen* and *Dr. Horrible's Sing-along Blog* find ways to deconstruct comic books. Though Alan Moore and Joss Whedon contrast in styles, meaning, and content, the authors echo in their handling of the setting, characters, ending, treatment of women in their stories, and the impact that each story made on their respective industries. They celebrate their shared genre, while simultaneously subverting, deconstructing, and criticizing the elements within.

PART SEVEN

Marvel's *Runaways*

• • •

Brian K. Vaughan created the Runaways as teen Marvel heroes. Upon discovering their parents are the Los Angeles supervillain team the Pride, they abandon them and go on the run, adopting one another in a "chosen family" of the type Whedon is so fond. In fact, there are a few *Buffy* jokes as the creator is a fan. Later, Whedon wrote the Runaways arc *Dead End Kids* while Vaughan wrote the *Buffy: Season Eight* arc *No Future for You*.

The teens all have their superpowers: Nico, the leader, has the Staff of One, which can cast each spell only once. Chase Stein has a telepathic bond with the dinosaur Old Lace, a gift from Gert, the dead Runaway whose absence creates a hole in their lives. Karolina and Xavin are in love, though she has rainbow-powered flight while Xavin is a Skrull, with powers of all the Fantastic Four. Little Molly has Hulk-strength, while Victor Mancha is a cyborg, cloned from his human mother and built by the robot Ultron. Like any family, they squabble and disagree, as several members fall in and out of relationships. Still, through it all, there's love. Whedon's run introduces several new characters including Klara Prast, later called Rose Red, who joins the team. In his arc, the Runaways travel back to 1907 and meet gangs of early heroes and villains, all while discovering the definition of teenagerhood.

Don Tresca examines different kinds of belonging and attachment, from star-crossed romance to biological and chosen families in "Dancing in the Sky: The Value of Love in *Runaways*," cleverly connecting the comic to the larger Whedonverse.

Dancing in the Sky

The Value of Love in Runaways

Don Tresca

• • •

In Joss Whedon's television work, one of the constants is the value of love, whether it be for family, friends, romantic partner, or (occasionally) an inanimate object. In Joss Whedon's six-part story arc in the Marvel comic *Runaways*, "Dead End Kids," we see love reflected throughout the text in a myriad of ways, running the gamut from the appealing and (seemingly) unconditional love between Karolina and Xavin or the familial bond shared by all of the young heroes to the less appealing church-sanctioned "love" between Klara Prast and her husband. The budding romance between Victor and Lillie and the impact of this relationship both to the 1907 past and the modern-day adventures of the teen superheroes binds the story together in a way that clearly defines the value of love within the narrative. Whedon's use of this theme within *Runaways* is an extension of its appearance within his work in other media, including television (*Buffy the Vampire Slayer, Angel, Firefly, Dollhouse,* and *Agents of S.H.I.E.L.D.*), film (including *Toy Story, Serenity, The Avengers,* and *Much Ado About Nothing*), and web series (*Dr. Horrible's Sing-Along Blog*). The various types of love apparent within each subplot of the *Runaways* text reveals much about the different varieties—from the strength of platonic and adoptive families to the pitfalls of romance and threat of suffocating parental affection.

First, I will provide a little background on the history of the Runaways team for those of you unfamiliar with the text. The Runaways are a group of teen superheroes, the children of a team of supervillains known as The Pride who operate out of Los Angeles. The original team of six included

Alex Wilder whose "powers" were restricted to an advanced knowledge of logic and strategy; Nico Minoru (codenamed Sister Grimm) with the power of sorcery which was aided by her bond to a mystical artifact known as the Staff of One; Molly Hayes (codenamed Bruiser and Princess Powerful), the youngest of the team at nine years old, with mutant powers of superhuman strength and invulnerability; Chase Stein (codenamed Talkback) with technological prowess (inherited from his mad-scientist parents); Karolina Dean (codenamed Lucy in the Sky) who discovers she is an alien with the powers of flight and light manipulation (allowing her to create lasers, force fields, and concussive blasts); and Gertrude Yorkes (codenamed Arsenic) who shares a psychic link with a genetically-enhanced deinonychus named Old Lace that her time-travelling parents brought back from their journey into the prehistoric past. The six become estranged from their families after learning of their parents' villainous identities when they witness the Pride sacrificing a teenage girl to their masters, a group of giant aliens known as the Gyborrim. They decide to all run away together and form a team for the sole purpose of defeating their parents' evil plans for world domination. As the series progressed, Alex was revealed as a mole within the team who was secretly working with the Pride, and he was eventually defeated, dying in battle against the rest. Likewise, Gertrude fell in battle against a new version of the Pride, sacrificing herself to save Chase and revealing her true feelings for him at the moment of her death while simultaneously transferring her psychic link with Old Lace to Chase in order to save the dinosaur from death. Two other characters joined the team as permanent members: Victor Mancha, the son of the villainous Ultron who was born with the ability to control electromagnetism, and Xavin, an alien from the Skrull race who was betrothed to Karolina and eventually used his shape-shifting abilities to transform himself into a female after he learned that Karolina is gay.

The Runaways continue to interact with other characters within the Marvel Comics Universe, primarily Cloak and Dagger, the Loners, and the Young Avengers, and eventually flee to New York City after a battle against Noh-Varr, a Kree alien in the employ of S.H.I.E.L.D., who has been charged with capturing the teen heroes for refusing to register as superhumans during the Civil War storyline. Once in New York, the teens, now aged 10 or 11 to 18, arrange to meet with the villainous Kingpin (aka Wilson Fisk) in order to seek his assistance in avoiding the Avengers or other superhero teams in the city that may be hunting them. It is at this point that Whedon's storyline within the *Runaways* text begins.

At its roots, the *Runaways* storyline is a variation of the 19th-century coming-of-age texts about children or young teens who embark on a journey of self-discovery, leaving behind their family and their childhood to venture into the unknown outside world, bravely facing the adult world of responsibility. Unlike monomyth protagonists, these child-heroes embark on a hero-journey of their own making, rather than a mythic quest that is foisted upon them (Makishima 1). Whedon, with "Dead End Kids," seeks to expand upon that initial concept by forcing each of the teen (and preteen in the case of Molly) protagonists to face the complex emotional turmoil of adult romantic relationships by literalizing the concept: He takes the team back to 1907, a time which bridges the gap between the 19th and 20th centuries. They begin the story in need of protection, a typical childhood need, so much that they meet with a notorious supervillain, the Kingpin, to obtain that security. The team begins by attempting a show of force, seeking equal footing with Kingpin by claiming they "represent the Pride" (*Runaways* #25), but Kingpin knows better. He sees the group for what they are, "children," which Chase immediately objects to by demanding, "You can stop calling us that any time, Shamu" (*Runaways* #25). While they try to present a united front, their squabbling suggests they are not as united, or as adult, as they wish to appear.

When Kingpin offers the team a deal, to steal an artifact from a local office building in exchange for his protection, we get our first look at the schism in the team's familial love for one another caused by this compromise of their heroic ethics. While Nico and Xavin find the deal a necessary evil in order to guarantee their survival, others, like Victor, feel that working for Kingpin will undermine their efforts to be "super heroes" (*Runaways* #25) and question the team's leadership (under Nico) if their ethics can be compromised so easily (*Runaways* #25). The fluidity of the team's heroic ethics and the subsequent shattering of the team's familial bonds lead to disaster during the commission of the theft itself. Chase and Old Lace are nearly killed. Immediately, the team fall into despair and squabble, as Nico insists, "This is our life! We try to do something right, we mess it up, we die, we frikkin *die*, and we blame someone and then we do it all over again" (*Runaways* #26). The team's mourning of the seeming death of the two, and the joyous discovery of their survival, reunites the team and reinvigorates their heroic disposition. While they continue to disagree and question Nico's leadership even as Nico questions herself, they support each other fervently. They unanimously agree not to deliver the stolen item, a piece of technology Chase immediately identifies as having been created by his parents (*Runaways* 26). The team fight in unison and defeat the Kingpin and his soldiers; however, the Kingpin calls in backup who forces them to use the stolen item in an escape attempt only to be thrown back in time to the year 1907.

In 1907, as the Runaways combine forces with the young metahuman gang called the Street Arabs, Victor meets Lillie McGurty, known as the Spieler for her ability to fly when music is being played. As they dance on air together, they find themselves the central romantic relationship within the text. Romantic love is an emotion that requires a singular object— that is, the lover can only be devoted to a single individual at one time, forsaking all others. This type of love is not "fungible," that is, no substitute object of the emotion can replace the primary object of the romantic love. Herein lies the central conflict of Whedon's tale: while true love requires the love of one and only one other, loving only in this singular fashion does not allow one to obtain a wider and more robust scope of love with the rest of the world and without that in one's character and experience, the lover loses the ability to connect with the rest of the world (Korsmeyer 168). Buffy obsesses over Angel to the point at which she neglects her duties and friends in "Bad Eggs" (B2.12). Ward kidnaps Skye so they can be alone together, isolated from their team. Despite the overwhelming passion Victor and Lillie feel, they must ultimately reject one another in order to achieve their individual destinies as heroes. He cannot leave his family to stay in the past, and she fears being helpless in the future. As she protests, "What if I don't like it? What if you don't like me? What if I can't dance?" (*Runaways* #30). While both Victor and Lillie grieve over the loss of their love, Lillie's grief seems even more heavily dramatized than Victor's. This is likely to do with the fact that Victor still has the love of his chosen family to fall back on, which we clearly see in many Whedon texts is a strong foundation, stronger than almost any other love humans can experience (Battis, *Blood Relations* 27). Lillie, on the other hand, lacks that foundation. She is left foundering, constantly berating herself for her decision not to accompany Victor, and obsessing for many years to the point of hatching an elaborate scheme to be reunited with her lost love, a scheme which sets Whedon's storyline in motion. Although as an old woman Lillie attempts to drag the Runaways into the past in the hopes of rewriting the star-crossed romance with a happy ending, she learns to her detriment that, for Whedon, the love of the chosen familial bond is stronger than the one-to-one romantic relationship Victor and Lillie share. The strength of the chosen familial bond is evident not just in *Runaways* but in many of Whedon's other texts including *Buffy the Vampire Slayer* in which the chosen familial bond between the Scoobies proves even stronger than the traditional family bond of the Maclays (in "Family," B5.6) and the Summers (in the "alternate reality" of "Normal Again," B6.17, in which Buffy chooses her friends over a "normal" life with her biological parents) and *Agents of S.H.I.E.L.D.* in which Skye chooses allegiance with her S.H.I.E.L.D. team over relationships with the now-evil Ward or her own biological father, Calvin Zabo.

A counterpoint to Victor and Lillie's drama appears in Nico, Victor's ex-girlfriend, who generously sends him to court his new flame. As she notes, "They were in love. Like stupid, first-sight, courtly head-over-heels Romeo and Juliet love. Everybody knew it." As such, she cares enough about Victor and the magic of love to support it. Tristan, a handsome 1907 boy who has always adored Lillie, completes the tangle of romance. He is seen serving her decades in the future, still adoring, as he selflessly aids her in her quest for his romantic rival. Thus Nico and Tristan lose in the game of romance, but both discover new levels of maturity and self-sacrifice, as they help their beloveds find true love with someone else.

Surprisingly, especially given Whedon's occasionally contradictory views of queer relationships in his narratives (see Muscat 3 and Tresca 162–163), the strongest romantic relationship in the *Runaways* text is the homosexual love between Karolina and Xavin. However, like Willow in *Buffy the Vampire Slayer*, Xavin hesitates to fully accept her lesbian lifestyle. As an alien shape-shifter, Xavin has a very fluid gender identification. Despite maintaining a female appearance to sustain a lesbian relationship with Karolina, Xavin frequently appears as a male character. In Xavin's initial appearance during the dinner meeting with Kingpin (*Runaways* #25) and then again later in 1907 New York (*Runaways* #27–28), Xavin claims that his male form shows strength and power, a typical response in most media representations of homosexual teenagers, which frequently focuses on disempowerment and social rejection (Ford 95). Xavin's early inability (or, more precisely, unwillingness) to choose a male/female gender identification continues what many consider Whedon's "fairly ambivalent stance towards homosexual relationships, as if [Whedon is] unwilling to fully commit a major character to a completely gay lifestyle" (Tresca 162). Xavin's gender switching is the subject of multiple jokes from the Runaways, as well as intrusive comments from a judgmental Nico. Nonetheless, the pair's story finds closure when Xavin reveals to Karolina that she considers herself female—Karolina is dating, not a shifting identity, but the "real her." As in *Buffy*, in which Whedon "attempted to make lesbianism more a force for good than evil" (Tresca 162) by focusing on the positive aspects of the Willow-Tara relationship, it is telling that the two lesbian characters are outsiders on multiple levels. In *Buffy*, the lesbian characters are magic-using witches; in *Runaways*, they are extraterrestrial aliens living amongst humans on Earth. As Edwina Bartlem states, the characters' status as otherworldly beings depicts lesbianism "as being beyond the material world, outside the physical body, and beyond reality. This approach insinuates that lesbian desire and sexuality are anomalies that exist beyond the normal world" (22). Karolina and Xavin are "aligned with unstable, otherworldly powers. To relate lesbian sexuality to powers that cannot be understood by general society is to leave room for lesbianism to be interpreted as something that is unnatural, unfamiliar, scary, and possibly evil" (Wilts 48), the exact reaction Klara has upon seeing Karolina and Xavin (in her female form) kiss in *Runaways* #29.[1]

The irony inherent in Klara's response to the Karolina-Xavin relationship lies in her own backstory of being the seemingly willing victim of a turn-of-the-century child predator. Klara has been sold into virtual slavery by her mother, forcing her into marriage to a middle-aged man known only as "Mr. Prast." Klara is, from a psychological perspective, a normal preteen girl child, one who is vulnerable and easily manipulated into engaging in activities that, from the modern perspective of outsiders like Molly and Karolina, are abnormal and perverted. In fact, Molly tells Klara that in the future, child rapists like Mr. Prast are thrown in jail. The relationship between Karla and her husband is extremely unequal and problematic in that he has all of the power due to his status as an adult authority figure (Cocca, "First World 'Jail,' Second Word 'Bait'" 5).

He punches her in the face and spends the money she earns as a factory worker on liquor. From Klara's limited perspective, the relationship between herself and her husband is a normal part of life.[2] However, Klara's reaction to the lesbian kiss between Karolina and Xavin in which she describes the kiss as "a sin," something "disgusting" and "unnatural," while simultaneously claiming that she has been "ungrateful. I have a duty to my husband" proves that what is considered "perverted" love is very much a product of an individual's perspective, culture, and time. While in Whedon's work, pedophiles are seen as frequently monstrous and evil including Marcus, the vampire torturer in the *Angel* episode "In the Dark" (A1.3) and the Ghost, a kidnapper and sexual predator in the *Dollhouse* episode "Ghost" (D1.1), practitioners of ephebophilia (or those with sexual desires for adolescents and teenagers as opposed to prepubescent children) are almost seen as normal with characters like Angel, Willow, and Xander portrayed as having such desires with no significant judgments from Whedon and his writers or the audience (Tresca 147–149).[3] Molly's reaction to Klara's comments regarding the "unnatural" nature of the relationship of Karolina and Xavin and the "natural" relationship between Klara and her husband echoes the sentiment of all contemporary readers of the text, with Molly claiming that she thought Klara would "be one of us," meaning an enlightened twenty-first-century young person without realizing that Klara is in fact a product of her own time. The general acceptable nature of pedophilia compared with the rejection of homosexuality as corrupt and sinful in the early twentieth-century era shows the ways in which definitions of acceptable relationships transform.

Klara's narrative is that of the child-hero described by Keiko Makishima who must confront a darkness within her own life and then move forward into a new completely alien environment, which will include a potential conflict involving an adult same-sex antagonist (3). This conflict leads to the child venturing on a journey that will lead her into becoming more assertive and ultimately integrating the elements of the new environment into her personality to become a healthier and happier whole person, usually with the help of individuals considered outsiders in her "normal" world (Griswold 7). She eventually makes a return to her first life, which then becomes an "accommodation of two lives," their past and present selves, which resolves their issues of identity (Griswold 7). Klara's narrative progression over the course of the "Dead End Kids" storyline adheres closely to the progression of Griswold's "Three Lives of the Child-Hero": she begins as a virtual orphan separated from her original family and "adopted" (or in her case married) into a surrogate family; although she is miserable with her marriage and her life as a factory worker, she laments the loss of that "vanished happy time" by claiming that her denial of that life is a "mistake" and that she has "been ungrateful" for shirking her "duty of my husband" (*Runaways* #29). She then must make a journey and fight powerful antagonists in order to reconcile her fragmented identity, which Klara does through her experiences with the Runaways (Griswold 5–9). The element that allows Klara to accomplish this goal is her acceptance into another surrogate family; the Runaways themselves.

For Whedon, the Runaways as a family are the "dramatic embodiment of a family ideal that does not neglect the common good, an ideal of a family founded, not primarily on blood, self-interest, or patriarchal control, but instead on love, mutual responsibility, and a mission to serve and save others in need" (Locklin 10). This idealized embodiment of a family is based upon non-hierarchical structures and individual freedom of choice. Despite the fact that many of the relationships may entail inequality (such as the Slayer/Watcher dynamic between Buffy and Giles in *Buffy the Vampire Slayer* and the military-style command structure inherent in both *Firefly* (between Malcolm Reynolds and his crew) and *Agents of S.H.I.E.L.D.* (between Coulson and his team), typically the characters in these relationships treat each other as equals with plenty of mutual respect and trust (Zhang 403). This is clear from early in the *Runaways* narrative when, despite everyone on the team acknowledging Nico as the leader, each individual, including Molly, has a say in determining whether or not they accept the Kingpin's offer of protection (*Runaways* #25). However, when the expected equity of these relationships is violated, it is highlighted within the text as extremely problematic and genuinely unacceptable, such as the episode "All the Way" (B6.6) in *Buffy the Vampire Slayer* in which Willow uses her powers to violate Tara's memories or the scene in *Serenity* in which Mal pulls rank on the rest of his crew to demand they use the bodies of their fallen friends to disguise their ship as a Reaver vessel. In the follow-up conversation between Nico and Karolina in *Runaways* #25 after the group has discussed their decision to assist the Kingpin, Nico uses her knowledge of Karolina's vulnerability to challenge her relationship with Xavin out of petty jealousy, showing how easily such relationships between alternate family members can be violated in this manner within the world of the teen superheroes. When Karolina offhandedly comments that Xavin is "such a guy sometimes," Nico quickly retorts, "Is she? I mean … does she really change, or … I mean, as a Skrull was he—she born with … please make me stop" (*Runaways* #25).

The Runaways form a support network for one another, providing each member with vital practical and emotional support. This need for this kind of alternative familial structure reflects a particular stage in adolescent development, when young people turn to their peers for support, cease to confide in the adult members of the family, and, in extreme cases, break with it (Burr and Jarvis 14) as the Runaways were forced to do early in their "superhero careers" when they broke ties with, and ultimately became literal antagonists to, their parents when they learned that of their family legacies as supervillains. The importance of each member of the Runaways reiterating their familial bond and their love and concern for one another's well-being and happiness, which occurs with regularity in each issue of Whedon's story arc, cannot be underestimated. The familial bond proves even stronger in many ways that the erotic, romantic bond between characters like Karolina/Xavin and Victor/Lillie by revealing how the family unit, with its emphasis on responsibility for others beyond oneself and group cooperation, are more important than the individualist pleasures of romance because of its ability to keep the members integrated into the whole of humanity rather than trapped in personal pursuits. This is clearly evident in Lillie's story arc in which she becomes so obsessed with her romantic desires for Victor that they essentially consume her life, forcing her into deep isolation to the point where she can think of nothing else but being reunited with her love, even when she becomes an old woman in the "modern" storyline.

Lillie's obsessive love for Victor points out another concern inherent in Whedon's work: the doomed romance (Chiat, "Giant" 348). There are many examples of doomed romance within Whedon's television and film work, including Buffy/Angel and Giles/Jenny Calendar (in *Buffy the Vampire Slayer*), Wesley/Fred (in *Angel*), Zoe/Wash (in *Firefly/Serenity*), Echo/Paul Ballard and Topher/Bennett (in *Dollhouse*), and Ward/Skye (in *Agents of S.H.I.E.L.D.*). Both of the early antagonists, Kingpin and Punisher, in Whedon's *Runaways* story arc are significant because they both suffer from the loss of loved ones to the deadly machinations of the criminal underworld. Kingpin's wife dies twice in the course of his Marvel Comics appearances. First, she dies of multiple organ failure caused by the guilt of being forced to murder her own son, Richard, after he attempts to assassinate his own father in order to take over his criminal empire (*Daredevil*, volume 2, #92–93). She is later resurrected and brainwashed by the criminal organization the Hand in a plot to destroy Kingpin in order to take over his criminal operations in New York. Initially, when Vanessa attempts to kill him, Kingpin refuses to fight her and tries to reason with her; however, he is eventually forced to snap her neck when she lunges at him with a sword. He discovers too late that she was not actually aiming at him, but at a second assassin who was approaching him from behind in order to deal a killing blow (*Savage Wolverine* #8). Likewise, the Punisher's family, both wife and children, are murdered during a botched mob hit at a local park (*Marvel Premiere* #2). The loss of loved ones turns both men into vindictive and bloodthirsty killers with little to no remorse or moral compass.[4] The theme of lost love becomes increasingly significant as "Dead End Kids" progresses, with characters Chase, Victor, Nico, and the Yorkes either being motivated by or ultimately suffering a tragic loss of a loved one, either through death (as in the case of Chase and the Yorkes) or permanent separation (as in the case with Victor and Nico).

Ultimately, not all familial connections in *Runaways* are positive ones. The traditional, biological family is portrayed throughout Runaways as "dysfunctional, if not evil and dangerous, and as oppressive" (Burr and Jarvis 6). The biological family fails its members in practice by being inadequate and corrupt and never living up to the ideals inherent in the alternate family model. Unlike the alternate family discussed earlier, the biological family unit is undemocratic, totalitarian, and based entirely on inequality, especially for young people and women. It is for this reason that the younger generation look to each other for support, care, and respect the way the Runaways do, core necessities that their biological families do not provide (Burr and Jarvis 10–11). In *Runaways*, no adult authority figure can be trusted, especially not parents or other family members. The group is completely on its own, with only the other team members to depend upon (Chiat, "Joss Whedon 101" 321). When they do turn for protection to an adult authority figure, such as Kingpin, the disastrous results lead the team into deep danger. The Yorkes, supervillain parents of deceased Runaways member Gertrude Yorkes, appear from before their deaths thanks to their power of time travel. The villainous masterminds behind the 1907 street gang the Sinners, they exist as a primary example of the selfish nature of the family unit. When Chase tells them of Gertrude's act of self-sacrifice to save the lives of her alternate family, instead of feeling pride for the nobility of their daughter, they immediately seek a way to undo her good deed for their own self-serving needs. They decide to sacrifice the New York City of 1907 in order to guarantee their daughter's safety by destroying her alternate family and then going forward in time to save her before she commits her act of self-sacrifice. Mr. Yorkes specifically frames this as a war against all the young people, saying, "We'll kill them all. Them, the Street Arabs, all the kids in this time and place. They'll die for her pain. Then we'll go back and put things right" (*Runaways* #28). Ultimately, however, the Runaways manage to band together and prevent the Yorkes' bomb from detonating. Nico's final spell, "The Show Must Go On," forces the Yorkes to retain the memory of both their daughter's demise and their own but be unable to prevent either, the ultimate symbol of the futility of a love based solely on self-interest (*Runaways* #30).

Another character who shows the occasionally dark nature of biological familial bonds is the 1907 sorceress known as the Witchbreaker. Viewing Nico, her descendant, as weak and undeserving of her power, she sees no wrong in torturing Nico unmercifully in order to remake her into someone more in keeping with her image of her family: "The more pain you learn to take, the more power you will control. I won't have my great-granddaughter live at the mercy of her humanity. I can make you better. Or kill you, if I'm wrong about your potential" (*Runaways* #29). Given the subtext within the Runaways suggesting Nico's bisexuality (a subtext stressed intensely by Whedon in the early scene in *Runaways* #25 between Nico and Karolina after the team's meeting with Kingpin), the Witchbreaker's torture of Nico in an effort to make her conform suggests

Anthony Giddens' claim of inequality within the biological family unit for those young people of "non-normative sexuality" (Giddens 130).[5] Nico responds by accepting the testing with the words, "Hit me," battling through her ordeal to become far stronger. She arrives to save her friends by floating through the air (a new power) with a remade staff, quipping to the villainous Sinners, "You guys have *got* to grow up" (*Runaways* #30). While accepting her ancestress' training, Nico leaves her once the lesson is learned. Nico rejects the biological family as exploitative and controlling and is able to tap into her previously unknown reserves of magical strength by virtue of protecting her friends, not because of her desire to conform to her biological family's expectations (*Runaways* #30).

As the story ends, Klara leaves her abusive husband and travels to the twenty-first century with the team, while a frightened Lillie remains behind (apparently closing the time travel loop, which has her living with regret for decades then setting the time travel scenario in motion each time). Karolina (in many ways the team's maternal figure) comforts Victor by reminding him that he stayed with his family. Meanwhile, Chase time travels to see a young Gert before she became a Runaway and died, describing his glimpse of his star-crossed lover as "beautiful" (*Runaways* #30).

As the story winds down, Chase sums up what he liked about the last century—no one treated them like kids. Indeed, while they battle gangs of adults and team up with a gang of superpowered teens, 1907 is most significant to their story because there was no adolescence concept—anyone who could do a man's work or bear children was an adult and treated as such. "Teenagers haven't been invented yet" as Victor tells Molly (*Runaways* #29). When they join the grandiose superhero battle through the city or choose their romantic destinies, they make the choices as adults. As Chase concludes, "Age doesn't make grown-ups." Immediately, young Klara mentions that that was what her husband always said, and Chase cringes. As he says to forget he was talking and Karolina assures him they always do, their family bond continues to thrive. The value of love in Whedon's story arc in the Marvel comics *Runaways* series cannot be underestimated.

The entire storyline revolves around all the various aspects of love that are inherent in the human experience, from the Runaways' chosen family and destructive parents to a star-crossed couple, a strong couple, and supportive ex-lovers to an abusive relationship from America's past. Each type of love is explored, examined, and evaluated, with the entire spectrum shown to range from positive and nurturing to negative and destructive. Love, however, in Whedon's worldview is something worth fighting for. It is the one emotion that allows humans and superhuman alike to care enough about themselves and one another to risk their life and limb to protect each other. And, ultimately, no matter what the time period or no matter what the world is like, love is the one constant that helps bring everything into proper perspective and allows everyone to join together for the fight.

Notes

1. Klara Prast, a girl Molly's age from 1907, is an original creation of Whedon's, like Lillie and Tristan.

2. The marriage between a grown man and a young girl child was not unheard of in the late nineteenth and early twentieth centuries. According to statistical data, thirty percent of statutory rape cases from 1896 to 1926 sought to resolve the case by marriage or financial payment (Mintz 9).

3. In fact, many *Buffy the Vampire Slayer* fans consider the ephebophiliac relationship between Angel and Buffy to be the one great romance of the entire series and one of the great love stories of contemporary television.

4. The Punisher is seen as a hero (or anti-hero) as opposed to Kingpin's villain status primarily because he only kills criminals and those seeming deserving of death. The Punisher spares innocents and actively seeks to protect others. The Kingpin, on the other hand, has no moral compunction about killing innocents and will willingly put innocents in danger in order to gain an advantage over superheroes seeking to apprehend him.

5. Given Whedon's past metaphoric connection of lesbianism and magic (Willow and Tara in *Buffy the Vampire Slayer*), the connection between Nico's status as a magic-wielding superhero and her status as a bisexual woman within Whedon's artistic sensibility is not all that great a stretch.

Part Eight

Marvel's *X-Men*

• • •

Whedon boasts a long history with *X-Men*. While he read the comics as a child, he also did a treatment on the first film, though little of his work appeared onscreen. (Fascinatingly, an early draft suggests Rogue would have taken Mystique's powers to stop Magneto and save the day, rather than requiring Wolverine to rescue her while she was a chained-up pawn).

In Whedon's world, spunky, powerful Kitty Pryde was queen. As he explains in his forward to *Fray*, there were few girls in comics worth admiring before she arrived in Chris Claremont's regime. He calls her a figure of "such affection and identification" that it's unsurprising his own X-Men comics starred Kitty as main character. In fact, he arguably rebooted her to the Claremont years, even flashing back to her arrival at the school. Kitty inspired Buffy herself, and other spunky young heroines that followed.

From 2004 to 2008, Whedon wrote *Astonishing X-Men* vol. 3 (#1–24) and a final comic for *Giant Size Astonishing X-Men #1*. These were reprinted in four *Astonishing X-Men* trade paperback collections: *Gifted, Dangerous, Torn,* and *Unstoppable.* While Professor X is on Genosha, Scott Summers leads the team of Beast, Wolverine, Colossus, Lockheed, Kitty, and Emma Frost. Whedon introduced several characters to the X-Men franchise in these issues, including Agent Abigail Brand and her new organization S.W.O.R.D., the Danger Room turned sentient, and new X-Men Blindfold and Armor (both young Asian women). His Dr. Kavita Rao and the mutant cure plotline reappeared in the film *X-Men: The Last Stand*.

This collection's X-Men essays are all comparisons: Fernando Gabriel Pagnoni Berns and César Alfonso Marino link the new costumes and their statement of heroism with *Tales of the Slayers*, while Melissa C. Johnson sees River Tam as a hybrid of Wolverine, Dark Phoenix, and Kitty Pryde. I examine Kitty's heroine's journey, alongside others, later in the collection.

Embracing Goodness (and Colorful Costumes) Amid a World of Gray

Fernando Gabriel Pagnoni Berns
and César Alfonso Marino

• • •

In our current postmodern world, good and evil face the philosophy of relativism, which turns them into "fragile preferences of a particular social group at a certain place and time" (Pollefeyt 129). Good and evil are not, we know, essences but social constructions (Geertz 52). That, united with the desire to make our superheroes more human in a new millennium loaded with serious global problematics (Gray and Kaklamanidou 1) and gray ethical areas, is what prompts the creation of "realistic" superheroic fiction.

Joss Whedon, in his tenure as lead writer of *Astonishing X-Men*, plays with the dichotomy of good/evil, not to undermine it, nor to legitimize it, but to make it more complex. To do this he uses the figure of liminality as explained by Victor Turner, understood as alternative, as an in-between state. Still, by no means does this indicate any purpose on Whedon's part of denying the concrete existence of values such as virtue and immorality.

This brings a second topic in the Whedon universe: the uncompromising defense of an ethical position will alienate the person who embraces it. X-Men are lonely people much like Buffy, the most famous character created by Whedon. In fact, the embrace of ethics as a one-way road towards alienation is perfectly illustrated in the series *Tales of the Slayers* (Dark Horse, 2002), which narrates, through the centuries, the loneliness and pain of the women charged with defending their communities from the vampires.

Thus in *Gifted* and *Tales of the Slayers*, Whedon tears down simplistic dichotomies. Good and evil do indeed exist, but in connection with Estate. The lonely heroes who stand up for their ethics act as deviant subjects from the community and since each societal group "provide[s] its own definitions of deviant behavior" (Erikson 5), both the female Slayers and the X-Men are social pariahs, liminal characters in constant interplay with the boundaries that define good and evil. In the end, Whedon's comic-books, so widely read by teenagers, display under the format of adventures a complex dialectic of the need to hold fast to one's ethics even when that results in exclusion—a metaphor for the adolescent experience.

Gifted and the Embrace of Super-Heroics

With the coming of heroes to TV and cinema as never before, adaptation issues oblige creators to make certain changes that in a cursory glance appear as superficial. One of the most noticeable is the lack of costumes. This obeys the belief that, as Coogan argues, what looks good in comic-books—incredibly over-complicated costumes—looks simply silly on screen (9). Still, under this simple truth lies another one, more complex: the replacement of colorful costumes by more "civilian" clothes frames the new superhero subjectivities—that of moral ambiguity filtered through realism. Costumes respond to the old paradigm of absolute good vs. evil and in current sensibilities, this moral simplicity is replaced by gray for both heroes and villains.

This highlights the importance of Cyclops' simple request (to Wolverine's dismay) of returning to the use of bright yellow costumes rather than black leather which "made people nervous" (*Gifted* #1). This mention of the "black leather" answers the *X-Men* film series by Bryan Singer and its realistic approach to superheroes. In the 2000 film, all the main X-Men go on their first rescue mission in black leather uniforms. Hilariously, Wolverine (Hugh Jackman) complains about them, and Cyclops (James Marsden) replies that they are better than "yellow spandex," in clear reference to the bright colors that the classic X-Men have used through history.

The film emphasizes Rogue and Wolverine's humanity, as (respectively) a frightened runaway teen and a loner whose past has vanished, desperately seeking answers. Though both find acceptance among Professor Xavier and his friends, Rogue remains a student, and Wolverine ends the film driving off into the distance in his original leather jacket—they remain more human than their comic book counterparts. Meanwhile the other characters spend more time onscreen as teachers and students in civilian clothes than superheroes. The main storyline ties in with the United Nations and political spin, adding a layer of realism. Ambiguity stands out in the film, as Magneto, a Holocaust survivor, truly (and possibly correctly) believes he's protecting his people from genocide, and he and Professor Xavier acknowledge each other as "old friend."

Historically, the X-Men wore blue and yellow uniforms in the comics from 1963 (their debut) until original artist and co-creator Jack Kirby's departure. In 1975, Chris Claremont took over. His stories are some of the most beloved: long complex epics weaving together many storylines. He created Kitty Pryde, Dark Phoenix and many more iconic characters that inspired Whedon. *The Uncanny X-Men* offered fan favorite storylines that arguably inspired all the films, from *The Wolverine* to *X-Men: Days of Future Past*. In the seventies, when many superhero comics took on drugs and war, his were pure entertainment. His X-Men wore modest yellow and black costumes, emphasizing their blend of bright yellow with dramatic darkness.

The costumes used in *X-Men* (2000) inspired new black leather uniforms seen in the Grant Morrison comic-book run from 2001 on. Morrison's stories were dark and subversive, bringing Emma Frost into the lineup. In issue #115, the island of Genosha and its inhabitants, including Magneto, are completely destroyed. In his "New Worlds" (#127–133, illustrated by John Paul Leon and Phil Jimenez) the X-Men are revealed to the public and struggle to broker peace during rising human/mutant tensions. Under Morrison's authorship, good-boy Cyclops has a psychic affair with Emma Frost that destroys his marriage. With treachery and murder from within the X-Men ranks, no one can be trusted.

Whedon succeeded Morrison, emphasizing a need to return to the earlier time of Claremont's earnest, righteous teens with yellow and black. In this way, Whedon looks for a return to the classic values now retold in new scenarios, with his voice is embodied in Scott Summers' decisions. Following Cyclops's thinking, the X-Men are superheroes and for that, they must use costumes. If the black leather represents a realistic approach (as it's less outrageous and more practical for intimidation or battle), the return to a colorful wardrobe means the embrace of idealistic virtue against the "all-too-human" approach. In this scenario, it is not surprising Wolverine is always complaining about this seemingly minor detail. His character, both in comics and on onscreen, is closer to an anti-hero than a true savior. Thus, he is the one most uncomfortable with the idea of embodying of "pure" goodness. Whedon utilizes him as an excellent counterpart to his tired and disheveled version of Cyclops. In this sense, the realistic drawings of John Cassaday help to create characters in which the internal stresses to remain strong in their convictions can be observed (e.g., Cyclops's tired face, the sharp features in the face of Emma Frost). This new incarnation of the X-Men decide to present themselves to the world, leaving aside any ambiguity, as clear archetypes of superheroes. This can be seen as a cynical move on Cyclops's part, especially since the X-Men new modus operandi includes giving press conferences about their actions (*Gifted* #2). Even so, Scott accepts the mission that the X-Men, as superpowered beings, have in this world. In his first chat with the team, he asks for acceptance of their calling as saviors, even when this world hates them. As he explicitly says in the first issue, they are a group of superheroes and it is time to behave as such.

Something has to remain clear: Whedon is not advocating for a return to a Manichean concept of absolute evil and goodness. In Whedon's world, gray areas and ambiguity indeed exist within human beings (Lavery and Burkhead 186). He even introduces the "mutant cure" plot that devastates the mutant community with the temptation to be "normal" and in some cases fix the devastations of their lives, a plot adapted into the film *X-Men: The Last Stand*. Nonetheless, his team must take a moral position in life. X-Men have elected to save the world, and for that, they choose to embrace altruism and sacrifice, especially in the wake of emotional devastation—Cyclops has lost Jean Grey, Kitty Pryde has lost her father, and the mutants have lost millions of their brethren on the island of Genosha. Despite their grief, while they do not choose the dark side (and they are, certainly, free to do so), they must behave as heroes.

In this sense, it is not by chance that former-villain-turned-hero Emma Frost teaches ethics in the school for mutants, to Kitty Pride's astonishment and anger (*Gifted* #3). Whedon makes this move explicitly to muddle the characters' moral certainty. Frost as teacher of ethics is an ironic gesture. Though she tries to embrace the team's virtues, she is smart enough to know that she risks falling into villainy again. For that, she has requested Kitty's presence since Emma perfectly realizes that Kitty Pryde hates her and thus will watch for slips. Kitty responds: "Whenever I think about evil, whenever I think about the concept of evil, yours is the face that I see." As she adds, "I don't have to 'watch you,' Miss Frost. I can smell you." For Kitty, Emma is the embodiment of evil in pure form and this cannot be altered. This rivalry is one of the highlights of Whedon's run (Kaveney, *Superheroes* 223).

Embracing a moral position is to take ethical values which cannot always be framed within relativism or subjectivity. In 1944, C. S. Lewis wrote *The Abolition of Man*, a book that denounces the dangers inherent in the idea that values exist only within persons and therefore, have no entity outside subjectivities (5). Ethical values indeed exist outside human embodiment. Concepts such as good and evilness cannot be taken just as trivial subjectivities. Lewis argues for the objectivity and materiality of moral values as concrete concepts representing concrete universal actions (Duriez 66). There is free will to choose certain paths, but when chosen, the person who has done so must stand for these values, even when this determinacy to sustain ethical issues alienates him or her. In this scenario, the X-Men are the perfect subjects since Scott Summers has chosen to embrace super-heroics and goodness even when he and his team know that humanity hates mutants. This is part of Whedon's philosophy: ethical values result in rejection from the world. Nonetheless, this is part of what takes to embraces goodness in a world of gray.

This topic of alienation is a big part of Buffy mythology both in TV and in comic-book form (Stanley 253), since she is a girl trapped in her mission of saving the world, even when this means that she cannot carry on a normal life. *Tales of the Slayers* aims especially for this concept.

Tales of the Slayers and the Loneliness of the Hero

Tales of the Slayers is a graphic novel whose action takes place within the Buffyverse. The book's storyline consists of eight stories written by Joss Whedon and his top writers, which tell of different members of the Slayer lineage.

The stories are presented in chronological order and offer brief moments or tales of Slayers throughout history, from the First Slayer to Melaka Fray, a Slayer from the future. The overarching theme of the graphic novel is about the loneliness that comes with the duties of being a Slayer.

The book opens with the First Slayer battling demons in some uncertain primeval era. The first words that appears in the book are "I am alone" and are pronounced by the Slayer herself, establishing the tone of the whole book. After the Slayer kills the demon, a little child who represents the village that has been saved approaches the Slayer and gives, as an offering, a basket full of food. Then she asks the Slayer to leave the place since the villagers fear her monstrous nature.

This first tale is only six pages long and those are enough to showcase all the topics that respond to Whedon's philosophy. The Slayer is a lonely creature feared by those whom she must protect and despite this, she (and her subsequent sisters) will continue doing so. This marks a clear connection with the universe of the X-Men that Whedon has developed so well:

the hero as pariah who has taken the mantle of savior with all the toils and virtues that come with it, and acts in consequence. Another issue unites *Tales of the Slayers* with the *X-Men*: the quality of liminality. In this first tale of the Slayers, the little child mentions the reason behind her community's fear: she is half human/half demon. As Victor Turner argues, the attributes of a liminal persona are ambiguous since the people who have them "elude or slip through the network of classifications" within a society (Turner 147). This way, society, community and State cannot exert any real power upon a person who rejects being classified. To name or classify is a hermeneutic way to control based upon a dichotomy constructed around artificial meanings of normalcy and abnormality. Thus, both Slayers and X-Men, as mutated humans, as liminal beings (both humans and something more) can avoid total control by the State, a fact that turns them into dangerous beings. For Whedon, the maximum difference recognized between the representatives of the moral and those segregated by them is that the former have an institution that supports: the State. For Whedon, State is the border which marks the difference between what is permitted and what not. Consequently, State needs to continuously create very clear parameters of normalcy so to obliterate or negate any alternative and appear fully unquestioned. In this system, Whedon finds in the liminality of the heroes the fissure needed to display the contradiction.

Liminality is not present only in the first story, but is a continuous subplot through the graphic novel. In the story set in Victorian England ("Presumption"), the Slayer passes as a man. Only disguised can she go to places forbidden for women, and thus, be more effective in her mission to exterminate vampires. Again liminality appears since she is both a woman and a man according the circumstances. It should be noted that, for the Victorian society, exaggerated mobility of women in the public sphere without proper (male) permission was a defiance of propriety (Becker 35). Here we find, then, an example of how each society and each historical moment enacts its own conceptions of what is right and what is wrong.

Mixed blood and lack of belonging illustrates liminality in the tale taking place in "The Glittering World." It is not by chance that the Old West is chosen as the setting for this tale since popularly, this space and time offered very simplistic representations of good and evil, leading to the clearly-labeled "Black Hats" and "White Hats" referenced in *Buffy* and other Whedon projects. In "Righteous," the tale taking place during the Inquisition, the Slayer who saves the community is accused of witchcraft. Even when rescuing her neighbors, she is feared because of her powers and strong values. For the community, she is human but also demonic. The title of the story implies that she has some objective value by her side, even when she dies burned at the stake in the end. Again, the philosophy of Lewis seems to frame the adventure: ethics are objective values (rather than just subjectivities) and must be carried on to the very end. In fact, as Mark Pike signals, "righteousness" is a word very valuated within Lewis' philosophy (Pike 18).

But is "Sonnenblume" that most perfectly encompasses the topics of righteousness and evil as existent entities rather than subjectivities prone to relativism. Sonnenblume is an adolescent living in Nazi Germany. Even being so young, she is already an expert killer of demons. But she understands "pure evil" as a quality inherent only in supernatural beings. Outside the supernatural sphere, all is relative. In front of her eyes, Nazi atrocities begin. Even so, Sonnenblume remains doubtful and idle. She kills monsters but, even with superior strength, she does nothing to help those arrested by the Nazis, even when they are her friends. Even more, she starts to despise Jews. She can start to stop the Nazis only after she accepts that evil indeed exists as an entity that affects monsters and humans as well. Then, she begins to fight "Evil" as an objective value, not just an idea embodied in supernatural monsters. If the girl has her doubts about the true nature of evil and good, the end of the tale shows that Whedon "is not a nihilist about ethics and value. There are objective standards" (Baggett 23) indeed. And those standards are what heroes, as representatives of goodness, must carry.

Conclusions

In *Gifted* #4, Scott Summers presents himself and his team as "heroes" and not vigilantes. When the mission gets personal and thus, subjective, he separates himself from heroism, explaining: "This night, we are not heroes" but rather, civilians, even if they are using the inspirational costumes. This means that the civic persona and the heroic are not one and the same; that, when heroes, they embrace additional ethical values.

In our contemporary world filled with moral ambiguity, the "old" hero/villain binarism seems to have no place, as it is much too simplistic for the complexities of the new millennium. Joss Whedon works with this dichotomy and plays with the complexity of gray areas, but he understands moral and ethics values as objectivities, no mere abstractions. Standing up for values of goodness (or evil) will generate social oppression and isolation, as the Slayers can testify. Even so, someone must do so in order to inspire the world.

River Is Wolverine

Whedon Performs a Sex-Change

MELISSA C. JOHNSON

• • •

As I was sitting in the audience at a panel on *Firefly/Serenity* at the Slayage 2 Conference at Gordon College in 2006, I had an epiphany. The speaker—whose name or topic I'm afraid I can't recall—was showing a clip from the film *Serenity*, which featured River's fight with the Reavers. The image of River, standing over the corpses of the Reavers with her two weapons dripping blood and her body both relaxed and poised to continue the fight with the advancing Alliance troops, struck me as very familiar—the lighting, her posture, the weapons in her hands, the way her head was tilted down as she looked up at the camera through her hair. Clearly there were overtones of Buffy and the scythe and Buffy poised on the platform with the hammer in "Anne" (B3.1), but what I really saw was Wolverine of the *X-Men* with his claws extended and dripping blood—an image from the *X-Men* films that I had recently been watching. That flash identification between River and Wolverine led me to pursue the parallels between them and to discover that River is not just similar to Wolverine in her origins and relationships with the rest of the crew, but is really an amalgam of the qualities of three *X-Men* characters—Wolverine, Kitty Pryde, and Jean Grey.

Roz Kaveney, in both her paper at Slayage 2, and in her book *Superheroes!* points out how Whedon's work has been influenced by "his comics obsession" in both positive and negative ways (202). She identifies this influence as one of the many that contributes to the "thick texts" created by Whedon and other "fanboy creators" (203) and traces Whedon's "obsession" with the figure of the superhero throughout his career. She notes in an aside that River is in the process of becoming a superhero and her character has many of the same superhero qualities as Buffy's—"powers, bad relationships with the authorities, and liminality"—but does not pursue this analysis of River or connect her specifically to any superheroes from the *X-Men* comics (212). However, she does note the influence of the Chris Claremont period of the *X-Men* comics on Whedon's work in general—an influence Whedon himself has often acknowledged, and a story which he has taken over in his writing of the *Astonishing X-Men* comics. Whedon has identified Kitty Pryde (Shadowcat) as an inspiration for Buffy Summers, and Kaveney notes that both Kitty Pryde and Jean Grey/Dark Phoenix are obvious influences on the characterization of Willow (*Superheroes* 214). In addition, River's character is also influenced and shaped by the *X-Men* comics, in several ways significant for Whedon scholarship and particularly for gender studies and feminist approaches to the Whedonverse.

River Tam of *Firefly* and *Serenity* is exceptional—both mentally and physically. As her brother Simon tells the crew in the pilot: "River was more than gifted. She ... she was a gift. Everything she did, music, math, theoretical physics—even-even dance—there was nothing that didn't come as naturally to her as breathing does to us" ("Serenity," F1.1). These gifts lead her to a government-sponsored school where she is brutally weaponized through surgical experimentation on her brain by Alliance doctors and scientists. While the procedures heighten and magnify her gifts, the cost is River's sanity. In the film, *Serenity*, she is described by Dr. Mathias to Simon Tam, who is posing as an alliance official, "River Tam is our star pupil. She'll be ideal for defense deployment ... even with the side effects." Those side effects are, in addition to River's obvious anguish as she dreams, being unstable and having a fragmented "reality matrix," but Matthias assures Simon, "She's not just a psychic. Given the right trigger, this girl is a living weapon."

In both the series and the film, Simon rescues her and they become renegades, hunted by the Alliance and disowned by their parents. Under her brother's care and in the safe womb of Serenity, River slowly begins to recover and to gain control of her psychic, physical, and mental powers. A small, feminine, graceful, and childlike presence, River Tam is also a force with which to be reckoned. As she says after shooting three men who threaten her and Kaylee in "War Stories," "No power in the 'Verse can stop me" (F1.10). Because she is usually taciturn, speaks in riddles on the rare occasions she does speak, and behaves erratically and sometimes violently, the other crew members fear her and see her as risk—particularly Jayne. After she slashes Jayne and his Blue Sun shirt with a butcher knife in

"Ariel" (F1.9) and is found with Jayne's loaded gun in "Objects in Space" (F1.14), Kaylee reveals River's prowess with a gun to the crew. Mal sums up the situation at the crew's conference thusly: "What we got here to deal with is the larger issue. And that larger issue is we got someone on board this ship might be a danger to us. Ain't a question of whether we like her" (F.14). His solution is to confine her to her room. The same trajectory is reflected in the film after she is triggered by the Fruity Oaty bars advertisement in the Maidenhead, beats up everyone in the bar, and nearly kills Mal. He says to Simon, "You had a gorramn time bomb living with us! Who we gonna find in there when she wakes up? The girl? Or the Weapon? Despite their fear of her, River utilizes her extraordinary abilities to save her fellow crewmembers and gains back the crew's, and particularly, Mal's trust. In both the series and the movie, Mal welcomes her back to the ship as the ship's "little albatross" and as a little sister. While the other crew members experience crushes, love, sexual adventures, and marriage, River remains alone. When she expresses a desire to marry Simon, her brother, in a deleted scene from "Our Mrs. Reynolds," this is seen by him and others as a part of her psychosis or a child-like imitation of Mal's marriage (F1.6). The partner she chooses is unacceptable to that person and to others. Thus she's symbolically isolated, as well as troubled, extraordinary, and marked in irrevocable ways by those who experimented upon her, seen as a kind of ghost by herself and others.

Her story bears marked similarities to Wolverine's, while keeping in mind that Wolverine is a very complex and long-lived character who has been written in many different, and sometimes contradictory, ways over his history. The best-known version comes primarily from the first three *X-Men* films—Joss Whedon was an uncredited script writer on the first, while his "mutant cure" plot from "Gifted" inspired the third. Another popular source is Wolverine's origin story told in "Weapon X" by Barry Windsor Smith which appears in *Marvel Comics Presents* #72–84 from 1991. Windsor-Smith replaced Chris Claremont, who had written the comic for sixteen years and made it extremely successful. Claremont described the character of Wolverine in an interview in 1982 in this way: "In the beginning, Len crafted him as a crazy man, and I took that and embellished on it, making him crazier. Problem was, I never really liked craziness, so Dave and I began making him more rational, and John and I continued that process" (Sanderson 2). However, Jim Shooter, the editor-in-chief of Marvel, complained that Wolverine was becoming a "sissy" and indicated that "he wanted Wolverine to be as much of a potential danger to the X-Men as to other people" (49). A mutant with extraordinary healing abilities, strength, and sensory perception, Wolverine (or Logan) is kidnapped and experimented upon by Canadian scientists. These scientists manipulate his memories and fuse adamantium to his skeleton, including his claws, which makes him even more formidable as a warrior. In his first appearance in *The Incredible Hulk* 181 in November of 1974, he is described as "The World's First and Greatest Canadian Super Hero." Within the comic, an officer at a secret Canadian military complex explains Wolverine's skills: "The Government has spent a great deal of time, effort, and money developing that mutant's natural born speed strength and savagery into the skills of a professional warrior—and despite the few kinks still remaining in his psychological makeup, I think we've done a pretty good job." Those "few kinks" cause Wolverine to lose his identity and much of his memory. After escaping, he lives for a time in the forest in a feral, mad state—a bit like Lancelot. Sometime after his recovery, he joins the X-Men, but he remains a distrustful loner, and is viewed by others as too volatile. He is known, in particular, for his uncontrollable "berserker rages," in which he kills indiscriminately and irresistibly, despite great odds. He falls in love with Jean Grey, who is married to Cyclops and therefore an unacceptable partner. While he slowly recovers his memory and befriends various younger X-Men recruits, including Kitty Pryde, Wolverine remains essentially a recluse who is often resented and feared.

In the continuation comics *Serenity: Leaves on the Wind*, a more stable River searches her mind for the secrets she's forgotten and discovers she was one of many similar victims. Like Wolverine in the film *X-Men 2*, she goes back to the facility where she was made, seeking answers. Both meet their elderly creators, who respond with pride. River's calls her "such a special girl. Such a unique mind. A work of art. Can I tell you a secret? You were always my favorite" (#4). Then, like his X-Men counterpart Stryker, he sets his other creations to attack. While Wolverine kills his female counterpart in the film, River manages to save Iris, an altered woman much like herself. Both stories force the heroes to weigh their curiosity about their pasts against their responsibilities to the team, emphasizing how both have become part of a community, albeit one of outcasts. These stories also offer another level of responsibility in the "cause"—the New Resistance in *Serenity* and the cries of "Mutant Freedom" for the X-Men, as even the loners must take a stand in the larger world.

It is clear that River Tam shares many characteristics with Wolverine, but there are significant differences between the two which may reflect their gender differences. She is more airy sprite and he more earthy animal. She is more philosophical and cerebral and he is more visceral. She is a teenager and he is at least middle-aged, perhaps even older. Many of the characteristics which differentiate River from Wolverine are those she shares with two female X-Men: Jean Grey and Kitty Pryde.

Jean Grey, like River, is highly intelligent, psychic, and hyper-feminine. They are both unable to fully control their gifts in the beginning and often must be protected by other members of the teams. River seems the innocent damsel and protectee of the group in her first appearances, as early Jean Grey has the most subtle power, compared with the physical violence of her male teammates. Both women comfort their teams with clever insights, pithy wisdom, and heartfelt sympathy. Jean Grey's early appearances as love interest and demure student are almost as passive as River's, curled naked in a shipping crate for her brother to protect. Of course, both young women grow exponentially in power. In late appearances, River defeats an army of Reavers while Jean ascends into near-godhood, almost destroying the universe as the Phoenix before tragically sacrificing herself. Finally, both women pose a serious threat to their teams as their power eclipses their control. In fact, River's "sleeper" persona, activated in *Serenity*, is a dormant alter-ego of incredible destructive force, much like the Phoenix.

River shares many more characteristics with Kitty Pryde. Kitty was created by Chris Claremont and John Byrne and first appeared in *Uncanny X-Men* #129 in January of 1980 as a thirteen-year-old and the youngest ever member. She is described in the *X-Men Companion II* as "the newest of the X-Men, the one who best embodies the essence of the group. She is a girl who has only recently passed puberty and entered into her teens, and who has left home and parents for the first time in her young life" (8). Kitty's mutant power is phasing—the ability to move herself and others into and through solid objects and people. While River doesn't possess this gift, she does a good job of imitating it in "Objects in Space" when she convinces Jubal Early that she has become the ship. In addition to this mutant ability, Kitty Pryde is a genius, a computer expert, and a gifted dancer. Later in her history, she masters martial arts when she is possessed by a demon ninja Ogun in the *Kitty Pryde and Wolverine* six-issue series written by Chris Claremont in 1984. Initially lacking in confidence and often fearful, Kitty Pryde goes on to become a valued member of the X-Men. As an adult, she is brought back by Joss Whedon in the *Amazing X-Men*. Whedon has spoken often of his attraction to this character, calling her in the Foreword to *Fray* "such a figure of both affection and identification." While his affection for River is clear, Whedon writes her in ways that go beyond Kitty Pryde, making her much more formidable and far more damaged with the addition of characteristics from Wolverine and Jean Grey.

Why does it matter that Joss Whedon seems to have based the character of River Tam on characters from the X-Men? First of all, as Kaveney points out, the influence of comics, and particularly the *X-Men*, on Whedon's creations is far more pervasive than just this single character. The ensemble casts of *Buffy*, *Angel*, and *Firefly/Serenity* all reflect the unusual ensemble nature of the X-Men team in their shared responsibilities, interdependence, and status as "chosen" families as Jes Battis calls them in her book *Blood Relations* or families of the heart as Kaveney terms them (*Superheroes* 9). The mutants in *X-Men* are othered by mainstream society as are the vampires, demons, witches, petty criminals, whores, lesbians, and geeks who populate the Buffyverse and the Fireflyverse. It is also significant that Whedon has chosen to make his Wolverine figure a girl. This "sex-change" offers another avenue for exploration in the ongoing scholarly conversation about Joss Whedon's feminism and the success or failure of his characters and plots to challenge the patriarchal status quo.

Chris Claremont's run on the *X-Men* was recognized for its feminism, while his commentary on his powerful female characters is often quoted. As he said: "It always seemed to me there was never any reason why a character should be any less heroic, courageous, intelligent, aggressive, simply because that character was a woman" (Sanderson 21). If crazy and damaged also appear on that list of adjectives, Whedon's rationale for the character of River Tam appears—creating yet another strong, complex female character as an alternative to the limited and stereotypical images of women in comics, film, and television. River, like Buffy, Faith, and Willow before her and Inara, Zoe, and Kaylee in the same series, both taps into and subverts sexist literary and pop culture images of women and girls. More significantly, River Tam is a further evolution of the morally justified woman warrior that Whedon created in Buffy Summers. As Frances H. Early argued in "Staking Her Claim: *Buffy the Vampire Slayer* as Transgressive Woman Warrior," Buffy is such a warrior, but complicated beyond a "compensatory fantasy for young women" (18). According to Early in a later, revised edition of the same essay, Buffy's woman warrior persona exhibits many of the qualities of male warriors in her strength and enjoyment of her bodily power, but the show's plots and characters also parody and interrogate traditional ideals of male warriors and soldier-heroes and offer an "incipient pacifist critique of the inevitability of war and the violence it engenders" ("Female Just Warrior Reimagined" 58–59). We can see River Tam's character as an evolution of this transgressive or subversive woman warrior when we examine the ways in which River's characterization, representation, and story arc differ from Buffy's.

As many scholars have demonstrated, River reflects an array of ancient and contemporary literary female tropes or stereotypes—witch, Cassandra, mad Ophelia, hysterical girl, and "weaponized woman."[1] Alyson R. Buckman observes that Whedon engages with these stereotypes in order to destabilize them and "deconstruct masculine discourse" ("Much Madness" 41). Buckman also argues that one of the ways in which Whedon does this is through his "resistance to sexualizing River" ("Much Madness" 46). This resistance as well as clearly identifying the causes of River's psychological damage, disordered behavior, and deadly combat skill as external to her own agency and biology, lies at the heart of Whedon's success in making River Tam a new kind of feminist heroine—not just another kickass shero who can beat the boys in a fight and also make them swoon. As noted earlier, River is an ineffective warrior until the end of the series and the end of the film. Unlike Buffy, she does not take the stage with control of her powers or as an object of male sexual desire. She only enacts violence when her programming is triggered or to protect the crew of the ship, her real and chosen family, not out of a sense of moral righteousness. While both the series and the film ultimately end with River gaining sufficient control of her innate intellectual gifts and Alliance-engineered powers to save the crew from Jubal Early and the Reavers respectively, the real triumph is Whedon's creation of a character who demonstrates the damage that patriarchy does to humanity as a whole. River Tam is unpredictable, difficult, and dangerous because she was made that way by the Alliance, not because she is a woman or because she is burdened by special powers or responsibilities. She survives and protects the crew because she is brilliant, brave, and loving, but also because she has been weaponized. The enemies she fights are humans who have, like herself, been damaged or co-opted by the Alliance, rather than demons. In a world without the Alliance and the oppression and horrors created by their desire to control and to conquer, she might never have been capable of or had to resort to violence. By delaying River's emergence as a "big damn hero," by making the audience frustrated with that delay, Whedon forces his audience to confront their own complicity in a frontier mentality and perhaps even in our own military-industrial complex.

Note

1. For a discussion of River as a witch see Alyson R. Buckman, "'Much Madness in the Divinest Sense': Firefly's 'Big Damn Heroes' and Little Witches," *Investigating*

Firefly and Serenity: Science Fiction on the Frontier, eds. Rhonda V. Wilcox and Tanya R. Cochran (London: I.B. Tauris, 2008), 41–49. For a discussion of River as a witch and a Cassandra figure, see Karin Beeler, "The Transformation of River Tam: Psychic Warrior, Female Prodigy and Anti-Hero in *Firefly and Serenity*," *Seers, Witches and Psychics on Screen: An Analysis of Women Visionary Characters in Recent Television and Film* (Jefferson, NC: McFarland, 2008), 38–48. For a discussion of River Tam as the latest in a series of "weaponized women" in the Whedonverse, see Michael Marano, "River Tam and the Weaponized Women of the Whedonverse," *Serenity Found: More Unauthorized Essays on Joss Whedon's Firefly Universe*, ed. Jane Espenson with Leah Wilson (Dallas: BenBella, 2007), 37–48.

An earlier version of Melissa C. Johnson's "River Is Wolverine: Whedon Performs a Sex-Change" was previously presented at SC3: The Slayage Conference on the Whedonverses. Henderson State University. Akadelphia, AR, June 7, 2008.

Part Nine

Whedon's Other Comics

• • •

Whedon's love of dystopia linked well with the twenty-first century post-apocalyptic comics as he created Melaka Fray, a Slayer operating in the ruins of Manhattan centuries after Buffy. *Fray* (2001–2003) was Whedon's first comic, though the character reappears in *Time of Your Life* (B8.4) and *Tales of the Slayers.* The cast is simple: a punk dystopian teen Slayer. Her demon mentor and mutated fish-boss. Her evil twin brother and bossy older sister. The vampire that killed her brother four years ago. And the little girl sidekick she longs to protect. In a world that's never even *heard* of vampires, she'll have to find her courage.

Sugarshock! (2009) is Whedon's stand-alone, a lighthearted intergalactic romp published in *Myspace: Dark Horse Presents #1.* Dandelion Naizen, a magenta-haired vixen with a deadly hatred of Vikings, leads the Sugarshock band. Tall L'Lihdra in pink pinstripes plays guitar, while plump Wade plays drums. Phil the robot completes the team. A mysterious invite to a battle of the bands (or some sort of battle anyway) falls from the sky and the team eagerly accepts.

Whedon has done more with Marvel and DC. His script for a *Wonder Woman* movie, while never filmed, has since been released online. He wrote the brief "Teamwork" for *Giant Size X-Men* #3 (2005) and two pages of *Superman/Batman* #26, to honor the untimely death of a staff writer (2006). He also penned "Some Steves" to celebrate the 65th Anniversary of Stan Lee's employment at Marvel for *Stan Lee Meets The Amazing Spider-Man* (2006).

One of my essays examines Whedon's heroine's journey through *Fray, X-Men,* and *Buffy: Season Nine*'s *Willow: Wonderland,* as well as his *Wonder Woman* script. The other examines his metacomics about fandom and conventions: *Angel: After the Fall*'s *Last Angel in Hell, Stan Lee Meets the Amazing Spider-Man,* and *Sugarshock!*.

The Heroine's Journey from Fray to Wonder Woman

Valerie Estelle Frankel

• • •

Call to Adventure

In *The Myth of the Superhero,* Marco Arnaudo proclaims: "No contemporary genre exhibits the specific qualities of epic so much as the superhero comic does," and goes on to compare the two forms through twenty tropes (118). Indeed, the episodic nature of comics reflects the growth of identity found in the classic hero's or heroine's journey, even as demigods battle evil incarnate and save the world each time.

It's appropriate that Whedon's first graphic novel, *Fray,* is a perfect heroine's journey in itself, paralleling Buffy's path but in only eight issues. Besides his monomyth pattern in the *Buffy* film and show (to say nothing of Echo, River, Cordelia, and Skye's mythic evolutions onscreen), Whedon wrote more heroine's journeys in the comic worlds of *X-Men* and *Wonder Woman* (though this last was only in script form). His production, *Buffy: Season Nine,* contains multiple personal journeys, including the spinoff comic *Willow: Wonderland* by Jeff Parker and Christos Gage. All of these follow the classic heroine's journey step by step, celebrating and illustrating the path of the chosen one.

Fray opens in grand epic style, in a world of demons, shattered graves and a blacked-out sun. "She is discovered.... No one has been called for two hundred years. The signs are dim," a disembodied voice proclaims. As the perspective shifts to a tunnel of corpses, the voice warns that the cycle must not "begin anew." However, Fray's destiny as chosen one defies the demons' plans.

Melaka Fray begins her story alone. As a Grabber, she steals for various criminal elements of the community, especially the fish-man Gunther.

In her first scene, she's falling off a roof after fellow thieves have pushed her. Still, this is all in a day. Fray "is hard, defensive, vulnerable, goofy, and yes, wicked sexy," Whedon says ("Foreword," *Fray*). Athletic and agile, she wears big boots and baggy pants, with a scar stretching from top lip to her left cheek, a nose stud, and multiple gold hoop earrings. She has dark nails and lipstick, though her most distinctive feature is the magenta highlighting in her black hair.

She stands out as unique in her world, not for her adornments but for her humanity. As she explains, "There's so many been mutated by the sun's radiation—whether by direct exposure or by their parents'—that you more or less get used to living in a side show." Her little friend Loo, with one arm and one working eye, is as endearing and sad as a three-legged puppy.

Fray's call to adventure is rather terrifying. A Watcher comes to her and announces, "You ... are the Chosen.... I am not worthy to come before you.... You will save us." Then he sets himself on fire and dies horrifically.

Wonder Woman's tale also begins in epic fashion, as a voiceover describes the all-powerful Amazons and their withdrawal from the world. "In the time of the ancient Greeks, the most powerful warriors on earth were the Amazon women.... Legend has it that Ares, the god of war, grew jealous of their power and had them imprisoned, their wrists bound in mystical chains." The Amazon queen prayed to Athena for deliverance and the goddess carried them all far from the world. On her home of Paradise Island, the queen's daughter, Diana, visits Athena's temple each night to ask what she's supposed to be. "I was meant to be more, I know it. To do something worthy." The desire to quest seethes within. Her mission arrives with Steve Trevor, a human she decides is worth saving, though the Amazons condemn him to die. She battles her mother and wins his safety ... and a chance to go with him.

Kitty Pryde's beginning is less apocalyptic. At the start of Whedon's run on *Astonishing X-Men*, she returns to the school as a teacher, not a student. In the newly rebuilt hallway, she reflects how, as she puts it, "nothing has changed." As she notes, she's "a kid again, out of my depth—completely overwhelmed by everything here, and it isn't the Sidri, or the Sentinels, or the Brood that surround me.... /It's the smaller pieces./ Shards/ Of me" (*X-Men: Gifted*).

Willow: Wonderland is a magic quest straight from Oz or Narnia. Willow explains:

> Music, poetry, everything's going bad. This isn't just me not liking new trends. No one can hit a note, everyone's auto-tuned. Coke doesn't taste

right anymore. I see examples everywhere. It's not just that there suddenly aren't witches and the occult around now. Suicide rates are moving up every day. It's the inspiration, the dreams. All the things that make life so wonderful. It's just not quite ... *there* like it used to be. So I'm setting out to do something about it. To bring magic *back* [*Willow: Wonderland*].

Willow takes Buffy's broken scythe and creates a portal into as she puts it, "wherever." This act of pure faith is rewarded, as it opens bloodlessly and whisks her to a new universe. There she quests for a Deeper Well that can restart earth's magic. As she travels, she is tentative, fearing the reappearance of Dark Willow or her magic addiction. Nonetheless, she's determined to try.

Mentor and Talisman

The monstrous Marrak, giant and crimson with goat horns, meets Willow upon arrival. He describes himself as a human conjurer, transformed into his beastly appearance by someone's spell. Stranded since the death of magic, he knows a great deal about the world, while Willow appears a naïve innocent by comparison.

After battling monsters, the pair find respite at a pure, cool spring. There lives the Caterpillar, straight from *Alice in Wonderland.* As Willow drinks from the pool, which he calls a "spring of memories," she sees her friends: Oz, Tara, Buffy and Xander, and feels the guilt of every mistake she made, every time she let them down. She fills her canteen there nonetheless. Water is a feminine symbol, appearing in grails and cauldrons and representing the font of life. This source of abundance and fertility also evokes the heart and lifeblood of the carrier (Cooper 76). Man quests for it, but woman carries it with her.

Fray's mentor is the demon Urkonn, who, much like Marrak, "resembles Giles in speech and Giles' Fyarl demon shape in appearance" (Frankel 276). He trains Fray as traditional Watchers do and gives Fray the scythe, saying, "It is your sword and scepter. Let it proclaim you the hero—and the monster—that you will need to be." Forged in ancient days (and drawn by Buffy from a stone), it's shaped like the Death Goddess's crescent or waning moon. It symbolizes death but also the following rebirth of the harvest, and thus echoes "the destructive and creative powers of the Great Mother" (Cooper 146). Fray's tattoo, intriguingly, is a triple crescent. Three moons are a goddess symbol, reflecting the three aspects of the moon (waxing, waning, and full) and three ages of womankind (mother, maiden, crone), as well as the feminine polarity of the universe.

Leaving *Fray* without prophetic dreams emphasizes the heroine's dividedness and isolation but also aligns her story closer with comic book tropes. Buffy may fight her destiny but she gives in soon enough to the pressure of slayer dreams (and even willingly goes to her foretold death in "Prophecy Girl," B1.12). Only in the comics medium of Season Eight does Buffy reject a new universe that's been building for millennia, with the words "I *never* do what I'm meant for" (*Twilight*, B8.7). By Season Ten she's writing prophecy instead of obeying it. Fray, completely unburdened by the pressure of slayer dreams, is free to choose slaying or not. In epic, prophecy is immutable. "In the superhero world, which is centered on the secular concept of freedom of the individual to pursue his own destiny, prophecies of a future predetermined by greater forces and external to individual will often take a negative, ominous, and suffocating tone" (Arnaudo 125). In their comics, therefore, Buffy and Fray ignore the universe's dictates.

In a nod to this philosophy, Whedon's Diana begins her story praying for guidance and eager to accept Steve Trevor's coming as a sign. However, after his sarcastic response to this ("So my imminent death is, wow, all about *you*"), Diana stops worrying about fate and leaves the island for a world of reality, not predestination and rule by the distant gods.

Diana's first mentor is her mother, who gives her the Lasso of Truth. She adds, "Remember who you are. They will take everything from you but that"—wise words that save Diana at the climax. As experienced, world-weary queen, Hippolyte cares deeply for Diana, though she's sure she knows best, for her and for the Amazon people.

Symbolically, the lasso is a mythic weapon "created in divine realms" and imbued with the power "to penetrate the human soul" (Arnaudo 126). As such, it corresponds to the gods-given weapon on the hero epic, like Excalibur. Further, it is a feminine weapon. "Goddesses traditionally use distance weapons—the bow of Artemis or the weather magic of the deadly Irish Morrigan" (Frankel 31). Hecate wields a long whip, as does Xena on occasion. String or cord is also a feminine symbol, like Ariadne's ball of yarn unraveling through the labyrinth. This too symbolizes enlightenment and the unity or continuity that binds the world together (Cooper 170). It also marks a source of connection between the wielder and those around her. "The cord is ambivalent as being both the agent of binding and limitation and also the possibility of infinite extension and freedom" (Cooper 42). Wonder Woman indeed embarks on a quest to break bonds but also make those she chooses, tying herself to a new community.

Kitty Pryde's gift is disappearing. Like Wonder Woman's invisible plane, this is a power of apparently harmlessness, but actually unseen defense of one's self and others. "While her ability to phase through solid objects initially may make her seem like a mysterious wallflower when she disappears through barriers, with this power, Pryde actively challenges notions of stability at their most basic, physical level" (Galvan 47). She saves her friends, phases through computers (destroying them), and dances through walls fast as a fairy.

This appearance-based power is also linked with the costume-transitions Kitty and Wonder Woman undergo. Superheroes "have multiple identities, with many that alternate between being a regular person and a hero. This narrative device can be perceived as a symbolic reflection ... of the radically different stages that an individual can go through" (Arnaudo 134). Thus the characters change costumes as they mature. Fray swaps baggy olive cargo pants for tougher red ones like late-season Buffy. Meanwhile, Scott Summers orders the X-Men back into cheerful yellow and black costumes to appear more approachable, while Wonder Woman switches between starry armor, heavy with royal gold, to a demure suit, bun, and glasses as "Diana Prince" on a spy mission. After her descent and metaphorical rebirth, her mother sends her the invisible plane and a new iconic costume, as Whedon's script notes describe it: "Only it's a little shinier, the tiara a little more intricate. The colors vibrate—Diana is a superhero now."

Lover

While hero's journey writer Joseph Campbell sees the female lover inspiring the male hero or protecting him from afar (like Arwen, Ariadne, or the Lady of the Lake), the male lover brings rationality and wisdom to the partnership close-up. Traditionally he contrasts with the heroine, offering skills she doesn't possess herself that can lead her to enlightenment. "As the heroine grows, her Animus matures, or is replaced by a wiser Animus when she's ready for his more developed stages: initiative and planning, rule of law, and wisdom" (Frankel 70).

Whedon's Steve Trevor offers a practical skepticism, in contrast with Diana, who trusts in gods and signs. He constantly warns her to be cautious, reminding her of the civilians who could be endangered by gunfire. He also slices through her illusions, reminding her that she is more bored debutante than hero: "Has there ever been a day you didn't have everything you wanted? Have you ever been hungry? Been cold? Worked twenty hour days underground for no pay, been spat on, stepped on, shot at...." She is too privileged for him to respect as a role model or icon—at least at first.

In an alien prison cell, Kitty finds Peter Rasputin (Colossus), her first love, who had recently died in a heroic sacrifice. This is an emotional devastation for the young heroine. "You have to know that if you're a clone or a robot or yeah a ghost or an alternate universe thingie, I can deal ... but if you are some shapeshifter or illusionist who's just watching me twist, I will kill you, I will kill you with an axe," Kitty tells him (*X-Men: Gifted*). Kitty, young and rational, a computer expert and noncombatant, must tap the primal fury within herself to become a champion. Her angry words upon meeting him suggest she's already taken her first step. Peter in turn has undergone torture and experimentation by the alien force until there's little left of him but anguish and fury. He screams, "I am made of rage" and devastates the enemy, offering a passion to augment her rationality.

Willow, too, is pragmatic. Her lover thus is magic incarnate, a shapeshifting trickster she chose as mentor in the Season Eight comics. Aluwyn, also called Saga Vasuki, greets Willow and guides her to the Wellspring, a beautiful waterfall where she and many goddesses of magic live in a "supercoven." There Willow finds "a place to belong" something she's always craved. Paradise, an enclosed garden for most cultures, represents "primordial perfection and the Golden Age" as well as the innermost soul (Cooper 126). There in the center of things, a fish woman takes her under the ocean, where Willow has a vision that her light and dark sides must balance. Under the surface, she says, enlightened, "I don't understand the universe ... but I feel where I *belong* in it." Her new friends repair the Scythe, source of feminine magic. They also garb her in mystical grey robes, symbolizing her state between dark and light.

Aluwyn and Willow wile away their time romantically, as Willow dozes through dreams of beautiful clouds (with suggestive breast shapes). It's a place of nurture, comfort, and happiness, an illusion like that created by Greek nymphs and sirens for the unwary hero. As she dreams, Marrak invades her sleep and tells her the supercoven is providing a never-ending high that has made her forget her friends. She wakes, and discounts his warning. However, a sip of the memory water awakens her and she realizes how Aluwyn has tricked her. The water, as well as offering memories, offers healing and grounding. In another feminine symbol, it is a mirror to the real self, unclouded by illusion. She leaves paradise and resumes her quest.

Like Buffy, Fray discovers the one she loves most has become a soulless vampire determined to destroy the world. This is not her lover but her twin brother Harth. "I always said we were two halves of the same person" he comments. He is her equal and opposite, her mirror: "I don't think the Slayer's supposed to have a twin and he got ... the memories, the heritage.... I just got the strength," she explains (B8.4). He is the dreamer, while she is the warrior—a pattern that appears in many heroine's journeys from Eowyn and Faramir to mythic Artemis and Endymion or Atalanta and Hippomenes. However, he also threatens all she values: "I am more than beast. I am the one who will lead.... I will open the gateway and bring the old ones back. And everyone you love will die screaming."

When someone is hurt or damaged, "such people usually have a very vulgar hidden power complex which comes out in the shadow—an infantile attitude toward life through which those around are tyrannized" (Von Franz 54). Harth is childlike, much like the Trio on *Buffy*—a petty schemer who only craves power and a lesson he can teach anyone stronger. "I guess you shouldn't have gotten me killed," he tells his sister, like the inner voice expressing her buried guilt. By battling through their confrontation and facing this inner voice, Fray gains strength. This casts him as beloved but also (though he is the other gender) as her shadow.

Shadow

The shadow archetype, described by Jung's philosophy, is the characteristics of the self we most detest, projected onto another person of the same gender, as the hidden, repressed, and undesirable aspects of the personality. While often repellent and evil, it has much power to offer. The hero's traditional enemy is the world-dominating tyrant like Darth Vader or Sauron. While Wonder Woman faces this force as the monstrous Strife, the heroine's traditional opposition comes from the same-sex: her sister or most often the wicked witch.

Besides Harth, Fray has additional shadows: Erin, the third sibling, is a police officer who lives a civilized life above the grid and hunts criminals like Fray for a living. Bossy, blonde, and older, with crisp uniform and tidy ponytail, she's all sloppy, careless Fray isn't. "You took him on a grab [thieving job] and you got our brother killed," she lectures. Their relationship echoes Buffy and Faith—good girl and bad girl. Diana (in the comics) has a similar foil in Artemis, the "bad Amazon." Both she and Faith shore up the heroines "as 'proper' female warriors but can also be read as challenging what it means to be a 'good' superheroine" (Cocca, "It's about Power and it's about Women" 220). As such, they challenge the heroine on her deepest level of identity.

Fray meets yet another shadow when Buffy arrives in *Time of Your Life*

(B8.4). Buffy, now leader of thousands of slayers has lost sight of the compassion that sends Fray saving individual lives. "'Big picture.' That spin's for govvers. Not slayers," Fray says dismissively.

> The two slayers find themselves fighting midair in a full page spread, long hair thrashing, each clutching her identical Scythe. Though slayers, they're on opposing sides; Buffy wants to return to her world and Fray fears that will cause her own to end. Buffy, defender of twenty-first century earth, beholds Fray's world without magic and sees the threat of the future—a magicless, dystopic world she will cause [Frankel 278].

Thus they battle. "Vampires gain strength from each other. Slayers, ultimately, don't," Dark Willow, the true villain of the comic, smirks (B8.4). Dark Willow is rage incarnate, and also a voice of experience. Gwyneth Bodger, examining the show's constructions of femininity, notes that after Tara's death "Willow's transition into the 'crone' phase, and all its unpleasant associations, come with the loss of her magickal 'fertility.'" She is the story's wicked witch, tormenting the maiden heroines from Dawn on the show to Buffy and Fray in the future. Buffy realizes this, and destroys her.

Meanwhile, Willow and Marrak travel into a neighboring dimension of charred ruins. She lets the magic guide her to a plane of its choosing, this one a barren desert. Standing in the blazing sun, she resolves to "shed all my burdens. My worldly concerns. Just become the light…." This is an encounter with the ultimate reality, with the font of creation, the source.

The desert is "a place of contemplation, quiet, and divine revelation" (Cooper 50). There are no distractions there, no illusions, only starkness. In the emptiness, Willow sips more of the water and wonders whether she can birth the earth's new magic or whether she risks turning evil. "Light and dark are not so easily disentangled," a flashback of the Caterpillar warns her. All at once, Dark Willow appears. Dark Willow of Season Six "has the power to end the suffering of others, but she does so as an Antichrist, destroying the good as well as the pain" (Richardson and Rabb 102). She planned to destroy the world, just as Willow on her quest intends to save it.

Willow rejects her at first, then reconsiders, saying, "That's my mistake. Acting like you're a separate person. Something I can close off or away from." She accepts the other side of herself and absorbs her, becoming whole.

Diana's nemesis, Strife, has an earthly representative in Arabella Callas (a soundalike for "callous"). She cold-bloodedly insists, that for war, "You need an acceptable level of poverty and ignorance. Despair, rage, religious fervor, and above all, fear." Whedon describes her as "very blonde, very patrician, unflappable and icy smooth. As lovely as she is untouchable." By contrast, Diana is her inverted mirror, as an exotic, dark Grecian beauty, raised on a tropical island—unworldly but passionate. The same contrast appears in their personalities and goals: Callas covers up their crimes when Strife tears down a building, while Diana fights to save the people within.

However it's Kitty's shadow that predominates her story: sexy, worldly Emma Frost. A former villain, Emma is tall and blonde with enormous cleavage as well as, as she puts it, "superpowers, a scintillating wit and the best body money can buy" (*X-Men: Gifted*). Smaller, darker, Kitty, in concealing street clothes, feels out of place. Emma, who stresses "control" of student powers over Kitty's empathy and stirring speeches, is the ice queen. In her welcome speech, she warns that normal humans "will always hate us" and they must never be trusted. Kitty notes that to her, Emma is the face of immorality: "Whenever I think about evil, whenever I think about the concept of evil, yours is the face that I see" (*X-Men: Gifted*). Her powers are showy and strengthening, as she reads minds, controls bodies, and transforms into flashy, impenetrable diamond. Kitty's power is literally vanishing. By facing this shadow, Kitty comes to understand these traits she's never tapped: sensuality, self-reliance, pride, and power, all of which she must harness to save everyone in her charge.

The Hellfire Club, with Emma as its unwilling catalyst, attacks telepathically. They envelop Kitty in her greatest fear: that she will drift away into the center of the earth. In the darkest place of all, Kitty faces her deep fear—never mattering, vanishing completely. However, "It is not a matter of Pryde leaning to do away with that sense of fragmentation, but learning how to responsibly embrace it" (Galvan 54). Kitty forces herself to beat the delusion through sheer willpower and go after the villainess behind it. Up above, Emma gazes at herself in the mirror. "You. Did you really think you could hide in there?" she asks (*X-Men: Torn*). Literally and metaphorically emerging from her own reflection, Kitty yanks her through and pummels her. Kitty wins the fight and phases Emma into a rock, telling her, "I'm gonna let you stay down here and think about what you've done" (*X-Men: Torn*). Like Faith in "Graduation Day" (B3.22), the villainess is "nailed down," unable to run. This withdrawal in order to reintegrate "looks like complete stagnation, but in reality it is a time of initiation and incubation when a deep inner split is cured and inner problems solved," Von Franz explains (106). As the adventure ends, Kitty forgives Emma and the two are somewhat reconciled, symbolizing a new teamwork within Kitty's uncertain mind.

Belly of the Beast

"Initiation usually requires a 'decent into hell' to overcome the dark side of nature before resurrection and illumination and the ascent into heaven" (Cooper 88). The hero's and heroine's path does likewise. Arnaudo describes the epic hero's mythic descent into the underworld as "another theme that recurs in superhero comics more than in any other contemporary genre" (124–125). The hero may explicitly visit, as Wonder Woman does in the comic collections *Land of the Dead* or *Odyssey*. The other more implicit version is metaphor:

On discovering the vampires have killed her friend, Fray dives into the sewers below the city, scythe in hand, and slays. There, alone in the darkness, with only a group of vampires and their cringing victim to protect, Fray's instincts take hold:

> I'm pissed like this rutting beast can't conceive—I'm a lifetime of pissed, of strong, of muscle built over bruise, I'm slick with power and feel the fight as it changes...
> As it flows...
> ...Everything into place, perfect, and I finally do what I was born to do. I slay.

In the emptiness, with only a helpless woman who reflects her innocent vulnerable side, Fray battles the enemy and saves the innocent. "I feel like I'm beginning," she tells Urkonn as she climbs from the water. Campbell called the descent into the darkest place of all the "Belly of the Beast," an echo of a hero's death-and-rebirth initiation.

For the heroine, it can take a different turn.

> In "Becoming Part Two" Buffy enters Angelus's mansion—not an underground lair but more of a vampire's fortress where Angelus can play father to Spike and Drusilla. This is the castle of the patriarchy.
> Journeying here represents the heroine leaving the place of her feminine power to ascend to the prince's tower or mountain, where she faces her greatest trial far from her unconscious realm of magic. The Little Mermaid leaves the ocean and Demeter leaves her fields as both journey into the man's world—human civilization. If Buffy's school library or home is invaded, that suggests an assault on Buffy's self. But when she journeys into the enemy's sphere, she's alone and vulnerable, cut off from her strongest supports [Frankel 109–110].

Agent Brand, who works for S.H.I.E.L.D.'s new partner S.W.O.R.D., swoops up the X-Men and takes them to the alien Breakworld, a planet of warriors all filled with hatred for the Earth. As Brand says, "The Breakworld believes we as a species need to be put down" (*X-Men: Dangerous*). This is a place where the X-Men have no power.

They crash on the planet and are split up—Kitty and Peter find themselves sheltered by the only compassionate citizens. Their leader Aghanne offers a night's safety, a moment as he describes it to hear the silence and discover a third path for themselves other than kill or be killed. Kitty and Peter take advantage of the pause to be together. The vulnerable side Kitty discovers here and nurtures is not just love but inner hope. As she puts it:

> Everything is so fragile. There's so much conflict, so much pain ... you keep waiting for the dust to settle and then you realize this is it; the dust is your life going on. If happy comes along—that weird, unbearable delight that's actual happy—I think you have to grab it while you can. You take what you can get, 'cause it's here, and then ... gone [*X-Men: Unstoppable*].

This respite before the great battle is seen in most stories, as in *Buffy* all the couples find a moment of closeness in "Touched" (B7.20). After grounding herself and preparing for the final battle, Kitty discovers a missile the aliens have aimed at Earth and slips inside. However, like the prison that held Colossus, it's made of a super-dense metal resistant to her phasing that saps her strength. "I'm in the cage I freed Peter from," she realizes, coming full circle (*X-Men: Unstoppable*). She finds herself collapsing.

"We need a hero. Not a demigod sent from on high to lecture us about potential," Steve Trevor insists. "We need someone with no advantage, no hope, who's still out there trying." In the moment Diana is most devastated by the harsh censure, Strife attacks. He vows to kill Steve Trevor unless Diana submits to him and accepts the chains that once bound the Amazons, the ultimate symbol of degradation and slavery to the patriarchy. She gives in.

Triumphant, Strife abandons Diana in the South American jungle without her powers. There she's caught in the rain, tumbles helplessly down a hill, and starves, all while bound in chains. This is a place of stillness and transition for the heroine. "Living in the forest would mean sinking into one's deepest nature and finding out what it feels like," away from the rules of civilized life (Von Franz 97). Found by a village, Diana shakes with fever and when asked who she is, she can only respond, "It doesn't matter," much like a miserable, identity-less Buffy in "Anne" (B3.1).

A little girl firmly tells her that Diana must remember who she is because no one can take that away. Upon hearing the words, Diana galvanizes. The girl represents the innocent voice of her subconscious and also her watching mother. "If the Self appears as a young person in a woman's unconscious productions, it means the newly and consciously discovered Self" (Von Franz 170). An older woman, like Diana's mother or Buffy's Primitive, suggests the deeper self that has always existed far below the strutting Ego.

Like Buffy's wandering in the wilderness of "Restless" (B4.22) and "Intervention" (B5.18), Diana's journey is a moment of withdrawal—a time to face the self without worldly concerns. As well as binding, chains symbolize the links that tie humankind to existence and to one another, a link she's just begun feeling (Cooper 32). For the first time, Diana experiences poverty and pain. For the first time, she's not a princess or a superpowered goddess. And for the first time, she discovers her inner strength. She proudly names herself and prepares for battle.

Climax

Far in the future, the vampire Icarus, Harth's sire, towers over Fray. "You really think you can put *me* down, girl? What have you got besides a shiny new axe?"

"Faith," she replies. And discards the weapon.

Suddenly, an entire flying car crashes on Icarus, and Erin emerges with the words "That's for my brother, Dickhead." The sisters have united against their common enemy, symbolizing a unity of purpose and a new strength. A massive battle begins, with aid from the poor of Fray's community and the lawmen of Erin's.

However, Harth and his allies intend to open a portal to the demon world. Urkonn warns, "It will be the destruction of *everything*." A dinosaur-like monster appears, with its womb the portal that will birth the demons. It swallows Fray, dragging her literally into the belly of the beast, but she smashes her way out, destroying the gateway. Her descent and rebirth have saved the world.

Without warning, Marrak attacks Willow. He reveals he's really Rack, the magical drug dealer from Season Six, determined to drain her as she once did to him. However, he is attacking in the magical plane, her place of power, not his own. She calls him "A leech I thought I squashed" and picks him up—he's only the size of her hand. By knowing herself, this light-and-dark woman can squish patriarchal force like a bug.

Rallying for a greater attack, Rack summons a great tentacle beast from another dimension, which swallows Willow. This monster symbolizes "primordial chaos or the fearsome and terrifying powers of nature"

(Cooper 62). On *Buffy*, the monster lurks beneath the school, and the Scoobies battle it at the behest of the Watcher's Council. However, as a gateway of nature and mystery, the symbolism is all female. "The threat of the Hellmouth is the same as that of the vagina dentata; the capability to devour, engulf and consume.... Essentially then, Buffy can be read as little more than an agent employed by patriarchy in order to combat and allay fears of the castrating woman" (Bodger).

The Leviathan, however, is framed as a more benevolent female monster. While its antibodies destroy Rack, the unwelcome male intruder, the beast acknowledges that Willow "has caused no harm." Unlike Fray's beast or journeys into the Hellmouth, this descent into the feminine body is a moment of peace, joining and completion—a welcoming into the female world as Aluwyn's wellspring was. Willow wonders if it's an embodiment of magic, but it instead says it's "an embodiment ... of myself." It is perfectly centered and self-knowing, as Willow quests to become. As magic itself speaks to Willow, it shows her her own complexity, illuminating her veins, muscles, and chakra. It counsels her that new magic "must come from within. From the heart" and gives her a seed. By wanting to restore the world for others, not for herself, Willow has earned the approval of magic incarnate. She has learned to be a selfless savior at last.

Similarly, rather than battling her patriarchal surroundings, Kitty embraces them, allowing herself to bond deeper with the alien missile aimed at Earth. Emma links with her and pushes her to escape with the same savage strength she's always shown, calling her a "weak kitten" and demanding she save herself. But Kitty tells her the alien metal has become part of her—there's no fighting to escape. In their mental link, Emma and Kitty accept and understand each other in a way they never have before. Again, the sides of the heroine unite.

> **EMMA FROST**: Kitty ... I ... I can put you somewhere else. I can make you less afraid.
> **KITTY PRYDE**: Nah. Nah, I'm gonna see this through. Peter should know ... well, he should already know, so don't worry about it.
> **EMMA FROST**: This was never meant to ... not you.
> **KITTY PRYDE**: Yeah, I was supposed to take you out, as I recall. Disappointed Ms. Frost?
> **EMMA FROST**: Astonished, Ms. Pryde. (*X-Men: Unstoppable*)

Using all her will, Kitty turns the entire bullet insubstantial and it passes safely through the Earth. Kitty, the smallest X-Man, uses the quietest of powers and saves everyone. The story ends with the bullet careening into space, Kitty still merged with it, perhaps forever.

Diana climbs out of the pit where she's been thrown and battles the petty druglords terrorizing the South American village. She grapples with one in the mud, using only her human-strength hands and then finds a shovel. Finally, using her strength of hands and will, she shatters her chains. As a reward, her mother sends the invisible plane. With the technological magic of her birthright, Diana returns to the city. There, she battles Strife's monstrous Khimaera. As she raises her sword to slice off its head, Strife appears for a duel. Diana whacks him into construction and finally impales him with a spear, defying his uncle Ares when he too appears. She vows she will defend the people whenever he comes and that she will help them turn away from war.

Conclusion

At story end, with the villain beaten, Diana kisses Steve. He takes her to a temple of Athena, where she receives guidance, though she refuses to divulge its nature. She finishes the script at the cliff's edge, noting that it would be lovely to fly.

> **STEVE**: Okay. You're a hell of a woman but ... Diana. You can't fly.
> **DIANA** [smirking]: "Can't?"

Throughout the story she has always ignored what others say she can't do. Now she has one more opportunity.

The embodiment of magic returns Willow home, her own power restored, brimming with the wisdom of how to heal the world. She must share her magic with each person she meets, "up close and personal," and thus enrich everyone's lives until the world grows brighter. She reunites with her friends in *The Core* (B9.5) in time to save them, then all of existence.

Fray returns to thieving but adds slaying to her life. She ends her comic crouching protectively over the city, her city now. As she thinks:

> Come on, guys. I'm just *one* girl. No big hero, no protector of justice, not even a bona fide one-hundred-percent slayer. So what are you waiting for?
> Take me on.
> Hurt my world.
> I dare you.

Of course, the comics medium, unlike film, means the story isn't really over, only the issue. Fray makes a short appearance in *Tales*, as she stumbles into a library of Watcher's Diaries. The room, with the image of a scythe on the floor, marks itself as her destined home. Unlike the male hero, the female finds herself bonding with a place as her tool: her city, headquarters or house. "I am the only one in the world ... but I am not alone," Fray realizes. Like Willow and Wonder Woman, Fray is poised for many more adventures.

In later comics, Magneto restores Kitty, though she has been rendered permanently insubstantial and requires more intervention to return to herself. This is the rocky path back to wholeness, as difficult for Kitty as Season Six is for a traumatized Buffy. However, Kitty has grown through facing death and saving the helpless, evolved from girl to woman, student to teacher, adolescent to lover, pawn to savior.

"The superhero universe, so charged in tone and action, fosters the possibility of seeing the struggle between the basic forces of the human soul behind its stories, whether in terms of archetypes in the psychological sense or, more broadly, in the sense of narrative form" (Arnaudo 118). Harth represents Fray's inclination towards evil, as Emma Frost does for Kitty, Dark Willow does for Willow, and Strife does for Diana. All four heroines descend into darkness and discover that all alone, they have the power to accept the evil within as a necessary part of the self that, controlled, can offer endless power. They emerge far stronger than ever before, as champions and as powerful women of the Whedonverse.

Comic-Con, Consumerism and Chaos

Reflecting the Fans in Last Angel in Hell, Stan Lee Meets the Amazing Spider-Man *and* Sugarshock!

VALERIE ESTELLE FRANKEL

• • •

> **JED, MAURISSA, ZACK**: Without these things you spit upon, you'd find your fame and fanbase gone.
> **MAURISSA**: You'd be ignored at Comic-Con. ("Heart Broken," *Commentary! The Musical*)

Indeed, Whedon loves San Diego Comic-Con and attends each year. The event has grown into an annual pop culture event that influences every form of entertainment and is attended by over 140,000 people. It is arguably the most important cultural event in comic book society, a way for fans to connect and debate while discovering new franchises and exciting upcoming projects. Famed comic book author Grant Morrison calls it "the world's largest pop media culture marketplace fringe madness festival, and every year it grows larger" (372).

Whedon celebrates this gathering through his documentary of the convention, *Comic Con Episode IV: A Fan's Hope*, covering many of its diverse attendees. Presented by Stan Lee and Joss Whedon, and directed by Morgan Spurlock, *A Fan's Hope* follows five attendees as they pursue their dreams, from becoming an artist to winning the masquerade to making the perfect geeky marriage proposal at the 2010 convention. As comic book publishers like Dark Horse critique a budding artist's comics at Comic-Con, the film becomes incredibly self-referential.

Critic Christian Sager identifies the fans-as-creators, there to bring portfolios to the comic book reviewers and "exhibit their creative endeavors as devotees of comic books" as the most fervent type of fan, those who love products so much they have expanded the genre (159). Andrew on *Buffy* reaches this level, as he creates a documentary in "Storyteller" (B7.16). In fact, Willow writes fanfic, Xander collects memorabilia, and Anya buys and sells it. Grant Morrison notes that the *Buffy* years coincided with an era of unheard-of geeky expansion, as the counterculture of the outside "became the inside." He adds:

> For just a moment, there on the hinge of the millennium, it seemed as though the whole world wanted what we'd got. They'd seen how much fun we were having with our aliens, our Tantric sex, superhuman dreams, and glossy vinyl clothes, and they all wanted to join in [312].

There's a geeky current pervading the different Whedonverses, one that the fan-driven metacomics explore more deeply, pondering the nature of the Whedon audience.

While Buffy never attends Comic-Con herself in her stories, Angel does in the wrap-up to *Angel: After the Fall*, which follows Whedon's outline for the proposed Season Six. Whedon's other comics celebrate fandom, as he sends the band Sugarshock into space for an intergalactic battle of the bands and follows a fictional comic book dealer to Interdimensional Comic-Con where he meets Stan Lee. In *Comic-Con and the Business of Pop Culture*, Rob Salkowitz describes 2011 (just a few years after these three comics arrived) as "peak geek" a time of total fannish saturation. "Just about all the changes that industry watchers had been predicting for years seemed to be manifested simultaneously, while the past melted inexorably away" (4). How fitting then that Whedon's characters should attend. As Whedon explores merchandising, cosplay, groupies, and above all, the nature of heroism, one thing is certain—this won't be a typical Comic-Con!

Boys and their Toys

Angel #26 and #27 from IDW: "Boys and their Toys" parts 1 and 2, written by Brian Lynch with art by Stephen Mooney, are reprinted in the collection *Angel After the Fall: Last Angel in Hell*. The tale begins with a scene from every slash fan's dreams: Angel is saving L.A. ... and his blonde

Poster for the movie *Last Angel in Hell*, starring Nicholas Cage as Detective Angel Cartwright. Brian Lynch (writer), and Stephen Mooney (penciller). "Boys and their Toys." *Angel Vol. 6: Last Angel in Hell*. San Diego: IDW, 2010.

girlfriend Spike is by his side. As LAPD Detective Angel Cartwright (who looks suspiciously like Nicholas Cage) strides off to show Lucifer what hell really feels like, a snarky voice interrupts him, saying, "Speaking as someone who's seen all your sides, I gotta say, there's not really one I don't fancy, Luv." In moments, Angel and Girl-Spike are kissing.

"Whoa. Is it hot in hell or is it just them?" asks Gunn (played by Jose Garcia). Betta George is a dog; Lorne is the "evil Overlorne," and Illyria is merged with Gwen. The film *Last Angel in Hell* has Angel save the city and get the girl, by way of many guns and a nuke as well as his reimagined friends. The new catchphrase is "Let's go the f#@k to work." With the world's cheesiest banter, Angel and Spike's epic quest to save L.A. has been reduced to an action flick with plenty of smooching:

> **MOVIE SPIKE**: Is that a cursed hell-dagger in your pocket or are you just happy to see me?
> **MOVIE ANGEL**: Both baby. Both.

In fact, the real Angel is sitting in the movie theater, watching the movie adaptation of his exploits with chagrin. "Los Angeles went to Hell. Every third person in LA is a screenwriter. Sooner or later someone was going to write a movie about what happened. They could have gotten one fact correct. Just one."

As it's soon revealed, Connor has sent Angel and Spike to "San Diego ScifiCon" seeking an actual magical sword that's disguised as one of the more expensive movie props on auction. While the conference is described as a "Comic-Con knockoff," its relation to the original is clear. Matthew J. Pustz notes in *Comic Book Culture*, "As in other forms of storytelling, breaking the 'fourth wall' in comics allows creators to comment on the form itself and its restrictions" (124). Joseph J. Darowski, author of "When You Know You're Just a Comic Book Character" adds it's a short trip from cracking pop-culture references to actually questioning the nature of comic-book existence. Angel and Spike first watch themselves on screen (as readers enter an additional layer of fiction) then charge into the convention, prepared to deconstruct.

At the subcultural space of the con, there are movie previews, with the Spike actress signing autographs in Artist's Alley. Fans appear dressed from *Star Trek, Star Wars, Battlestar Galactica, Transformers,* superhero comics, and much more. The flaming sword is on sale alongside the hover board from *Back to the Future 2,* a green lantern, autographed pictures, a *Batman* belt, and a Thundercats sword. There's an ongoing product placement gag with *Last Angel in Hell* prequel comics, a breakfast cereal, action figures, and apparently a sequel awkwardly titled "Last Angel in Hell 2: Next Last Angel in Hell." Doublemeat Palace is making "Angel fun meals." Back in the theater, a fan obsesses over whether the movie's prequel comic should be considered canon in a perfect parody of the fans themselves. Outside the con, vendors are selling t-shirts of demon overlords and an agent later offers to put Angel on lunchboxes and make action figures of him (*Angel: Immortality for Dummies*). Even the apocalypse won't stop consumerism.

Outside the movie preview, Angel and Spike come across Jeremy, Lynch's character from an earlier comic, who's defending Spike with all his fannishness. He says: "My name is Jeremy Johns, I lived in San Diego but I do business in LA. Spike saved my life a bunch of times. He saved everyone he could and I'm 95% sure he was a dude!" Jeremy, Spike's fanboy and a character much like Andrew Wells, is Angel and Spike's convention guide, down to his all-knowing wizard costume. As he gushes about Angel and Spike's relationship, he's very much a stand-in for the readers.

Pustz explains that the shop or convention closes the culture off to most Americans. "Although the shop may function like a clubhouse for regular readers, for most others it is so intimidating that new readers, especially women, can find it difficult to become involved." Here Spike and Angel contrast with Jeremy, a longtime fan for whom "the environment is normal and sometimes even comforting" (23). "Many fans feel comfortable in this world, where they are the experts. This sense of expertise is no small thing for people who may feel powerless, at the mercy of parents, teachers, and classmates. As the labyrinth of this comics world grew, it became increasingly difficult to navigate, requiring explorers to becomes even more expert in their mastery of the minute details of the superhero universe" (Pustz 114). The fannish trivia appearing through the comic takes care of this. Meanwhile in this traditionally boy's paradise, the women and nonwhite characters are absent altogether.

Noted genre critic Henry Jenkins admits, "Most of our stereotypes about comics fans start from the idea of arrested development, that is, that the fans have somehow sought to pull themselves out of life processes and to enjoy the same kind of iterative existence as the guys and gals in tights" ("Death-Defying Heroes" 296). If so, unaging Angel and Spike are paradigms among the human geeks who only imitate true superpowered heroes. Nonetheless, for the length of a comic, the heroes find themselves outmatched and the fans take the chance to become the heroes.

Groo the barbarian warrior (who for once fits into his setting perfectly) takes the convention regulations to heart, forbidding "cutsies" and horseplay in the halls. As the voice of order, he's something of an incarnation of the convention in himself as a spontaneous volunteer. He also reflects the fans who go about their daily lives dressed as Klingons or Jedi, finally discovering themselves in a place where they can fully fit in and express their nonstandard personas without judgment. Groo destroys a pack of teddy-bear demons with the flaming sword and adds a hover-board to his ensemble, making himself the epitome of geeky role-play.

Sager sets consumers apart from artists and creators, dropping hundreds of dollars on collectable models and fannish t-shirts they simply could have ordered online. "The convention, in effect, provides an experience for consumers to associate with their purchases ... [Comic Con International] is an event about consumption first and marketing second. Fandom comes after both of these motivating factors" (159). Certainly, Groo, Angel, and Spike are there to shop and enjoy rather than become media creators. A subtle criticism appears as fans eagerly snatch free costumes and so become victims of their eagerness for swag.

Several plots jumble together as Groo warns that "there are numerous otherworldly bounty hunters here in deceptively cheerful costumes"—red-skinned demon assassins who are hunting Angel in giant teddy bear suits. To escape, Angel and Spike disguise themselves in costumes ... only to discover the free costumes offered by a ninja and a fat Superman are actually costumes like Ethan Rayne's from "Halloween" (B2.6). Angel discards his mask and rejects that chance to suddenly become an inversion of himself, but Spike keeps his on and transforms ... into a second Angel!

Chaos and parody ensue: The bounty hunters are instantly transformed into their cuddly teddy bear disguises. Jeremy takes a free costume and changes from wizard to ninja. People in zombie costumes attack. When Spike becomes Angel, he announces that fact, with the name written as the television show's logo in a specifically comic art form of parody. Spike uses his awareness of Angel to parody him, trying to redeem everyone and encourage them to join his misfit team. As he adds, "I usually fight and then mope. But then I realized, I could save time if I mope while I fight!" Spike as Angel insists, "I make it my mission to help the hopeless. I am so good and boring." He decides they must all walk in a line "slow, proud, sullen, important," showing a knowledge of the credits even as he mocks them.

Many fans at conventions construct identities: all based on one's costume, one may be called Captain Jack Sparrow, asked to pose with other pirates, and encouraged to buy Disney souvenirs. The next day, in a Spock costume, a new fannish identity appears. Fans congregate based on the identifying shirts, bags, costumes, jewelry, and other accessories, to the point where, far more than a Halloween costume, it *becomes* identity. In Whedon style, the metaphor becomes literal, to the point at which costumers believe their own fantasies as they gain superpowers or ninja skills. There are parallels with a beloved 1940's hero, by day the ordinary newspaper boy Billy Batson, who could transform with a magic word into the mighty adult Captain Marvel. As such, all the fanboys, especially Jeremy, find themselves reveling in newfound power. The comic convention has become, metaphorically to literally in the words of Grant Morrison, "a twenty-first century theme park where everyone will be a superhero forever" (372).

A group of aliens call a bemused Groo "earthling" and tell him their backstory as Groo insists there's no planet "Scrum" or ships that run on potassium. All the convention geeks who came dressed as superheroes now have superpowers and an obsession with their own origin stories. One is "half man, half other man," while one has two origin stories for twice the power. As seems all too believable, the scene deteriorates into arguments over canon and superiority, ignoring the actual magical threat.

In the midst of the fannish squabble, Angel uses his knowledge of genre to manipulate those around him and save the day: He locks the assassin teddy bears in the bathroom to practice cuddling, a mission they eagerly accept. He finally enlists Spike's help, managing to establish his identity as the real Angel but offering a partnership. On the intercom, Spike urges the superheroes to destroy the Janos statue causing the chaos. In self-aware fashion, Angel notes this is the message all the superheroes have sought: "A call to arms. An actual mission. A chance to be a hero." Angel asks a wizard (the all-powerful mighty Linus, roughly age ten) to shortcut the process and instantly summon the item. The boy refuses, until Angel bribes him with the promise of an expensive convention souvenir. Meanwhile, a real demon invades and Angel can smell the difference, though he thinks the man "dresses straight-to-video." Angel takes the villain down with a pen, suggesting comic book writers are the true power of this world. At the convention, the true power comes from the one who knows how stories work and can twist them to advantage. Angel knows what geeks want, sending a message to the comic book readers that he's truly one of them.

There are many meta-nods that shatter the fourth wall—hardly surprising in a comic about *Angel* characters at Comic-Con watching the movie of themselves. Spike insists his cigarette is part of his original costume—certainly an accurate fact for James Marsters, if not for Spike himself. Groo calls Spike-as-Angel "Spangel," a nod to fanfiction writers and shippers, even as Angel recoils in horror. The bespelled costumes are compared to doing a J.J. Abrams-style reboot of the series ... while this is clearly a *Star Trek* reference, the comics themselves are a sort of *Angel* reboot, and the characters are about to reboot themselves as well.

> Tactics like this can force the audience to consider the text more deeply than if they are focused on the narrative. Furthermore, this postmodern technique can highlight elements of a medium that are normally processed unconsciously and can thus bring to light intricate interactions that are often overlooked. Metafiction also raises ontological issues. Acknowledging the falseness of the narrative's reality encourages readers to ponder existence [Darowski 111].

A metacomic is a comic about comics—how they are structured and the type of hero that dominates them as well as the nature of narrative itself. The self-relating here is more than a cute wave to fans—it's a serious question, as in *The Cabin in the Woods,* of which kind of readers are participating in the story and which rules of the story are moral or immoral. Whedon and Lynch's Comic-Con fans get the opportunity to become what they pretend to be—heroes rather than geeks in costume. They all rise to the opportunity (except the villains), emphasizing the valor of ordinary people—Jeremy the fanboy, all-powerful mighty Linus, and all the other audience stand-ins. As such, the comic urges fans to become true heroes, not just people who play at it.

Angel guides readers to this realization as he's hyper-aware of what heroes long for, as well as villains (having been both in his time). He understands Spike-as-Angel, and encouraging him to help others reminds him of his mission, grounding him after the confusion and suffering of the *Angel: After the Fall* plot.

The completely goofy story does bring some closure, especially to the Angel and Spike relationship. Jeremy (as a stand-in for Spike fans everywhere) tells Angel that Spike considers him a big brother (Spike snarks that he must have been high on hell fumes) and Jeremy mentions that Spike used to ask what Angel would do in his position. Finally himself again, Spike asks Angel about heroism:

> **SPIKE**: Is it always like that for you? Freaking out over the safety of every single person?
> **ANGEL**: So you're claiming you're not the same way? I've seen you in action, Spike. I know you and I hate to admit it as much as you'll hate to hear it, but...
> **SPIKE**: Get this straight Angel, I'm not you. What I mean, is ... I lend a hand if I'm bored, but ... but.... Never gets any easier, does it?
> **ANGEL**: I really want to say yes Spike. I really do.

They leave the con, transformed by their experience, and prepared to keep fighting the good fight, more a team than ever. Behind them, Linus hugs his new stuffed duck, Groo duels to protect the flaming sword (and his new hoverboard!) and Jeremy debates kung-fu lore (which he will presumably keep, upgraded much like Xander the soldier). Heroes may grow and change, but the fandom will always continue.

Stan Lee Meets the Amazing Spider-Man

Whedon's other big foray into Comic-Con widens the story to altworlds at Interdimensional Comic-Con. Celebrating Stan Lee's 65 years at Marvel, the company put together a comic book anthology called *Stan Lee Meets the Amazing Spider-Man*, in which the beloved creator visits his creations. Whedon wrote the second comic in the collection, "Some Steves." In fact, this continues a great tradition as Stan Lee and Jack Kirby appeared in the tenth issue of *Fantastic Four*, welcoming readers into their studio.

This is a postmodern rarity as a comic about someone almost never seen within the books—the comic book retailer. Benjamin Woo, in his essay "The Android's Dungeon" on the comic book store as social space explains, "Comic book stores occupy an ambivalent position between the comics industry and its audiences; they are needed by both producers and consumers but are often treated only instrumentally, as facilitating the distribution of material goods rather than sustaining practices related to them" (134). The comic book dealers in this tale become gatekeepers and defenders of the art, with the central figure speaking up with Whedon's voice.

Steve Rennitz, an ordinary comic book dealer at Interdimensional Comic-Con, runs into multiple versions of ... himself! The Steves gush about *Time Cop* as stormtroopers and Batman characters pass. They also display the nerdish immaturity:

> **MAINSTREAM LIT STEVE**: I was gonna look for you last year, but ... I uh was checkin' out the Pornworld section.
> **FRIVOLOUS STEVE**: Went Pornworld.
> **EARTH STEVE**: I was over at the booth from the dimension where Anakin doesn't whine all the time. And then Pornworld.

Woo notes the simultaneous accuracy and caricature of Comic Book Guy on *The Simpsons*, explaining, "This picture—in its obsessiveness and fetishism, its pedantry and cliquishness, its homosociability and awkwardness, and its attendant air of despair—represents the very worst of comic-

Three versions of comic book retailer Steve discuss realistic comics "The Incredible Doctor Banner in a Bad Mood" and "Uncanny O-ppressed People." Joss Whedon (writer), and Michael Gaydos (artist). "Some Steves." *Stan Lee Meets the Amazing Spider-Man* by Stan Lee, et al. New York: Marvel Comics, 2006. 11–20.

book culture" (125). Much of this is reflected in the plural Steves, satirizing the very comic book culture the book is celebrating. In fact, this is a terribly insular and exclusive group—only one distinct person appears.

"The comic book shop is a meeting place, like the clubhouse at a country club or a small-town barbershop. It is a place for commerce, but, more importantly, it is a place for culture" (Pustz 6). As such, this chance meeting quickly transforms into literary debate. While our world's Steve chats with the others about the industry, he discovers that one alt-world Steve's comics are completely realistic: They include "The Incredible Doctor Banner in a Bad Mood," the "Normal Four," "Uncanny O-ppressed People," and the Punisher, who grounds the children for not making their beds (in a "reasonably exciting" lesson). In *Amazing Reality,* Peter Parker notes, "I still won't let an itchy spider-bite keep me from completing my science homework." When Gwen Stacy dies of shingles, he sues the doctors for malpractice.

"Some Steves" is drawn quite realistically by Michael Gaydos, in dark, simple colors. The older style primary color comics complete with grainy dot printing appear as comics within the comics as the Steves compare their products, presenting an amusing juxtaposition between classic and modern writings. There are two layers of comics here, with arguably six or seven worlds: three "realities" each with their own fictional Marvel comics, and beyond, the world of the reader (who can be said to live in the world of Normal Steve, though the reader is also observing this from outside). Metalepsis is the term for crossing storyworlds—arguably this only occurs as the fictional characters debate their bright colored comics, but in fact the reader is drawn into the argument. "This causes readers to step back from the false world they have been reading about in the comic book and acknowledge the reality that a writer did imagine everything that is on the page" (Darowski 111). As such, this story is a salute to Stan Lee indeed, a reminder that he is creator of all.

The two types of art also emphasize the debate that's existed from the earliest comics to today's better-respected graphic novels. Comics, of course, have until recently been considered trashy. As Stan Lee explains, when he started at Marvel "comics were so—I won't say hated—but were so disrespected in those days, most parents didn't even want their kids to read comics. If ever anybody over the age of twelve or thirteen was seen with a comic you'd think there was something wrong with him, and people just had no respect at all for comics" ("Afterward"). Thus he used a shortened form of his real name, Stanley Lieber, so he could use the latter name on his "Great American Novel" someday.

Today, comics have more respect, not only as big-budget movies but also as the subject of college classes and academic criticism (like this collection). Nonetheless, as our world's Steve battles the Steve who dismisses monsters and aliens as puerile, he's fighting the same battle for respect everyone in genre faces.

"The death of Gwen Stacy was really the birth of adult mainstream storytelling," the mainstream literature Steve insists. He sounds like the

"The Night Gwen Stacy Died" retold as a realistic comic, with cartoonish art indicating a book within the book. Joss Whedon (writer), and Michael Gaydos (artist). "Some Steves." *Stan Lee Meets the Amazing Spider-Man* by Stan Lee, et al. New York: Marvel Comics, 2006. 11–20.

literary snobs who dismiss works like *Firefly* and *Buffy* as less than artistic because they're based in genre.

In fact, the third Steve's comics are all that snobs suspect of genre, as Gwen Stacy airily declares that she'd be happy for Spider-Man to date her and MJ at the same time because "getting it on with Norman made me realize I've been *too uptight.*" *The Night Gwen Stacy Died* is now *The Night Gwen Stacy Lightened Up*, with all the angst and serious nature of the story dismissed in a blink. As the frivolous Steve from the world who created this comic notes, the point of comics is cosmic rays and the Eye of Agamotto, not storytelling. It's comic book writing without its heart as "With great power comes hot babes and money from wrestling." Once again, our world's Steve goes to battle, defending classic Marvel comics:

> **FRIVOLOUS STEVE**: Me-Guy, they're *heroes*. The whole *point* is they're not *us*. It's *fantasy*.
> **EARTH STEVE**: But the grounding is what *makes* it cool! What, do they just beat up the bad guys and have group sex every issue?
> **FRIVOLOUS STEVE**: Your point being?

Whedon, using the voice of our world's Steve, defends his art from both these perspectives. "It's the whole point of comics! Fantasy!" he protests. Still, comics also need the pain—"The consequences, the trials, you know, the things that make the heroes just like us."

Paralleling Whedon's examples, Jenkins explains the many ways comics help people deal with real-life trauma. He describes sitting with his terminally-ill mother, reading about the death of Bruce Wayne's parents and, as he puts it, "our common plight touched me deeply" ("Death-Defying Heroes" 295). His own illness made him tear through comics of "the death-defying world of the superheroes" who would never succumb themselves ("Death-Defying Heroes" 299). As he concludes, most children's literature explores violence, trauma, and death because "Literature helps us to cope with those fears at one level removed" ("Death-Defying Heroes" 303). Fantastical comics may be two levels removed, but the far-fetched, even goofy world provides additional comfort. Everyone returns to the comics of their childhood for security and for the writers who made imagination come alive.

When Steve discovers the two worlds of bad comics have no Stan Lee to write the comics, he rushes from the booth in despair. In the hall, he bumps into his idol, who only exists in Earth's dimension. As Lee explains, "There's a lot of amazing comic creators in the multiverse, kid … but there's only one Stan Lee." This comic is indeed a particular Stan Lee tribute. Like "The Wish" (B3.9) or "Birthday" (A3.11), this story focuses as a what-if tale—what if Stan Lee's beloved comics had no angst or no fantasy? Both versions are ridiculous parodies, inviting the reader to sympathize with the bewildered Steve from our world even before he meets his idol and turns gushing fanboy.

Comic-Con is more than an incidental setting. To many, it began as the home of comics, though now, much like the world without fantasy, many other worlds are intruding upon it. As sparkly vampires or television shows that sometimes aren't even genre take over the convention, many fans like Earth Steve feel pushed to defend the value of old-fashioned comics. Whedon describes herein the reason the stories—from *Spider-Man* and *The Fantastic Four* to *Buffy* and *Angel*—have such power for readers—the compellingly real trauma portrayed through monsters and magic.

Sugarshock

The Sugarshock band is introduced in a Battle of the Bands at "the South Fairville Hormer's Shrimp 'n' Taco Rock-Off." Riding off with their groupie, the band has their own fandom, albeit a tiny one. More interestingly, the band leader, Dandelion, shrieks with joy when their rival "sensitive guy" wins because his song gave her the tingles. Dandelion, the story's hero, is a true fan, who cheers her idols even when doing so doesn't profit her.

Dandelion's fannish t-shirts emphasize her participation in her chosen community (though the anti–Viking community is certainly a minority, even at conventions). Her hatred of Vikings (with no motive ever given) and anti–Viking t-shirts reflect obsessive fannish loves and hates—many fans will respond with knee-jerk reactions each time they hear references to Jar-Jar Binks or the end of *Lost*. At cons, especially, fans are known for labeling themselves with their shirts—the Season Eight comics celebrate this practice and wink at fellow fans as Andrew wears shirts from *The Punisher*, *Husbands*, and *Captain America*, while Kennedy wears *Homestar Runner*, *Watchmen*, and *Muppets*. Even Giles sleeps in a Sex Pistols t-shirt in *Retreat* (B8.6). In *The Avengers*, Tony Stark wears a Black Sabbath T-shirt, nodding to their own hit, "Iron Man."

Dandelion continues her fannishness with strange conspiracy theories that Lincoln freed the stoves, not the slaves, but these are likewise no stranger than fans' endless speculations on the real motivations of Emperor Palpatine. As she writes notes to the readers at the bottom of each comic, she spoils all of issue #3, quickly adding, "Uh, spoiler alert! Sorry." This metanarration winks at the readers, acknowledging Dandelion as storyteller as well as character, and also a fellow fan, in command of fannish language and behavior.

In a fan's dream come true, an alien plummets to earth clutching an invitation for a battle of the bands, or at least battle of some sort, which it bestows, dying, on Dandelion. She heads off into space with band members Wade (an alien princess), L'Lihdra (her bodyguard), and Robot Phil. Dandelion wins the day in the alien arena not by fighting but by singing the saddest song in the world: "Sort of like Samuel Barber's 'Adagio for Strings' if it was written by Leonard Cohen and Paul Westerberg for Emmylou Harris with a hint of the theme from that French film *Diva* in the underscoring and a bridge that feels like The Dead breaking into 'Morning Dew.'"

While more satire than serious, Dandelion does put an end to the

The Sugarshock team joins the intergalactic battle of the bands ... or some kind of battle, anyway. Joss Whedon (writer), and Fábio Moon (penciller). "Sugarshock." *Dark Horse MySpace Presents #1*. Milwaukie, OR: Dark Horse Books, 2008. 5–28.

war with her music, as the bodyguard defends her princess. If the frivolity of the heroes calls this into question, well, it's no worse than watching Buffy save the school with flaming hairspray. The Sugarshock band are true fans, loving music so much they continue gushing as fans of contrasting—and in this story—conflicting focuses. Dandelion loves the "Sensitive Guy" band more than her own. Wade loves handsome young men. Phil loves Dandelion (most likely) and L'Lihdra loves Wade ... enough to kill handsome young men that threaten her life plan. While *Buffy* and *Firefly* are the story of characters with disparate agendas (Spike, Anya, Jayne) working together, Sugarshock's mixed motivations appear to leaving them running about as haphazardly as characters in a Marx Brothers movie, and saving the day in spite of their chaotic goofiness.

As Wade's epic romance with a lost groupie plays out as quickly as a "what happens at Comic-Con stays at Comic-Con" affair, the alien overlord gratifies Dandelion by asking, "Sugarshockers, we honor your victory, your ingenuity, and your stabbing. We ask you ... are you ready to *rock our world*?" The next panel sees Dandelion anticlimactically negotiating all the subclauses of the band's contract before she is indeed prepared to rock anyone's world, emphasizing the business side of the fannish world. Robot Phil demands approval over plush toy likenesses. Dandelion wants free beer included. All is going well until the alien overlord decides hiring

"Sensitive Guy" will be less trouble. Dandelion calls this a "shocking betrayal," but to those accustomed to wrangling for gigs at the conventions, none of this comes as a shock. Even the narrator must point out that as shocking betrayals go, this one doesn't really count.

The constant interjections in the form of editor's notes, combined with Dandelion's epilogues, raise the level of metacommentary from the previous projects—the main character and "editor" are no longer critiquing other works of fiction but their own story. Stan Lee was famous for a similar series of editor's notes, particularly in *Spider-Man*. Grant Morrison explains, "With one caption, Lee became our friend, our confidant. He reminded us up front that we were reading a made-up story, then created with Ditko a story and characters so compelling, we were drawn in, despite its avowed fictional nature, in a display of showmanship" (96). Whedon, of course, does the same. As he and Dandelion speak directly to the reader, they emphasize how the reader's active participation is necessary. "Readers are invited to step back and consider their understanding of comic books and the manner in which they combine tests and images into a cohesive narrative. Readers then become aware of their collaborative work in creating a comic-book universe inhabited by fictional characters" (Darowski 112). Thus the metalepsis grows gigantic, in this case between Sugarshock world and reader's life.

Dandelion ends the comic with more advice for readers, advising them to "think a little bit about your own, less-amazing life ... get off your fat ass and learn some lathing already." She knows her comic-book fans all too well, and demands they learn artistic or life skills even if they're not about to win an alien battle of the bands as she has. With a final "Kissy th' face," she heads off on more adventures, as the ragtag passengers on a spaceship far beyond the stars.

Final Thoughts

In *Comic-Con and the Business of Pop Culture*, Rob Salkowitz describes the event as "an orgy of consumerism and commercialism and apolitical superficiality in the midst of a world full of serious problems" (8). The con may be a safe space of fannish fun, but one must recall the world waiting beyond. Dandelion's final message reminds readers to "think a little bit about your own, less-amazing life ... get off your fat ass and learn some lathing already." This parallels Angel's message in "Boys and their Toys— that everyone can be heroes, especially the fans. Instead of parading about in untouchably perfect outfits, they can use their powers for good and defend the helpless. Steve Rennitz does not become a superhero, but he defends the mix of fantasy and pathos that makes genre fiction come to life. Characters in all three stories battle (literally and figuratively) to defend the fannish gatherings they love so deeply, rewarding the fans who in turn have read all their adventures.

These meta-comics wink at the audience, acknowledging the value of geeks and all things geekery in the comic book world. For without the Jeremys, Steves, Dandelions, and Hammer groupies, there would be no Angel, Hammer, or Comic-Con itself. They gleefully join in a celebration of art, as Dandelion wins an intergalactic battle with her music but also cheers for "Sensitive Guy" and his songs. Steve gushes all over Stan Lee, creator of some of Whedon's favorite franchises. Angel, Spike, and Groo disport themselves at the convention, with costumes, previews, and a real superhero battle. Above all, these stories celebrate fandom across genre—especially the fans of Comic-Con.

Part Ten

The *Avengers*, *Agents of S.H.I.E.L.D.* and the MCU

• • •

The Marvel Cinematic Universe (MCU) launched in 2008 with *Iron Man*, as Marvel began making their own movies the way they thought superhero films should be done (*X-Men, Spider-Man, The Fantastic Four*, and other franchises were contracted elsewhere). More films followed: *The Incredible Hulk, Iron Man 2, Thor, Captain America*. Finally these characters united in *The Avengers* (*Marvel's Avengers* in some countries), written and directed by Joss Whedon (who also directed a few teasers and short videos called Marvel One-Shots). Opening weekend, *The Avengers* broke the record for the biggest box-office debut in film history. By the next week, it had grossed over one billion dollars worldwide. In "Authorship Assembled," Leora Hadas examines the film's branding and how it shaped the publicity of Whedon's involvement.

Following the film's incredible success, Marvel and Whedon created the ABC television show *Agents of S.H.I.E.L.D.* starring Agent Coulson (an original movie character first seen in *Iron Man*) with visits by Nick Fury and Maria Hill along with mentions and cameos of many other Marvel and MCU characters. Jed Whedon, Maurissa Tancharoen, and Jeffrey Bell act as the series' showrunners. Joss Whedon began among them but only wrote the first episode and then had to limit his involvement to work on *Avengers: Age of Ultron*. The series features a misfit team of Melinda May, a taciturn warrior and pilot; Grant Ward, who's concealing a deep agenda; Fitz and Simmons, adorable best-friend scientists; and Skye, a hacker with a mysterious origin and growing superpowers, all led by Coulson. For this collection, Gail D. Rosen compares May and Skye with Buffy and Willow, considering their adherence to men's laws.

Phase Two of the MCU, beginning with *Iron Man 3* (2013), is underway, concluding with *Ant-Man* (2015) before the MCU's Phase Three. With *Agents of S.H.I.E.L.D.* spinning off in the comics, the franchise is only expanding.

Authorship Assembled

Joss Whedon as Promotional Auteur in Marvel's The Avengers

LEORA HADAS

• • •

When, in 2010, Marvel Studios announced their intention to unite the characters of their various comics-based films—*Iron Man*, *The Incredible Hulk*, *Captain America* and *Thor*—in a single movie, journalists, fans and cast all voiced similar concerns. The film contained many more characters than standard superhero films, which have with few exceptions tended to be solo pieces. The crossover logic common in comics since the 1960s had never before been tried in film and its feasibility remained uncertain. Surprisingly, Marvel's choice for writer-director for the film fell on television creator and geek idol Joss Whedon. While an experienced showrunner, Whedon had previously directed only one film, *Serenity*, which disappointed at the box office. Although boasting a loyal cult following, he did not have the fame enjoyed by Christopher Nolan or Bryan Singer when they directed *Batman Begins* and *X-Men* respectively. In normally risk-averse Hollywood, the choice caused some puzzlement.

What Whedon offered Marvel Studios was a very particular *author brand*. Whedon had earned fame for a signature style—the fast-talking, quirky humour sometimes called "Buffyspeak"—and for the recurrence of themes, ideas and characters, such as feminism and empowerment, misfits and families, the mixture of fantastical and soap-operatic elements, and waifish yet deadly teenage heroines. His distinct voice, his history of clashes with network and studio executives, and the strong association of his writing with his personal identity as a feminist, geek and outsider all led his fans to celebrate him as an *auteur*. With *The Avengers*, however, Whedon was not working with original material that he could shape as he pleased according to his own style. Rather, Marvel Studios entrusted him with the culmination of an unprecedented experiment in franchise building; and this at a delicate time, with the studio very much concerned with establishing its own brand identity.

This chapter looks at how Marvel harnesses Whedon's auteur power in the promotion of *The Avengers*, even while carefully selecting which parts of Whedon's career to emphasize. The emergence of auteurist discourse as a strategy for media branding has brought to light issues of the discursive clash between the "authentic" artistic and the careful construction of marketing. The case of Whedon, Marvel and *The Avengers* demonstrates both the tensions in this strategy, and how they are negotiated and—albeit tentatively—resolved.

"Without reinventing the wheel": Utilizing the Whedon Brand

Whedon's name and face were not the only, nor even the most prominent features associated with *The Avengers* in the film's promotion. He shared the limelight with Kevin Feige, president of Marvel Studios and the studio's front man on all its previous productions. The division of labor between the two appears for the most part a question of target audience. The trade press, in publications such as *Variety* and *The Hollywood Reporter,* credits Feige as the driving force behind the film. Through him, industry discourse centers on the Marvel brand and particularly on Marvel Studios' success in franchise building. Though trade publications acknowledge Whedon's cult fame, it is Feige, rather, whom they portray as the devoted fanboy creating a passion project and lifelong dream. He thus frames himself and his involvement within an artistic as well as commercial discourse; his vision is as much a personal commitment as it is a business plan. In both capacities, he represents the studio's creative control over the film. His presence and his self-description as a fan all frame *The Avengers* as, above all, a Marvel movie, dreamed up and made a tangible reality by a Marvel devotee.

Conversely, Whedon—though he also holds his fan identity as important—serves to balance Feige by playing the role of the serious filmmaker of the enterprise. Actors, Marvel Studios personnel and Feige himself all describe him as the gifted writer and director who spent time and work mining the depths of the characters, giving the film a profundity in engaging with themes such as isolation, teamwork and war. For example, in a round-table interview by *Entertainment Weekly* with director and cast, the actors fall into a lengthy respectful silence while Whedon explains his ideas on community and togetherness and their expression in the film (Labrecque). Scarlett Johanssen (Black Widow) tells *The Los Angeles Times* that "you can't not [develop the character] working with Joss Whedon, he is so dedicated.... It's truly exciting to have someone like Joss Whedon to collaborate with, to build those layers with" (Kaufman). Even superstar Robert Downey, Jr. (Iron Man), in an article aptly titled *"Avengers*: Downey Says Whedon Brings 'Depths of Discovery,'" concedes that "Joss Whedon has really taken us to new depths of discovery for our characters" (Kaufman).

The divide works well for the film. As president and front man of Marvel Studios, present from the inception of the Marvel Cinematic Universe in 2008, Feige speaks for the franchise as a whole. A company man, he speaks to the industry in terms of branding, marketing and the studio's overall strategy and plays up *The Avengers* as an event movie and as the pinnacle of the MCU. Meanwhile in the more audience-oriented spaces of the popular press, Whedon takes a much more central role to discuss the film's individual identity and its claim for artistic merit. He clearly delineates responsibility on different aspects of the creative process, crediting Marvel and Feige for the (mass-produced, franchise-oriented) superheroic plot, and himself for the (authentic and artistic) humanity and realism of the characterization. As he tells *Entertainment Weekly*:

> [Marvel Studios] came to me and said, we have these basic action beats.... I'm like, "Great, because then I have my ends of each act ... now I just have to get from A to B." From that, getting from A to B meant how to be human.... Luckily, because enough [plot] is dialed in on a movie like this, most of my work has been just emotion, emotion, emotion [Breznican, "Crawl inside"].

As the keeper of *The Avengers*' emotional truth, Whedon appears in the film's promotion in two capacities. The first is the aforementioned character focus, which frames the film as more serious an undertaking than its summer blockbuster/franchise tentpole nature may otherwise merit. Whedon states, in Dave Itzkoff's interview "Joss Whedon on Assembling *The Avengers*," that he conceived of the film as a war movie, and elsewhere calls its heroes "broken and tortured and strange" (Itzkoff, "Superheroes Include the Director"), giving the colourful heroes a grimmer spin. This loneliness and strangeness of the heroes often features in trailers—Tom Hiddleston's villainous Loki calls them "lost creatures" and mocks their desperation—in cast interviews and in special features such as the aforementioned round table interview. Chris Hemsworth (Thor) highlights the director's instruction for the character dynamic, explaining: "Joss said it early on, the dysfunctional family" (Otto). Whedon's serious framing of the movie sometimes seems in need of limiting and repair lest it become *too* serious, as when Downey almost cuts him off in mid press junket to remark that "at a certain point you try not to take it too seriously—this is essentially a comic book movie" (Richardson).

Whedon's second function is to provide the cement that keeps *The Avengers* from flying apart or collapsing under its own multi-franchise weight, a mainstay of the film's promotion. In trailers and ad spots, Downey's Iron Man quips that he "[doesn't] play well with others" and Mark Rufallo's Bruce Banner claims, "We're not a team, we're a time bomb." For its marketing strategy, Marvel embraces the doubts, the question of whether a film on this scope with such a cast could work. One behind the scenes featurette is even explicitly entitled "Tension" (Marvel Entertainment). Though essential to superhero comics, the crossover logic of the MCU has never before been applied in film, and indeed a running theme of *The Avengers'* framing claims that the characters' team-up makes no sense and should not logically work. Not to worry, however, as Earth's Mightiest Heroes have on their side a man who has made his career out of defusing time bombs such as theirs; and hence, the tension and sometimes literally explosive conflict between characters appear in promotion as key elements of *The Avengers'* attraction. Whedon's credentials as a writer of ensembles and dysfunctional individuals forming functional teams, as in *Buffy the Vampire Slayer, Angel* and *Firefly*, gain prominence. Kevin Feige reassures the trade press that "Looking at Joss's body of work and the scripts that he's written and the TV shows, the characters never ever get lost," and the actors line up to promise that "Joss did such a great job of balancing the storyline" (Gilchrist and Simpson) and that "it's pretty incredible that he was able to weave all those stories together" (Gilchrist and Simpson).

In both of those functions, Marvel Studios utilizes specific elements of Whedon's author brand and incorporates them into the marketing of *The Avengers*. The film is promoted and framed as bearing Whedon's recognizable creative signature for his preexisting fans, so that it can be identified as Whedon's take on the Marvel Universe. Nonetheless, Whedon's talent is called upon in a limited and specific capacity here, to use his famed skills "without," as in Feige's words, "reinventing the wheel" (Barnes). Marvel craves not his reputation as a creative visionary, but an almost technical, perfunctory skill: the ability to write a good team movie. His brand qualities are distilled, some adopted and some discarded, so that they slot seamlessly into the value that the franchise might lack.

The film's promotional authorship, the "commerce of auteurism" to borrow Timothy Corrigan's term (96), is here usefully compartmentalized. Considering the dichotomy usually present in popular discussion of film, it is ironic that the "creative" Whedon—rather than Feige the "suit"—works as a commercial brand name. Instead of the appeal to originality and creativity that usually characterizes discourse around the creative genius, here the appeal is to expectation, standardization even. This appeal as the primary function of Whedon's name in the trade press shows how the logic of the brand as a guide and guarantee to the audience, which Paul Grainge already described as a powerful Hollywood marketing tactic, reaches back into the industry. Marvel uses Whedon's name not only to indicate to audiences that they will love *The Avengers*, but to reassure their *Variety*-reading Hollywood colleagues that the film will succeed.

"It just gives me layers": Auteurism Re-established

While Marvel mined Whedon's brand identity for appropriate meanings, Whedon retained his own interests that did not necessarily align with those of the studio. The standardization and predictability that served Marvel well could for him be a problem. Another risk came from the potential situation in which he would become most associated with a franchise not his own. Being somewhat of an under-recognized outsider had itself become a part of Whedon's brand. While a star at the WB, where *Buffy* was a flagship program, the early cancellation of *Firefly* and ongoing conflict surrounding his latter offering *Dollhouse* led to his expressing continued dissatisfaction with and distance from network television (Pappademas). Since independently producing *Dr. Horrible's Sing-Along Blog* during the 2007-08 writers' strike, Whedon advocated DIY media production, even taking the month's break between filming and editing *The Avengers* to produce an again independent adaptation of *Much Ado about Nothing*. With this underdog/independent status playing an important part in Whedon's creative identity, his association with Marvel Studios and its massive franchise film could prove seriously damaging. He indeed shows awareness of his position, tackling the problem outright with his usual ironic humor in one *New York Times* interview:

> "Where are the prestige pics? Where are the '70s, where are people taking chances?" Here in his blossoming rant, Mr. Whedon [...] had to smile at himself. He was delivering the tirade "while I'm making a giant, tentpole,

franchise, action, summer movie." ... With mock defensiveness, he added, "That doesn't make me a hypocrite, it just gives me layers" [Itzkoff, "Superheroes Include the Director"].

Throughout his appearances in the promotion of *The Avengers*, Whedon works to establish his genuine creative investment in the project. The same framing of the film as a story about isolation and community, which Marvel eagerly built into its promotional discourse, is expanded as a sign of this investment. Whedon characterizes *The Avengers* as the same kind of story that he always tells: "It's very much about people who are alone— because I'm writing it" (Breznican, "Joss Whedon"). "I'm talking about helplessness, I'm talking about aloneness, I'm talking about the gaining of strength and understanding of community. I'm always talking about those things. And no, I don't set out to do it" (Breznican, "Crawl Inside"). This is an auteurist statement *par excellence*, attributing the themes in his writing to a personal obsession that drives him even in his work on such an obvious commercial enterprise. He equates the experience of working on the tentpole franchise action movie to his independent work, as he tells *Entertainment Weekly:* "it's more like making an Internet musical than anything ... they handed me one of the biggest movies of all time, and I'm making it up as I go" (Breznican, "Crawl Inside"). While for Marvel, the description of the characters as "broken and tortured and strange" serves the attractive mark of the Whedon brand on the film, for Whedon himself, this made him "realize[d] that [he] could write those characters." What the studio spins as brand promotion, Whedon spins as auteurist authenticity.

Another tactic that sits a little less well with the studio is Whedon's constant use of ironic, self-deprecating humor in regards to the "gig" he's taken (PentaGon Pictures). Whedon uses this style regularly, echoing the style of humor in his writing, but here it serves to put a conscious distance between himself and the film and disrupt any perception of him as Marvel's loyal soldier. In press interviews, he speaks of accepting the project as something between a coincidence and a favor he'd agreed to do. "Sheer panic, maybe three times total," he says of his response to taking up the job, calling his initial relationship with Marvel Studios a "courtship" despite his previous work for Marvel Comics (Melissa). This attitude is clearest in his public appearances before the fannish crowds: in his 2010 San Diego Comic-Con panel he speaks about "the little intimate art film that I'm going to be shooting" (PentaGon Pictures). Before his fans, away from any Marvel colleagues or representatives, he reasserts his underdog position in the system: "I'll be in enormous trouble if it's not super good" (PentaGon

Pictures). In the same convention's Marvel Studios panel, Whedon let the crowd know that "I've had this dream my whole life and it was not this good, *and I am going to blow it*" (Zeitchik). It should perhaps come as little surprise that in their official clip from the panel, Marvel edited out that last sentence, Whedon's display of a little too much personal style.

Naturally, Whedon also relates his genuine devotion to the project through stressing his personal Marvel fandom, by which he can check and balance his disavowal. Here he utilizes an aspect of his own identity rather than his creative signature, making his investment personal as well as creative—an association further entrenched in auteurist discourse in which, as mentioned, artistic passions originate in personal histories and obsessions. Whedon's fan identity is most prominent when he speaks in fan spaces, where the audience can be best relied upon to understand and identify with it. Whedon relates the strength of his connection to the characters, and his ability to handle them in their great franchise vehicle without succumbing to Hollywood genericism, to his history with and love for the original comics.

> I'm a fanboy. I want to see what's up with Thor and Captain America and what he can do with that shield. All of those things have been in my DNA since I was a tiny child. I love all of that.... Obviously I look at The Avengers and go, this team doesn't make any sense at all, but I can work with that, because it doesn't make sense to them either. They're extraordinarily dysfunctional people. And they're in their own way very isolated. So just being able to tell that very basic story, isolated people who come together and become more than their parts, is a meaningful story to me [Melissa].

To the fans that comprise the target audience of this narrative, Whedon's previous work for the comics side of Marvel Enterprises, writing the critically acclaimed *Astonishing X-Men* in 2004-05, emphasizes his fannish credit and validates this narrative. With his work for Marvel Studios on a continuum from his work for the less glamorous, more niche Marvel Comics, Whedon can go on to reassert his devotion to working outside the mainstream and to the creation of narratives that he describes as "small, pure and odd" (Smith).

Marvel Studios happily allows Whedon to reinforce his auteur image in the popular press and in fan spaces, yet is careful to keep pace with this last spin as well. Just as the studio utilized the themes of loneliness and teamwork in the film's promotion—themes that comprise part of the Whedon brand, and which he himself frames in a discourse of art and auteurship—so do they take a similar approach to framing Whedon's comics and Marvel fandom. While for Whedon this identity expresses a matter of personal investment, to Marvel Studios, it is a means to reassure the most demanding segment of the audience that the franchise lies in safe hands. In a featurette on a special advanced screening of the film to an audience of costume-wearing, catchphrase-chanting fans, while the actors express amazement and fascination, Whedon expertly comments on how "it all starts with that kind of a fan's energy" (Alien Bee). The actors in turn inform the popular press of his credentials as a fan. Iconic guest star Samuel L. Jackson in particular says, "Joss has this relationship with comics…. He's always read 'em. And he understands the genre and how it works from the inside" (Clark).

The fannish identity that characterizes Whedon, according to Marvel, is a private one, focused on dedication to the text and not on any kind of affiliation with a fan community. Despite what one might expect, Whedon's status as cult idol does not feature as any part of *The Avengers'* marketing strategy; his long resume of cult achievements receives no mention even at Comic-Con, never mind in official interviews or in Marvel's press materials. No doubt Marvel Studios were aware of Whedon's fandom when they hired him, and equally aware that his name attracted many. But these many did not need much advertising. Devoted fans, they would watch the film one way or another. To emphasize that the pinnacle of the franchise came "from the creator of *Buffy the Vampire Slayer*" could very well have done it more harm than good among casual moviegoers, uncertain parents and, importantly, fans interested in the Avengers, not the Scoobies. Emphasizing Whedon's fannish love for comics reassures fans that he will handle their favorites well, while avoiding the impression that *The Avengers* is a cult film for a cult audience. It must be remembered that Marvel Studios created their brand hinging on movies that were based on comic books without being "comic book movies"; ones that actively reworked the genre to appeal to audiences beyond the fannish. Marvel aimed for "an awareness when people see the name, 'Oh, here comes another movie that I can enjoy as an adult and take my kids to,'" as says Rob Moore, vice-chairman of *Iron Man* distributor Paramount Pictures (Boucher). This once more demonstrates how a creator's brand qualities may be picked and chosen, emphasized or sidelined or indeed re-contextualized by what the studio chooses to forefront or ignore.

Conclusion: Authorship in the Franchise Adaptation

Joss Whedon's case is not the only one to suggest a certain method in Marvel Studios' choice of directors for the MCU. Jon Favreau, director of the first two *Iron Man* films, could claim little clout as a director before being chosen on the strength of a pitch that conceived of *Iron Man* as a spy/thriller movie inspired by Tom Clancy, Robert Altman and the James Bond franchise (Fendelman). *Captain America: The First Avenger* director Joe Johnston had been a prolific director of children's adventure films in the nineties (*Honey, I Shrunk the Kids* in 1989 and *Jumanji* in 1995) only recently returned to Hollywood after a six-year break. Kenneth Branagh, director of *Thor*, had directed Shakespeare adaptations but never an action film. Their creative signatures could all stand for unique takes on their source materials—a Shakespearean director for the story of a feuding family of pagan gods; the director of *The Rocketeer* for a World War II era Nazi-stomping pulp-like hero—but *not so unique* that they would eclipse the source material. Along the same line, Marvel employed Whedon as a writer of funny, fast-talking team dynamics for a film whose most obvious weakness lay in its large cast of stars.

These choices can be traced back to Marvel Entertainment's greater branding strategy. The launching of the MCU was rooted in Marvel rebranding itself, to quote Derek Johnson, "not as a comic book publisher, but as a repository of licensable superhero characters with synergistic potential in other media" (66), as well as in its ongoing bid to centralize and secure maximal control over the development of its properties in such other media. Since recovering from bankruptcy in the mid–90s, Marvel increasingly sees its survival as dependent on the extension of its intellectual properties into other media, particularly film, an endeavor that requires "clear, consistent brand identity" across the system of corporate, product and character brands (Johnson 69). In 2004, Marvel Studios struck finance and distribution deals that allowed the studio to produce its own films instead of its previous practice of selling Marvel properties to other studios. It then became crucial to Marvel Studios to maintain control over their brand, to assure its consistency and cohesion, and at the same time to establish distinction that would allow the small studio to make the best of its resources. Marvel's role model was Pixar, another studio that, though starting small, attained great success by becoming associated with original, quirky, and creative takes on an undervalued genre, in their case children's animation. Hence, as Feige says, the idea was not to reinvent the wheel, but to make films that though distinct within the superhero genre, were still recognizably Marvel movies.

Within this context, Kevin Feige and Marvel Studios have used Whedon's name as a form of guarantee to their industry peers and a draw to their fan audience, and have incorporated his cues and approach into the framing of the film. Yet in the end, he remains a peg in the finely honed Marvel movie machine. Certainly, it is an important peg: Like Marvel's previous unusual directorial choices, Whedon holds the film's balance between creative innovation and faithfulness to the source material, making it distinctly *Marvel's Avengers.* Nonetheless, this demonstrates the complication of popular ideas of auteurism when they run up against Hollywood realities. Whedon is celebrated for his creative identity, an identity tied to his positive interaction with fandom, to his feminist politics, perhaps most importantly to his designation as that elusive, reified figure of the creative genius. At the same time, this identity is also a commodity, a commercial identity as consumer brands are. Its use in this respect creates a complex relationship with the branding efforts of media studios and corporations—one which, in Whedon's case, has only grown complex as he becomes more closely involved with the MCU (Hadas). With the franchise soon continuing in *Avengers: Age of Ultron*, there is no doubt ample room to continue research into this subject as well.

Whedon's Women and the Law

Parallels from Slayers to S.H.I.E.L.D.

GAIL D. ROSEN

• • •

Does the law have gender? How does a female approach differ from the male, especially for Whedon? In *Buffy the Vampire Slayer*, Buffy is bound by the rules of the Watcher's Council, and Buffy and Willow are bound by the laws of man. Similarly, in *Marvel's Agents of S.H.I.E.L.D*, Skye and Melinda May must adhere to the rules of S.H.I.E.L.D. In both television shows, these characters often confront the tension between the obligation to blindly follow the rules and the need to disregard them when justice and fairness demands.

In *Buffy the Vampire Slayer*, both Buffy and Willow (at different times) achieve the status of single most powerful person in the world. Yet both characters make most of their important decisions by consulting with their circle of friends. This group functions more like a family, and their love for each other informs their choices and allows them to sometimes create their own laws. This is also true of Skye and May in *Marvel's Agents of S.H.I.E.L.D.* The characters in this television show are family—much more than co-workers or even friends. Both Skye and May subvert the law and rules of S.H.I.E.L.D. in order to protect fellow members. In both *Buffy the Vampire Slayer* and *Marvel's Agents of S.H.I.E.L.D.*, the "family" becomes both the law and a court of equity—in both cases, due to Buffy, Willow, May and Skye with their ethics of care, equity and love.

In his book *Law and Literature*, legal scholar Richard Posner discusses Carol Gilligan's book *In a Different Voice*, which distinguishes between "ethics of justice" (masculine) and "ethics of care" (feminine). Gilligan uses a study of boys and girls about enforcement of rules in games.

She found that boys want to strictly enforce rules where girls want to look at contexts, relationships and feelings rather than formal rules/rule breaking. When adjudicating an infraction in the game, girls paid particular attention to preventing problems in the relationships (124). Posner also sees these same ideas in Susan Glaspell's "A Jury of Her Peers" (1917), (based on the 1900 murder trial of Margaret Hossack) in which two women hide evidence during a murder investigation in order to protect the accused wife. He concludes that women prefer to look at the circumstances of the case and do not feel the need to conform to neutral principles of law. Posner noted that women were virtually excluded from the legal system at time "A Jury of Her Peers" was written (122–124). For women, justice was not blind. But did ethics of care inform the way women view the law solely because women were excluded from legal processes? Is the ethics of care principle still relevant in world where women actively participate in all aspects of the legal system?

In "Myth, Morality; and the Women of the X-Men," Rebecca Housel sees Gilligan's "ethics of care" in Storm and Jean Grey (80–87). It appears that although times have changed since Glaspell wrote "Jury of Her Peers," the "ethics of care" has not. We can see this dramatically illustrated in the world of *Buffy the Vampire Slayer*, in which Buffy Summers and Willow Rosenberg, the two most powerful women in the world, continue to use ethics of care when applying laws.

Destiny has chosen Buffy to be the slayer. The slayer's mission is to kill vampires, demons and the forces of evil, following the dictates of Watchers' Council and their representative, Giles. Still, early on, Buffy shows that she is a woman who does not follow rules blindly. Buffy defies the Council on several occasions to save the lives of her vampire boyfriend Angel and her friend Willow. In the latter case, Buffy's new watcher Wesley and the Watchers Council oppose a hostage negotiation in which Buffy must trade the deadly Box of Gavrok for Willow. The Council insists it is better to save many lives than one. But Buffy ignores their commands ("Choices," B3.19). She's shown in contrast with the other slayer, Kendra, who eagerly follows rules. When Kendra insists that they check in with the Watchers Council before helping Angel, she cites procedure. Buffy objects to this, telling Kendra, "I don't take orders, I do things my way" ("What's My Line," B2.10). Buffy further explains to Kendra that she doesn't draw strength from rulebooks but "my emotions give me power."

Near the end of Season Three, in "Graduation Day Part 1" (B3.21), Buffy finally quits the Watchers Council when they refuse to find a cure for a poisoned Angel. Wesley justifies his actions, saying that, "It is not council policy to cure vampires." Even Giles, using the ethics of care principles adopted by Buffy and Willow, asks if Wesley explained to the Council that "these are special circumstances" ("Graduation Day Part 1," B3.21). Contexts, relationships and feelings are more important for Buffy than neutral principles of law; even if those laws have, as Wesley says, "existed longer than civilization." In the episode, Buffy quits the Council for good, declaring, "I don't think I am going to be taking any more orders from the Council. I am not working for them." When Wesley describes her actions as "mutiny" she replies, "I like to think of it as graduation" ("Graduation Day Part 1," B3.21). This strained relationship with the Council continues throughout the series.

As the series progresses, Buffy extends the ethics of care principles to others beyond her intimate circle. She makes exceptions to the "kill vampires, demons and the forces of evil" slayer mission for those certain beings (Spike, Anya, Clem and others) by examining the specific circumstances and considering the feelings of her friends. Even when Spike and Anya commit murder, she forgives them as part of her inner circle.

Unlike Buffy who begins the series as a slayer, Willow becomes more powerful magically each year. Willow's relationship to the law evolves as her power grows. Early in the first season, a shocked "good girl" Willow learns of the existence of vampires and suggests calling the police to help battle them. "They couldn't handle it. They'd only show up with guns," Buffy answers ("The Harvest," B1.2). Through the early seasons, she uses ethics of care, comforting Buffy through romantic troubles. When Angel (once murderous, now good) returns from death and Buffy conceals this fact, Buffy's friends stage an intervention. Willow explains that instead of making accusations, the group should express their feelings by making "I" statements. Willow, using ethics of care, begins by saying, "This isn't about attacking Buffy." The feelings of the group members (in this case Buffy) are more important than following the rules and punishing Buffy for breaking them.

Buffy and Willow move beyond looking at the feelings of those in their inner circle, and begin to apply the principles of equity to those they do not know. Equity dictates that strict rules of law should be applied with sensitivity, so that the intention is not sacrificed to the letter of the law, as with Portia's insistence in *The Merchant of Venice* that taking a pound of flesh will be murder and therefore unjust. Willow, more than Buffy, leads the charge for equity. In Season Two, a ghost, a former student who had an affair with and then killed his teacher and himself, is haunting the school. Willow investigates the ghost and empathizes with him. Thus,

Willow combines the principles of ethics of care and equity by looking at the circumstances of the ghost and advocating for equity in this case. Willow feels that the ghost is not an ordinary killer acting without remorse. She urges others to find out what the ghost wants, instead of trying to destroy him ("I Only Have Eyes For You," B2.19). Buffy is especially angry and only wants to kill it. Buffy says the ghost should be serving a long jail sentence and "making friends with Roscoe the weightlifter." Her anger prompts Xander to reply, "The quality of mercy is not Buffy." The reference to Portia and her quality of mercy speech shows how far apart Buffy and Willow are when it comes to equity in this case. When Buffy realizes that the ghost needs forgiveness to move on, she balks, but only because she cannot forgive herself for her relationship with the then evil Angel. In the end, Buffy accepts Willow's teaching that the best way to get rid of ghost is to forgive him and thus saves the school. Equity is not only the just solution, but the best solution to the problem of the murdering ghost.

An even stronger demonstration of equity can be seen in season four. During Thanksgiving, a Native American spirit from the Chumash tribe wants vengeance for his people ("Pangs," B4.8). Although the spirit has killed innocents, Willow spends time reading about the atrocities committed again this tribe. After this, Willow thinks they should be helping spirit redress these wrongs and should bring the atrocities to light, rather than stopping him. Even after the spirit gives Xander a disease, Willow continues to defend it. For Willow, the principles of equity are clear here. The many wrongs committed against his tribe mitigate the Native American spirit's crimes. Buffy has conflicting feelings, as she does not "like her evil mixed up with guilt and destruction of indigenous people" ("Pangs," B4.8). Buffy is finally convinced by Willow and tries to apologize to the spirit. When the spirit tries to kill all of them, Buffy is forced to destroy him—but she first tried for a more equitable solution.

In "It's About Power: Law in the Fictional Setting of a Quaker Meeting and in the Everyday Reality of *Buffy the Vampire Slayer*," Anthony Bradney posits that "Law in the latter half of *Buffy the Vampire Slayer* is arrived at through discussion with one's intimate friends and requires their assent. Law is connected with and supplemented by love" (15). This idea of Buffy's family as a court of law solidifies by Season Four. In "Pangs" (B4.8), a heated discussion takes place about the Native American spirit. When Xander asks the group when they will kill the spirit, Buffy replies, "That's sort of the question before the court" (B4.8). Historically, slaying was thought to be a somewhat solitary activity. Buffy signals a change to this when she includes her friends (her chosen family) and later her mother

Joyce and her sister Dawn in her battles against evil. In this scene, Buffy has firmly acknowledged that her chosen family will help her decide how to enforce the law.

But what happens if the monsters are human and the "criminals" are part of the family? The evil human Warren kills Tara and wounds Buffy. A grief-stricken Willow wants revenge. But Buffy is clear on the distinction between human monsters and non-human monsters. She firmly states, "We don't kill humans. That is not the way. The human world has its own rules for dealing with people like Warren" ("Villains," B6.20). Despite Buffy's disagreement with the edicts and authority of the Watchers Council, she firmly believes and respects the laws of man for punishing the crimes of man. However, the conversation in the family changes after Willow kills Warren. The "family" decides he may have deserved it. But this does not seem to be the family applying principles of equity or ethics of care. They change their mind because they love her and she is one of them. At the end of the episode, a completely evil Willow tries to destroy the family and the entire world. Nonetheless, the "family" in the form of Giles and Xander stops her and forgives her ("Grave," B6.22). While Giles offers law (not from the Watchers Council but from the gentle Wiccan group who sense a disruption in the natural world), Xander offers pure faith and love. After joining the Wiccan community to learn nondestructive magic, Willow is rehabilitated in the next season. Part of the reason Willow is forgiven is because she truly repents. In the end, Willow is an integral part of the family, and the family decides not to punish her. Love has supplanted law (Bradney, "It's About Power" 16).

This pattern continues in the Season Eight and Nine comics. In "Anywhere but Here," Buffy and Willow each discover the other has committed transgressions: Buffy is stealing and Willow has been cheating on her girlfriend with a magical tutor. Each forgives the other on the spot, after listening to the explanation. When Amy, Andrew, and Angel (to varying extents) betray the team, Amy, the outsider, is treated as an enemy. By contrast, when Andrew throws himself on Buffy's mercy and volunteers to sacrifice himself, Buffy calls him "part of the family" and forgives him (*Predators and Prey*, B8.5). She judges him on her own, but in this scene, she appears to speak for the family who would clearly rule the same way. In Angel's case, Faith insists on supervising his rehabilitation, vowing to care for him personally until he can live with himself because he's "the one person who never gave up" on her. She considers herself responsible and also practical for the job since "Buffy can't look at him" and "everyone else wants his head on a pike" (*Last Gleaming*, B8.8). Buffy, who stops herself and Xander from executing Angel (presumably because he'll always be an insider and her first love), permits this, and the "family" gives Faith permission. By contrast, one of the enemies of the season, General Voll, represents the hidebound patriarchy. He decides, based on the evidence, that Buffy and her friends are the enemy, and he orders them destroyed. He, like the Watchers Council, is bound by hierarchy rather than compassion.

In flashback, after teen Giles broke the Council's laws and summoned the demon Eyghon, his grandmother offered him a personal absolution:

> **EDNA**: You were a young fool who felt immortal, did remarkably ill-advised things, and it cost people their lives, eh? You bloody idiot. That doesn't disqualify you from being a watcher. It makes you perfectly suited to mentor a Slayer. They're young girls granted tremendous power. Who can relate to them better? A man like your father, who's done the right and proper thing his entire life? Or you?
> **GILES**: What I've done goes well beyond a misspent youth.
> **EDNA**: Oh, stop. I know all about Eyghon. Perhaps your soul is damned. Perhaps he'll claim it the moment you die and subject you to an eternity of torment. If you want to be selfish about it, a lifetime of good works may be the one way to save yourself from that fate. The only path to redemption. And if you genuinely want to atone for what you've done, it's your duty. Much as you despise the word. You feel you've done wrong? Then stop crying about it ... and start making amends [*Angel and Faith* 4].

While she is literal family, not metaphorical, she speaks on behalf of a chosen family—the Watchers Council themselves. She invites young Ripper to join and gives him a personal penance to undergo. She may be a personification of the law, but her speech holds ethics of care, as she insists Ripper seek inner redemption.

Buffy the Vampire Slayer aired from 1997 to 2003. *Marvel's Agents of S.H.I.E.L.D.* began its first season in 2013 and is in the middle of the second season as of this writing. We can already see parallels to *Buffy the Vampire Slayer* when examining the way Whedon's newest strong female characters relate to the law. While Buffy is clearly in charge of her group, Phil Coulson commands the S.H.I.E.L.D. agents. In a sense, he is like Giles in *Buffy the Vampire Slayer*, but with more power. Is S.H.I.E.L.D the law? S.H.I.E.L.D is similar to the Watchers' Council, but is also a government agency. Coulson and his team report to those in charge at S.H.I.E.L.D, but S.H.I.E.L.D also has legal authority, as least as the series begins.

When we first meet Melinda May, she seems an unlikely candidate to use the ethics of care principle in applying the law. May is a pilot and a fighter whose nickname is "The Cavalry." Wild stories circulate about how she earned the name, which May does not like to discuss ("0–8–4," AS1.2). Newest member of the team Skye thinks May is "all business" ("Repairs," AS1.9). This, along with her military background suggests a person who would strictly adhere to neutral principles of law and follow the masculine "ethics of justice" approach. However, May is more complicated than that. "May was different. Thought rules were made to be broken," Coulson explains of the old May before a traumatic incident ("Repairs," AS1.9). In the second episode of the season, Coulson tries to calm his bickering team, as they debate the best course of action after they are attacked in Peru. May responds to the heated discussion about the best way to proceed with a terse, "You guys talk a lot." Despite the fact that she expresses annoyance at their protracted discussion and her "all business" attitude, she wants to strengthen relationships. Later in the series, May plays a prank on the team and laughs ("Repairs," AS1.9). Her actions show that she is inclined to adopt the ethics of care approach when she must enforce rules.

Later in the first season, Agent Victoria Hand kicks Skye off the team's aircraft home when Skye wants to hack into some financial records in an effort to find a missing Coulson. Agent Hand asks May if Skye will "be of any use to us on this plane?" and May (choosing her words all too carefully) answers, "No." Near the end of the episode we learn that, using ethics of care, May wanted Skye free to find Coulson without the hampering of bureaucracy ("The Magical Place," AS1.11). Finding Coulson outweighs following orders from Agent Hand. In the very next episode ("Seeds," AS1.12), May agrees with Coulson's decision not to turn in a fugitive agent who protected Skye as a baby, a decision that better protects the team. Despite outward appearances, May is not one to follow rules blindly.

While May seems to slowly adopt ethics of care principles, Skye uses them right from the start. Skye doesn't believe one person always has the solution, but that sometimes it takes a group to figure things out ("0–8–4," AS1.2). Later on, Skye says that she wants to think "outside the box" and break rules to save Fitz and Ward, "two people we care about." She enlists the help of Simmons with the hack. Simmons shoots a guard with a stun gun and Skye breaks into a restricted area. "Are we just numbers?" Skye asks in defense of her decision to go break the rules ("The Hub," AS1.7). It is clear that her feelings for these two members of the team trump the rules. Even more than that, Skye convinces Agent Simmons to follow suit.

When telekinetic Hannah blames herself for the death of four people, Skye investigates the truth. She realizes that Tobias, a traveler between two worlds, wants Hannah. Coulson explains that Skye helped save Hannah by figuring out what the people around Hannah wanted, saying, "You know what makes people tick. You see the good in them" ("Repairs," AS1.9).

At first, May appears to have no real connections to anyone on the team except for Coulson. Even when she begins a sexual relationship with Ward, the more intimate act for May is revealing it to Coulson ("Seeds," AS1.12). In the second half of the season, the team suspects that May is a spy. She denies it and reveals that she is taking direct orders from Director Nick Fury, on a mission to protect Coulson from the aftereffects of his resurrection, an act she knew she couldn't do alone. May explains, "I assembled this team." In a sense, she chose a family for Coulson that would allow love to determine the way they enforce the law.

Later, May leaves the team because Coulson does not trust her. "I was here for Coulson, but he cannot get past me lying," she explains. May believes that the price of following orders has been too high ("The Only Light in the Darkness," AS1.19). Still, after May leaves the team, she still contacts Agent Hill to prove herself to Coulson and the team ("Nothing Personal," AS1.20). A defining moment for both May and Skye comes when Hydra infiltrates S.H.I.E.L.D. and Coulson and his group go into hiding. They turn from loyal soldiers to outlaws, but they remain intact as a family devoted to protecting the world, even in secret. Near the end of Season One, May returns with information that reassures Coulson about her loyalty and his own (as he fears he's been programmed by a Hydra agent) ("Nothing Personal," AS1.20). He forgives her and the episode ends with the reformed family lounging at a motel pool and awaiting their next assignment.

Skye's path towards the family also begins with Coulson. We learn early in the series that Skye is both an orphan and a loner. She does not know anything about her biological family, and when the series opens, she is a hacker living alone in a van. However, Skye is abducted by S.H.I.E.L.D. and begins to work with them ("Pilot," AS1.1). Early in the season, Skye crashes a party thrown by evil businessman Ian Quinn, and attempts to gain his trust. When Skye tells Quinn that she has been spending time with S.H.I.E.L.D., Quinn isn't surprised. He says S.H.I.E.L.D. preys on people like her—people with no family ("The Asset," AS1.3). Skye reveals to Ward that she never fit in with any of the foster parents she was shuffled to as a kid. There was one family in particular that she had hoped to join, but it never happened. Ward assures her S.H.I.E.L.D. won't turn their back on her ("The Asset,"AS1.3). Like Buffy, Skye will choose her own family.

Near the middle of the first season, Coulson tells Skye the truth about her family. Instead of being devastated to learn she was the cause of destruction and S.H.I.E.L.D. agents dying, Skye is relieved and hopeful. Coulson tells May:

> Her whole life, she thought she wasn't wanted, that she didn't belong, that every family that took her in didn't want her to stay, didn't care. But all that time, it was S.H.I.E.L.D. protecting her, looking after her. That's what she took away from the story ... not the family she'll never have but the one she's always had. Here I am, telling her something that could destroy her faith in humanity. And somehow, she manages to repair a little piece of mine ["Seeds," AS1.12].

After S.H.I.E.L.D. goes into hiding, all members of the team are given a lie detector test. They are all asked the same question by Agent Koenig: Why are they still fighting now that S.H.I.E.L.D. does not exist? Skye says that S.H.I.E.L.D is the only family she has ever known ("The Only Light in the Darkness," AS1.19). Her attachment to Coulson has grown to encompass the rest of the team—her chosen family.

The chosen family continues as a law-enforcing body. While Skye, May and the rest of Coulson's teams are fugitives as Season Two begins, Ward is imprisoned by S.H.I.E.L.D. after they discover he has been secretly working against them with Hydra. Skye and May do not forgive him, even when Ward offers to take Skye to her father ("Shadows," AS2.1). Unlike Willow, who seemed to have a real excuse for turning evil, Ward does not. While Willow was remorseful, Ward is not. Unlike Willow, Ward is rejected by the family, perhaps permanently. While Skye and May seemed so different from each other as the series began, by Season Two they seem to have reached the same place in their journey. Both May and Skye continue to protect Coulson above all others. May tells Coulson she will pull the plug on their mission if she senses things are too much for him, but she refuses Coulson's request to kill him if he becomes dangerous ("Face My Enemy," AS2.4). Skye protects Coulson from her own father, threatening to shoot him to protect Coulson ("What They Become," AS2.10). This chosen family is evolving into an entity quite like Buffy's chosen family. They will continue to act as a court of law, using love and family as a guiding principle.

In *Buffy the Vampire Slayer*, the journey for Buffy and Willow from ethics of care, to equity, to the family and love as law ends when the series ends. Buffy and her chosen family identify all of the females with the potential to be the Slayer ("Potentials," B7.12). These young women train with Buffy and her group and live together in Buffy's house. In the final episode, Buffy and Willow use a spell to activate the Potentials, making all of these women slayers ("Chosen," B7.22). No longer will there only be one Slayer. A powerful group of women will now fight evil together, and together they save the world. Skye and May discover a similar homecoming, as their team of six (Season One) expands to include a mercenary group and other lost characters like Trip, an agent without a team. Coulson insists they can rebuild S.H.I.E.L.D. the right way, from the ground up, and transform their little family into a mighty institution. Just like Buffy and her new army of thousands, Skye, May, Coulson and the rest of the group are determined to bring justice and protection to the helpless.

An earlier version of Gail D. Rosen's "Whedon's Women and the Law" was previously presented at "Buffy to Batgirl: Women and Gender in Science Fiction, Fantasy, and Comics." Rutgers University. New Brunswick, NJ, May 2–3, 2014, and at the Mid-Atlantic Popular and American Culture Association Conferences.

A Guide to Buffyverse Comics

• • •

These Dark Horse comics are supervised by Whedon—written or edited by him. They take place during the series or are flashbacks/flashforwards:

- *Buffy: The Origin*
- *Fray*
- *Tales of the Slayers*
- *Tales of the Vampires*

The following are officially "noncanon" (as Whedon didn't supervise them, so they may contradict "canon" materials) but they contain the canon *Buffy: The Origin*, Whedon's *Long Night's Journey* and original characters who later appear in the canon *Angel: After the Fall*. These comics mostly take place during the TV shows. This is the suggested reading order:

- *Buffy: Omnibus 1–7*
- *Angel: Omnibus 1&2*
- *Spike: Omnibus*

There's also a "best of" art book from Dark Horse, published in 2007, titled *Buffy the Vampire Slayer: Panel to Panel*.

Angel: After the Fall from IDW (2007–2011)

This series isn't called *Angel*: Season Six, but it begins moments after *Angel*: Season Five, so it could be. Whedon has declared the works canon, and adapted the storyline from his plans for Season Six of the show. These are IDW hardcovers in reading order:

Spike: After the Fall by Brian Lynch

Volume 1
1. *Angel: After the Fall* by Joss Whedon and Brian Lynch
2. *Angel: First Night* by Joss Whedon and Brian Lynch
3. *Angel: After the Fall* by Joss Whedon and Brian Lynch
4. *Angel: After the Fall* by Joss Whedon and Brian Lynch
5. *Angel: Aftermath* by Kelley Armstrong
6. *Angel: Last Angel in Hell* by Brian Lynch

Volume 2
1. *Angel: Immortality for Dummies* by Bill Willingham
2. *Angel: Crown Prince Syndrome* by Bill Willingham
3. *Angel: The Wolf, The Ram, and The Hart* by David Tischman
   (These three volumes are also available as *Angel: The End*.)

Spike: The Complete Series by Brian Lynch
Angel: Only Human by Scott Lobdell
Angel: The John Byrne Collection
Illyria: Haunted by Scott Tipton and Mariah Huehner
(The canon on these four is a bit more muddled.)

Dark Horse Collections

Buffy: Season Eight (2007–2011)
This follows *Angel: After the Fall*, but that could be explained by the slayers taking time to set up their base before the action begins. These are produced and written by Whedon and his staff.

8.1 *The Long Way Home* by Joss Whedon
8.2 *No Future for You* by Vaughan & Whedon
8.3 *Wolves at the Gate* by Drew Goddard
8.4 *Time of Your Life* by Loeb, Whedon & Moline
8.5 *Predators and Prey* by Jane Espenson
8.6 *Retreat* by Loeb, Whedon & Moline
8.7 *Twilight* by Meltzer, Whedon, & Moline
8.8 *Last Gleaming* by Whedon, Espenson, and Allie

Buffy: Season Nine and *Angel & Faith* (2011–2013)

Buffy the Vampire Slayer 9.1 *Freefall* by Joss Whedon
Angel & Faith 1: Live Through This by Christos Gage
Buffy the Vampire Slayer 9.2 *On Your Own* by Andrew Chambliss
Angel & Faith 2: Daddy Issues by Christos Gage
Buffy the Vampire Slayer 9.3 *Guarded* by Andrew Chambliss
Angel & Faith 3: Family Reunion by Christos Gage
Spike: A Dark Place by Victor Gischler
Willow: Wonderland by Jeff Parker & Christos Gage
Buffy the Vampire Slayer 9.4 *Welcome to the Team* by Andrew Chambliss
Angel & Faith 4: Death and Consequences by Christos Gage
Buffy the Vampire Slayer 9.5 *The Core* by Karl Moline
Angel & Faith 5: What You Want, Not What You Need by Christos Gage

Buffy: Season Ten and *Angel and Faith vol. 2* (2014–) are currently in production.

SERENITY COMICS

1. *Those Left Behind* by Joss Whedon and Brett Matthews
2. *Better Days and Other Stories*
   - "Better Days" by Joss Whedon and Brett Matthews
   - "Float Out" by Patton Oswalt
   - "The Other Half" by Jim Krueger
   - "Downtime" by Zack Whedon
3. *The Shepherd's Tale* by Joss Whedon and Zack Whedon
   - "Serenity: Firefly Class 03-K64—It's Never Easy" by Zack Whedon (Free Comic Book Day comic, free on the Dark Horse site)
4. *Serenity: Leaves on the Wind* by Zack Whedon

OTHER JOSS WHEDON COMICS

Dark Horse
- *Sugarshock!* 1–3 (reprinted in *Myspace Dark Horse Presents* #1)

DC
- *Superman/Batman* #26 (p. 20–21)

Marvel
- "X-Men: Teamwork" (in *Giant Size X-Men* #3)
- *Astonishing X-Men* vol. 3: (#1–24) & *Giant Size Astonishing X-Men* #1 (reprinted as the collections *Astonishing X-Men: Gifted, Dangerous, Torn, Unstoppable*)
- *Runaways* vol. 2 (#25–30) (reprinted as *Dead End Kids*)
- "Some Steves" (in *Stan Lee Meets The Amazing Spider-Man* #1)

OTHER ZACK AND JED WHEDON COMICS

Dark Horse
- *Dollhouse Volume 1: Epitaphs* by Andrew Chambliss, Maurissa Tancharoen, and Jed Whedon
- *Dr. Horrible and Other Horrible Stories* by Zack Whedon, Joelle Jones, Jim Rugg and Farel Dalrymple
- *Terminator: 2029–1984* by Zack Whedon and Andy MacDonald

Glossary

• • •

A1-A5: The *Buffy* spinoff television show *Angel*, seasons one through five.

Adaptation: The art of transferring a work from one medium to another.

Agents of S.H.I.E.L.D.: A television show (2013-) in the Marvel Cinematic Universe (MCU) featuring Agent Coulson and his team. Joss Whedon and his brother and sister-in-law are showrunners.

Alternate Universe, Alt-Universe: Genre that changes one or more elements of the source work, such as having Superman raised on Krypton or adopted by different parents on earth.

Anime/Manga: Japanese animated cartoons and comic books respectively.

Angel and Faith: Two short Dark Horse series, corresponding with *Buffy: Seasons Nine and Ten*.

Annual: Comics or collections published once a year.

ATF: *Angel: After the Fall*. An IDW comic run that takes the place of *Angel: Season Six*.

Auteur: The author brand, not necessarily the same as the actual writer.

B8, B9, B10: Buffy Seasons Eight-Ten are series of comic books rather than television, though Season Eight was developed into a motion comic as well. B1-B7 reference the show.

Blog: Short for "Weblog," an online journal often used to discuss pop culture.

Buffyverse: The world in which Buffy and Angel live, including their shows as well as canon and non-canon comics.

Camera shots: A method of describing comic books' point of view, as if they're a film.

Canon: This term refers to material designated "official" or "sanctioned by the author" contrasted with other authors' contributions to a franchise (the *Star Wars* movies, for instance, are considered canon; the spin-off novels and comics are not). While *Buffy, Angel,* or *Firefly* products produced by Whedon are considered canon (even with other authors writing the text), products he did not supervise are relegated to semi-canon or noncanon status. *Buffy* and *Angel* comics fall in both categories.

Caption: Small box of written text.

Comic book: A short collection of comic pages published in a magazine format, often serialized.

Comics Code: A set of self-censorship rules, dating from 1951 onward.

Con: Short for convention or occasionally conference. Many fantasy conventions use this term in their name, such as WesterCon or Comic-Con.

Cosplay: Short for "costume play." Wearing costumes and occasionally acting them out.

Crossover: Fanfiction, fan art, etc. that combines more than one series, such as *Buffy* and *Twilight*. Licensed crossovers often appear between characters in the Marvelverse or the Buffyverse.

D1, D2: *Dollhouse,* Whedon's contemporary dystopia show about mindwiping technology.

Dark Horse: The third largest producer of comic books, they produced the Buffy comics along with *Angel & Faith, Serenity, Fray, Tales,* and *Sugarshock!*.

DC: The publishers of *Superman, Batman,* and other top comics. Whedon's work for DC has been limited to a few pages in a special tribute copy of *Superman/Batman* #26. He wrote a Wonder Woman script for them, and experimented in the past with Batman and other stories, but these were never filmed.

Deconstruction Age: Mid–1980s-1990s. Comics from this time, like *Watchmen* and *Dark Knight Returns* questioned the nature of the superheroes themselves and their right to put themselves above others.

DH: *Dr. Horrible,* Whedon's superhero web musical

Fandom: Devotion to a particular franchise, in this case Joss Whedon and his worlds.

Fangirl, fanboy: This term suggests a truly obsessed fan, often lacking in social skills as he or she revels in enthusiasm and gushes to an extreme degree. Some fans humorously use this term to describe themselves. Doctor Horrible's groupies and possibly Spike's friend Jeremy Johns from the comics are examples.

Focalization: The perspective from which the story is told, though from a third person point of view.

Fridging/Stuffed into the Fridge: A woman hurt or killed to hurt the male hero. A common comic book trope, popularized by critic Gail Simone.

Golden Age: Comics produced between 1938 and the late 1940s. Superman is the most famous, joined by Captain America, Wonder Woman, and the Flash. These heroes were generally uncomplicated and good, altruistically fighting the forces of pure evil. Many major conventions of the genre were established around this time, as earlier comics had mainly been adventures or thrillers.

Graphic novel: This format became prominent in the 1990s. It suggests a comic book published all in one piece as a large story. Use of the word "novel" also elevates it to a higher art form.

Gutter: The space between panels.

IDW Publishing: Founded in 1999, this San Diego publisher did many of the *Angel* comics including *After the Fall*.

Independent comics: Comics from smaller, less mainstream houses. IDW comics are arguably this, though Dark Horse is growing in prominence to become the third largest producer.

Mainstream comics: Usually refers to Marvel and DC, the biggest houses.

Marvel: The publisher of *The Avengers, Agents of S.H.I.E.L.D., X-Men, Runaways,* and many other franchises. Whedon went from writing occasional comics for them to writing and directing some of their movies and television.

Marvel Cinematic Universe (MCU): This refers only to the movie universe of *Iron Man, The Avengers, Agent Carter, Agents of S.H.I.E.L.D.,* etc., excluding the more extensive comics.

Marvelverse: Anything that takes place in the fictional world of Marvel Comics, including *The Avengers, X-Men,* and *Runaways.*

Metalepsis: Crossing boundaries between the story world and real one or between two story worlds.

Metanarration: When the narrator references the fact that he/she is narrating.

Motion Comic: Still animations combined with voiceovers to make a comic book movie. Whedon's *Buffy: Season Eight* and *Astonishing X-Men* were adapted into this format.

Narration: A narrator may be depersonalized, or may be a character, may speak from within the narrative or without. Buffyverse characters in Season Eight and *Angel: After the Fall* specifically tell their stories directly to the reader on many occasions.

One-Shot: A self-contained, one-issue series.

Panels: The boxes in which pictures and words are located.

Quarterly: Published four times a year (every three months).

Ships, Shipping: Short for writing about or otherwise supporting a particular relationship between characters; a popular term used in fanfiction.

Silver Age: Comics produced in 1956 through the 1970s. The X-Men, Spider-Man, and the Hulk number among these. These superheroes were more conflicted and had to balance normal lives with their heroism.

Slash: Refers to homosexual relationships generally not canon in the series (such as Angel/Spike). This is a popular genre of fanfiction.

Social media: Facebook, LiveJournal, MySpace, Tumblr, Twitter, and other sites where fans can connect, blog, share photos and videos, and otherwise create *Buffy* communities.

Speech bubble: A character's words, written in a white bubble.

Speed line: Small lines indicating movement, force, and speed.

Spoilers: These bits of upcoming or recently-released information "spoil" fans' enjoyment of the plot by ruining the surprise.

Story world: The fictional world in which the narrative takes place.

Superhero: An individual with superhuman powers who fights to protect the innocent.

Trade paperbacks: Individual comics are often collected after individual publication in this format, making *Buffy*'s Season Ten comics 1–5 into the widely-distributed book *Buffy: New Rules*.

Transmedia: Works that appear across multiple medias, such as comics, online games, and video.

Twenty-first century comics: These have a tendency towards dystopia and self-reference, aware as they are of the decades that preceded them. *Buffy* and *Angel* comics can be counted among these, along with the *Avengers* movie franchise.

Web comic: A comic book released on the web, whatever its original format.

Wiki: A website like Wikipedia where users can add and modify content. These are frequently used as encyclopedias of fandom. There are many on the Whedon and Marvel series discussed here.

Bibliography

Films

The Avengers. Dir. Joss Whedon. Perf. Scarlet Johannsen, Robert Downey, Jr., Chris Hemsfield. Paramount Pictures, 2012. Blu Ray.

Buffy the Vampire Slayer. Screenplay by Joss Whedon. Dir. Fran Rubel Kuzui. Perf. Kristy Swanson, Donald Sutherland, and Rutger Hauer. 1992. 20th Century–Fox, 2001. DVD.

Comic Con Episode IV: A Fan's Hope. Wrekin Hill Entertainment, 2011. DVD.

Commentary! The Musical. Dr. Horrible's Sing-Along Blog. Mutant Enemy, 2008. DVD.

Dr. Horrible's Sing-Along Blog. Mutant Enemy, 2008. DVD.

Serenity (Widescreen Edition). 2005. Los Angeles: Universal Studios, 2005. DVD.

"Wonder Woman." *Scribd* 7 Aug 2006. http://www.scribd.com/doc/23644１０30/Wonder-Woman-by-Joss-Whedon.

X-Men. Dir. Bryan Singer. Perf. Patrick Stewart, Hugh Jackman, Ian McKellan, Halle Berry, and Famke Jannsen. 20th Century–Fox, 2000. DVD.

X-Men: The Last Stand. Dir. Brett Ratner. Perf. Hugh Jackman, Halle Berry, Ian McKellan, and Famke Jannsen. 20th Century–Fox, 2006. DVD.

X2: X-Men United. Dir. Bryan Singer. Perf. Patrick Stewart, Hugh Jackman, Ian McKellan, Halle Berry, and Famke Jannsen. 20th Century–Fox, 2003. DVD.

Television

Agents of S.H.I.E.L.D.: Season One. ABC. 2013–2014. Television.

Agents of S.H.I.E.L.D.: Season Two. ABC. 2014–2015. Television.

Angel: The Complete First Season. The WB Television Network. 1999–2000. DVD. Los Angeles: 20th Century–Fox, 2003.

Angel: The Complete Second Season. The WB Television Network. 2000–2001. DVD. Los Angeles: 20th Century–Fox, 2003.

Angel: The Complete Third Season. The WB Television Network. 2001–2002. DVD. Los Angeles: 20th Century–Fox, 2004.

Angel: The Complete Fourth Season. The WB Television Network. 2002–2003. DVD. Los Angeles: 20th Century–Fox, 2004.

Angel: The Complete Fifth Season. The WB Television Network. 2003–2004. DVD. Los Angeles: 20th Century–Fox, 2005.

Buffy the Vampire Slayer: The Complete First Season. The WB Television Network. 1997. DVD. Los Angeles: 20th Century–Fox, 2002.

Buffy the Vampire Slayer: The Complete Second Season. The WB Television Network. 1997–1998. DVD. Los Angeles: 20th Century–Fox, 2002.

Buffy the Vampire Slayer: The Complete Third Season. The WB Television Network. 1998–1999. DVD. Los Angeles: 20th Century–Fox, 2006.

Buffy the Vampire Slayer: The Complete Fourth Season. 1999–2000. The WB Television Network. DVD. Los Angeles: 20th Century–Fox, 2003.

Buffy the Vampire Slayer: The Complete Fifth Season. The WB Television Network. 2000–2001. DVD. Los Angeles: 20th Century–Fox, 2006.

Buffy the Vampire Slayer: The Complete Sixth Season. UPN. 2001–2002. DVD. Los Angeles: 20th Century–Fox, 2004.

Buffy the Vampire Slayer: The Complete Seventh Season. UPN. 2002–2003. DVD. Los Angeles: 20th Century–Fox, 2008.
Buffy the Vampire Slayer: Season 8 Motion Comic. DVD. Los Angeles: 20th Century–Fox, 2011.
Dollhouse: Season One. 2009. DVD. Los Angeles: 20th Century–Fox, 2009.
Dollhouse: Season Two. 2009. DVD. Los Angeles: 20th Century–Fox, 2010.
Firefly: The Complete Series. 2002. DVD. Los Angeles: 20th Century–Fox, 2003.

Books and Comics

Allie, Scott, Sierra Hahn, et al. *Buffy the Vampire Slayer Season 9 Volume 3 Guarded.* Milwaukie, OR: Dark Horse, 2013.
Armstrong, Kelley, and Dave Ross. *Angel: Aftermath.* San Diego: IDW, 2009.
Brereton, Dan, and Christopher Golden, writers. *Buffy the Vampire Slayer: The Origin.* Pencils by Joe Bennett. Inks by Rick Ketcham. *Buffy the Vampire Slayer Omnibus: Volume 1.* Milwaukie, OR: Dark Horse, 2007.
Brubaker, Ed, and Michael Lark. *Daredevil* 92. New York: Marvel Comics, December 27, 2006.
Brubaker, Ed, and Michael Lark. *Daredevil* 93. New York: Marvel Comics, January 31, 2007.
Chambliss, Andrew, Scott Allie, Sierra Hahn, and Georges Jeanty. *Buffy the Vampire Slayer Season 9 Volume 2: On Your Own.* Milwaukie, OR: Dark Horse, 2012.
Chambliss, Andrew, Sierra Hahn, Scott Allie, et al. *Buffy the Vampire Slayer Season 9 Volume 4: Welcome to the Team.* Milwaukie, OR: Dark Horse, 2013.
Chambliss, Andrew, Maurissa Tancharoen, and Jed Whedon. Pencils by Cliff Richards Inks by Andy Owens. *Dollhouse: Epitaphs.* Milwaukie, OR: Dark Horse, 2012.
Ellsworth, Fredric Whitney, et al. "The Case of the Costume-Clad Killers" *Detective Comics* v.1 #60. New York: Detective Comics, February 1942.
Espenson, Jane, and Georges Jeanty. *Predators and Prey*, Season 8, Vol. 5. Milwaukie, OR: Dark Horse, 2009.
Gage, Christos, Scott Allie, Nicholas Brendon, and Rebekah Isaacs. *Buffy the Vampire Slayer Season Ten*, Issue 7. Milwaukie, OR: Dark Horse Books, 2014.
Gage, Christos, Scott Allie, Nicholas Brendon, and Rebekah Isaacs. *Buffy the Vampire Slayer Season Ten Volume 1: New Rules.* Milwaukie, Milwaukie, OR: Dark Horse Books, 2014.
Gage, Christos, Scott Allie, and Sierra Hahn. *Angel & Faith Volume 4: Death and Consequences.* Milwaukie, OR: Dark Horse, 2013.
Gage, Christos, Scott Allie, Rebekah Isaacs, and Phil Noto. *Angel and Faith Volume 1: Live Through This.* Milwaukie, OR: Dark Horse, 2012.
Gage, Christos, Lee Garbett, Derek Fridolfs, and Rebekah Isaacs. *Angel & Faith Volume 3: Family Reunion.* Milwaukie, OR:Dark Horse, 2013.
Gage, Christos, Sierra Hahn, Scott Allie, and Rebekah Isaacs. *Angel & Faith Volume 2: Daddy Issues.* Milwaukie, OR: Dark Horse, 2012.
Gage, Christos, Sierra Hahn, Scott Allie, and Rebekah Isaacs. *Angel & Faith Volume 5: What You Want, Not What You Need.* Milwaukie, OR: Dark Horse, 2014.
Gischler, Victor, et al. *Spike—A Dark Place.* Milwaukie, OR: Dark Horse, 2013.
Goddard, Drew, and Georges Jeanty. *Wolves at the Gate*, Season 8, Vol. 3. Milwaukie, OR: Dark Horse, 2008.
Loeb, Jeph, Joss Whedon, and Karl Moline. *Retreat*, Season 8, Vol. 6 Milwaukie, OR: Dark Horse, 2010.
____. *Time of Your Life*, Season 8, Vol. 4. Milwaukie, OR: Dark Horse, 2008.
Lynch, Brian, Juliet Landau and Franco Urru. *Angel Vol. 6: Last Angel in Hell.* San Diego: IDW, 2010.
Lynch, Brian, and Franco Urru. *Spike: After the Fall.* San Diego: IDW, 2009.
Lynch, Brian, Franco Urru, Nicola Zanni and Stephen Mooney. *Spike: The Complete Series.* San Diego: IDW, 2012.
Marsters, James (w), Dan Jackson, Steve Morris, and Derlis Santacruz (i). *Spike: Into the Light.* Milwaukie, OR: Dark Horse, 2014.
Martz, Ron, et al. "Forced Entry." *Green Lantern* v.3 #54. New York: DC Comics, August 1994.
Meltzer, Brad, Joss Whedon, Georges

Jeanty, and Karl Moline. *Twilight,* Season 8, Vol. 7. Milwaukie, OR: Dark Horse, 2010.
Moline, Karl, Scott Allie, and Sierra Hahn. *Buffy the Vampire Slayer Season Nine Volume 5: The Core.* Milwaukie, OR: Dark Horse, 2014.
Moore, Alan, and Dave Gibbons. *Watchmen.* New York: Warner Books, 1987.
Moore, Alan, et al. *Batman: The Killing Joke.* New York: Warner Books, 1988.
Parker, Jeff, et al. *Willow: Wonderland.* Milwaukie, OR: Dark Horse, 2013.
Simone, Gail, et al. "Shattered." *Batgirl* v.4, #1. New York: DC Comics, November 2011.
Thomas, Roy, and Gil Kane. *Marvel Premiere* 2. New York: Marvel Comics, May 10, 1972.
Vaughan, Brian K., Joss Whedon, and Georges Jeanty. *No Future for You,* Season 8, Vol. 2. Milwaukie, OR: Dark Horse, 2008.
Wein, Len (w), Herb Trimpe (p), and Jack Abel (i). "And Now ... the Wolverine." *The Incredible Hulk* v.1, #181 (Nov. 1974), Marvel Comics.
Wells, Zeb, and Jose Madureira. *Savage Wolverine* 8. New York: Marvel Comics, September 18, 2013.
Whedon, Joss. "Some Steves." *Stan Lee Meets the Amazing Spider-Man* by Stan Lee, Joss Whedon, Olivier Coipel and Michael Gaydos. USA: Marvel Comics, 2006. 11–20.
Whedon, Joss. "Sugarshock!" *Dark Horse MySpace Presents #1.* Milwaukie, OR: Dark Horse Books, 2008. 5–28.
Whedon, Joss. *Tales of the Slayers.* Milwaukie, OR: Dark Horse, 2002.
Whedon, Joss. "Teamwork." *Giant-Size X-Men #3.* USA: Marvel Comics, 2005. 1–8.
Whedon, Joss. "Welcome to the Hellmouth." *Buffy the Vampire Slayer: The Script Book, Season One, Volume 1.* New York: Pocket Books, 2000.
Whedon, Joss, and John Cassaday. *Astonishing X-Men Vol. 1: Gifted.* New York: Marvel Comics, 2006.
Whedon, Joss, and John Cassaday. *Astonishing X-Men Vol. 2: Dangerous.* New York: Marvel Comics, 2007.
Whedon, Joss, and John Cassaday. *Astonishing X-Men Vol. 3: Torn.* New York: Marvel Comics, 2007.
Whedon, Joss, and John Cassaday. *Astonishing X-Men Vol. 4: Unstoppable.* New York: Marvel Comics, 2008.
Whedon, Joss, and Michael Ryan. *Runaways, Volume 8: Dead End Kids* (25–33). New York: Marvel Comics, 2009.
Whedon, Joss, and Scott Allie. "Always Darkest." *Myspace Dark Horse Presents #4.* Milwaukie, OR: Dark Horse Books, 2009.
Whedon, Joss, Andrew Chambliss, Sierra Hahn, and Scott Allie. *Buffy the Vampire Slayer: Season Nine Volume 1: Freefall.* Milwaukie, OR: Dark Horse, 2012.
Whedon, Joss, Ben Edlund, Jane Espenson, and Brett Matthews. *Tales of the Vampires.* Milwaukie, OR: Dark Horse, 2004.
Whedon, Joss, Jane Espenson, Scott Allie, and Georges Jeanty. *Last Gleaming,* Season 8, Vol. 8. Milwaukie, OR: Dark Horse, 2011.
Whedon, Joss, and Georges Jeanty. *The Long Way Home,* Season 8, Vol. 1. Milwaukie, OR: Dark Horse, 2007.
Whedon, Joss, Brian Lynch, Nick Runge, David Messina. *Angel: After the Fall, Volume 3.* San Diego: IDW, 2009.
Whedon, Joss, Brian Lynch and Franco Urru. *Angel: After the Fall, Volume 1.* San Diego: IDW, 2008.
Whedon, Joss, Brian Lynch, Franco Urru, and Alex Garner. *Angel: After the Fall, Volume 4.* San Diego: IDW, 2009.
Whedon, Joss, Brian Lynch, et al. *Angel: After the Fall: First Night, Volume 2.* San Diego: IDW, 2008.
Whedon, Joss, Brett Matthews, Will Conrad, Laura Martin, Michael Heisler, and Adam Hughes. *Serenity Volume 1: Those Left Behind.* Milwaukie, OR: Dark Horse Books, 2007.
Whedon, Joss, Brett Matthews, Will Conrad, Zack Whedon, Patton Oswalt, Chris Samnee, Jim Krueger, and Patric Reynolds. *Serenity Volume 2: Better Days and Other Stories.* Milwaukie, OR: Dark Horse Books, 2008.
Whedon, Joss, and Karl Moline. "Willow: Goddesses and Monsters." Milwaukie, OR: Dark Horse Books, 2009.
Whedon, Joss, Karl Moline, and Andy Owens. *Fray.* Milwaukie, OR: Dark Horse, 2003.
Whedon, Joss, Zack Whedon, Chris Samnee, Dave Stewart, Michael Heisler, and Steve Morris. *Serenity Volume 3: The*

Shepherd's Tale. Milwaukie, OR: Dark Horse Books, 2010.

Whedon, Zack, and Fábio Moon. "Serenity: Firefly Class 03-K64—It's Never Easy." Milwaukie, OR: Dark Horse Books, 2012. http://www.fireflyfans.net/mthread.aspx?tid=51833.

Whedon, Zack, Joelle Jones, Jim Rugg, Farel Dalrymple, and Eric Canete. *Doctor Horrible and Other Horrible Stories*. Milwaukie, OR: Dark Horse Books, 2010.

Whedon, Zack and Georges Jeanty. *Serenity: Leaves on the Wind*. Milwaukie, OR: Dark Horse Books, 2014.

Willingham, Bill, David Tischman, et al. *Angel: The End*. San Diego: IDW, 2011.

Windsor-Smith, Barry. "Weapon X." *Marvel Comics Presents #72–84*. New York: Marvel Comics, 1991.

Secondary Sources

Abbott, Stacey. *Angel*. Detroit: Wayne State University Press, 2009.

_____. "It (Re-)Started with a Girl: The Creative Interplay Between TV and Comics in *Angel: After the Fall*." *The Literary* Angel: *Essays on Influences and Traditions Reflected in the Joss Whedon Series*. Ed. AmiJo Comeford and Tamy Burnett. Jefferson: McFarland, 2010. 221–232.

Alien Bee. "Global Fans Assemble." Online video clip. *YouTube* 15 Apr. 2012.

Amy-Chinn, Dee. "'Tis Pity She's a Whore: Postfeminist Prostitution in Joss Whedon's *Firefly*?" *Feminist Media Studies* 6.2 (2006): 175–190.

Andrae, Tom, Geoffrey Blum and Gary Coddington. "The Birth of Superman." Interview with Jerry Siegel and Joe Shuster. *Nemo: The Classic Comics Library*. Ed. Richard Marschall. Stamford, CT: Fantagraphics Books. August 1983.

Arnaudo, Marco. *The Myth of the Superhero*. Trans. Jamie Richards. Baltimore: Johns Hopkins University Press, 2013.

Baggett, David. "*Firefly* and Freedom." *The Philosophy of Joss Whedon*. Ed. Dean Kowalski and Evan Kreider. Lexington: University Press of Kentucky, 2011. 9–23.

Barnes, Brooks. "With Fan at the Helm, Marvel Safely Steers Its Heroes to the Screen." *New York Times* 25 July 2011.

Bartlem, Edwina. "Coming Out on a Hell Mouth." *Refractory* (March 6, 2003). http://www.refractory.unimelb.edu.au/refractory/journalissues/index.htm.

Battis, Jes. *Blood Relations: Chosen Families in* Buffy the Vampire Slayer *and* Angel. Jefferson, NC: McFarland, 2005.

_____. "Captain Tightpants: Firefly and the Science Fiction Canon." *Slayage* 25 2008. http://slayageonline.com/essays/slayage25/Battis.htm.

Becker, Susanne. *Gothic Forms of Feminine Fictions*. Manchester: Manchester University Press, 1999.

Beeler, Karin. "The Transformation of River Tam: Psychic Warrior, Female Prodigy and Anti-Hero in *Firefly* and *Serenity*." *Seers, Witches and Psychics on Screen: An Analysis of Women Visionary Characters in Recent Television and Film*. Jefferson, NC: McFarland, 2008. 38–48.

Bell, Jeffrey. Audio Commentary. "Not Fade Away." *Angel: The Complete Fifth Season*. The WB Television Network. 2003–2004. DVD. Los Angeles: 20th Century–Fox, 2005.

Blanch, Christina, and Thalia Mulvihill. "The Attitudes of Some Students on the Use of Comics in Higher Education: Anthropology Students' Perceptions." *Graphic Novels and Comics in the Classroom: Essays on the Educational Power of Sequential Art*. Eds. Carrye K. Syma and Robert G. Weiner. Jefferson, NC: McFarland. 2013. 35–47.

Bodger, Gwyneth. "Buffy the Feminist Slayer? Constructions of Femininity in *Buffy the Vampire Slayer*." Special Issue on Buffy the Vampire Slayer. Eds. Angela Ndalianis and Felicity Colman. *Refractory: A Journal of Entertainment Media* 2 (2003).

Boucher, Geoff. "Marvel is on a Mission." *Los Angeles Times* 9 Mar. 2008.

Bradney, Anthony. "It's About Power: Law in the Fictional Setting of a Quaker Meeting and in the Everyday Reality of Buffy the Vampire Slayer." *Issues in Legal Scholarship* 1.8 (2006): 1–20.

Breznican, Anthony. "Crawl Inside Joss Whedon's Head as He Makes 'The Avengers.'" *Inside Movies. Entertainment Weekly* 13 Apr. 2012.

_____. "Joss Whedon: *The Avengers* Is Seen Through One Superhero's Eyes."

Inside Movies. Entertainment Weekly, 13 Jan. 2012.

Buckman, Alyson R. "'Much Madness Is Divinest Sense': Firefly's 'Big Damn Heroes' and Little Witches." Wilcox and Cochran 41–49.

____. "Wheel Never Stops Turning: Space and Time in Firefly and Serenity." Wilcox, Cochran, Masson, and Lavery 169–184.

Burr, Vivien, and Christine Jarvis. "'Friends Are the Family We Choose for Ourselves': Young People and Families in *Buffy the Vampire Slayer.*" *Young: Nordic Journal of Youth Research* 13.3 (2005). http://www.slayageonline.com/SCBtVS_Archive/Talks/Burr_Jarvis.pdf.

Campbell, Joseph. *The Hero with a Thousand Faces,* 3d ed. Navoto, CA: New World Library, 2008.

Carpi, Daniela. "Failure of the Word: Law, Discretion, Equity in *The Merchant of Venice* and *Measure for Measure.*" *Cardozo Law Review* 26 (2005): 2317–2330.

Chiat, Kevin. "Giant Dawn and Mutant Superheroes: Joss Whedon in Comics." Money 341–362.

____. "Joss Whedon 101: *Runaways.*" Money 320–324.

Clark, Noelene. "*Avengers* Samuel L. Jackson on His 'Master Manipulator' Nick Fury." *Hero Complex. Los Angeles Times,* 3 May 2012.

Cliffy. Weblog comment. Noel Murray. Rev. of "Power Play" (A5.21) and "Not Fade Away" (A5.22). *A.V. Club.* Avclub.com. 25 May 2012.

Cocca, Carolyn. "First Word 'Jail,' Second Word 'Bait': Adolescent Sexuality, Feminist Theories, and *Buffy the Vampire Slayer.*" *Slayage: The Online International Journal of Buffy Studies* 3.2: (10 Nov. 2003). http://www.slayageonline.com/essays/slayage10/Cocca.htm.

____. "'It's About Power and It's About Women': Gender and the Political Economy of Superheroes in *Wonder Woman* and *Buffy the Vampire Slayer.*" *Heroines of Film and Television: Portrayals in Popular Culture.* Eds. Norma Jones, Maja Bajac-Carter, and Bob Batchelor. Lanham, MD: Rowman & Littlefield, 2014. 215–235.

"Colossus and Kitty Pryde: The Rocky Road of Love." *Comicdom Wrecks* 18 Jan. 2011.

Coogan, Peter. "Comics Predecessors." Hatfield, Heer and Worcester 7–15.

Cook, Roy T. "Canonicity and Normativity in Massive, Serialized, Collaborative Fiction." *The Journal of Aesthetics and Art Criticism* 71.3 (Summer 2013. 271–276).

____. "Why Comics Are Not Films: Metacomics and Medium-Specific Conventions." Meskin and Cook 165–187.

Cooper, J.C. *An Illustrated Encyclopedia of Traditional Symbols.* London: Thames and Hudson, 1978.

Corrigan, Timothy. "The Commerce of Auteurism." *Film and Authorship.* Ed. Virginia W. Wexman. New Brunswick: Rutgers University Press, 2003. 96–110.

Daniels, April. "The Star Wars Expanded Universe Is Dead, Long Live the Star Wars Expanded Universe," *The Mary Sue* 2 May 2014. http://www.themarysue.com/star-wars-expanded-universe-canon.

Darowski, Joseph J. "When You Know You're Just a Comic Book Character: Deadpool." *X-Men and Philosophy: Astonishing Insight and Uncanny Argument in the Mutant X-Verse.* Ed. William Irwin, Rebecca Housel, and J. Jeremy Wisnewski. Hoboken: Wiley, 2009. 107–124.

Davidson, Donald. *Essays on Actions and Events.* Oxford: Oxford University Press, 1980.

de Beauvoir, Simone. "The Second Sex: IX. Myth and Reality." *The Norton Anthology of Theory and Criticism.* Ed. Vincent B. Leitch, et al. New York: W.W. Norton, 2001. 1406–1414.

Derrida, Jacques. "Afterword." *Limited Inc.* Evanston, IL: Northwestern University Press, 1988.

Descartes, Rene. "Discourse Concerning Method." *Rene Descartes: The Essential Writings.* Trans. John J. Bloom. New York: Harper & Row, 1977. 101–166.

Duriez, Colin. *The A-Z of C.S Lewis: An Encyclopedia of his Life, Thought, and Writings.* Oxford: Lion Books, 2013.

Early, Frances H. "The Female Just Warrior Reimagined: From Boudicca to Buffy." *Athena's Daughters: Television's New Women Warriors.* Ed. Frances Early and Kathleen Kennedy. Syracuse: Syracuse University Press, 2003. 55–65.

____. "Staking Her Claim: *Buffy the Vampire Slayer* as Transgressive Woman

Warrior." *Journal of Popular Culture* 35.3 (2001): 11–27. *Wiley Online Library*.

Edwards, Lynne. "Slaying in Black and White: Kendra as Tragic Mulatta in *Buffy*." *Fighting the Forces: What's at Stake in "Buffy the Vampire Slayer?"* Ed. Rhonda V. Wilcox and David Lavery. Lanham, MD: Rowman & Littlefield, 2002. 85–97.

Edwards, Lynne Y., Elizabeth L. Rambo, and James B. South, eds. *Buffy Goes Dark: Essays on the Final Two Seasons of* Buffy the Vampire Slayer *on Television*. Jefferson, NC: McFarland, 2009.

Eisner, Will. *Comics and Sequential Art.* New York: Norton, 2008.

_____. *Graphic Storytelling and Visual Narrative.* New York: Norton, 2008.

Erikson, Kai. *Wayward Puritans: A Study in the Sociology on Deviance.* New York: Macmillan, 1966.

Fendelman, Adam. "'Iron Man' Sits Indisputably in Club of Highest-Rated Superhero Movies of All Time." http://www.HollywoodChicago. 2 May 2008.

Flood, Alison. "Superheroes a 'Cultural Catastrophe' Says Comics Guru Alan Moore." *The Guardian* 21 Jan. 2014.

Fodor, Jerry A. "The Mind-Body Problem." *Scientific American* (244): 124–132.

Ford, Jessica. "Coming Out of the Broom Closet: Willow's Sexuality and Empowerment in *Buffy*." Money 94–102.

Frankel, Valerie Estelle. *Buffy and the Heroine's Journey.* Jefferson, NC: McFarland, 2012.

Frohard-Dourlent, Helene. "Buffy/Satsu: 'Pure Genius' or 'Out of Character'? Complicating Reader Responses to Modern Narratives of Sexuality." Conference paper. Whedon Studies Annual Conference 2010. Flagler College, St. Augustine, FL. 5 June 2010.

_____. "'Lez-faux' Representations: How Buffy *Season Eight* Navigates the Politics of Female Heteroflexibility." *Sexual Rhetoric in the Works of Joss Whedon: New Essays*. Ed. Erin Waggoner. Jefferson, NC: McFarland, 2010. 31–47.

Galvan, Margaret. "From Kitty to Cat: Kitty Pryde and the Phases of Feminism" *The Ages of the X-Men: Essays on the Children of the Atom in Changing Times*. Ed. Joseph J. Darowski. Jefferson, NC: McFarland, 2014. 46–62.

"Gay, Lesbian and Bisexual Issues." Counseling Center, Ball State University, 2014. http://cms.bsu.edu/campuslife/counselingcenter/newsfooteritems/diversityresources/diversityinformationandlinks/glbt.

Geertz, Clifford. *Available Light: Anthropological Reflections on Philosophical Topics*. Princeton: Princeton University Press, 2012.

George, David. "On Origins: Behind the Rituals," *Performance Research: A Journal of Performing Arts* 3. 3 (1998).

Giddens, Anthony. *The Director's Lectures: Runaway World: The Reith Lectures Revisited*. Lecture 4, 1 Dec. 1999. http://www.lse.ac.uk/Giddens/pdf/1.Dec.99.pdf.

Gilchrist, Todd, and David Simpson. "Behind the Scenes of Marvel's 'The Avengers.'" *The Hollywood Reporter* 5 Apr. 2012.

Glendening, Daniel. "Gischler Enters the Whedonverse with 'Buffy the Vampire Slayer: Spike.'" *Comic Book Resources*. 19 June 2012. http://www.comicbookresources.com/?page=article&id=39258.

Grainge, Paul. *Brand Hollywood: Selling Entertainment in a Glocal Media Age*. London: Routledge, 2008.

Gray, Richard, and Betty Kaklamanidou. "Introduction." *The 21st Century Superhero: Essays on Gender, Genre and Globalization in Film*. Ed. Richard Gray and Betty Kaklamanidou. Jefferson: McFarland, 2011. 1–14.

Griswold, Jerome. *Audacious Kids: Coming of Age in America's Classic Children's Books*. New York: Oxford University Press, 1992.

Gustines, George G. "Experimenting in Bed When Not After Vampires." Rev. of *Buffy the Vampire Slayer*, Season 8, Issue 12. *The New York Times* 5 Mar. 2008. http://www.nytimes.com/2008/03/05/books/05buffy.html?_r=0.

Hadas, Leora. "Authorship and Authenticity in the Transmedia Brand: The Case of *Marvel's Agents of S.H.I.E.L.D.*" *Networking Knowledge: Journal of the Me CCSA-PGN* 17.1 (2014).

Halfyard, Janet K. "*Hero's Journey*, Heroine's Return: Buffy, Eurydice, and the Orpheus Myth." Wilcox, Cochran, Masson, and Lavery 40–52.

Harris, Wendell V. "Canonicity." *PMLA* 106.1 (January 1991): 110–121.

Hatfield, Charles, Jeet Heer and Kent Worcester, eds. *The Superhero Reader.* Jackson: University Press of Mississippi, 2013.
Havens, Candace. *Joss Whedon: The Genius Behind Buffy.* Dallas: BenBella, 2003.
Hellmouth Central. "Interviews with Georges Jeanty Pt. 1." *Hellmouth Central* 9 Apr. 2007. http://buffycomics.hellmouthcentral.com/html/interviews/georgesjeanty.htm.
Hobbes, Thomas. *Leviathan.* London: Penguin, 1985.
Housel, Rebecca. "Myth, Morality; and the Women of the X-Men." *Superheroes and Philosophy: Truth, Justice, and the Socratic Way.* Ed. Tom Morris, Matt Morris, and William Irwin. New York: Open Court, 2001. 80–87.
Howe, Sean. *Marvel Comics: The Untold Story.* New York: Harper, 2012.
Itzkoff, Dave. "Behind the Mask." *New York Times* 20 Nov. 2005.
_____. "A Film's Superheroes Include the Director." *New York Times* 15 Apr. 2012.
_____. "Joss Whedon on Assembling the Avengers." *New York Times* 11 Apr. 2012.
Jenkins, Henry. *Convergence Culture.* New York: New York University Press, 2006.
_____. "Death-Defying Heroes." Hatfield, Heer and Worcester 295–304.
_____. "Transmedia 202: Further Reflections." *Confessions of an Aca-fan: The Official Blog of Henry Jenkins.* 2011.
JMP. Weblog comment. Noel Murray. Rev. of "Power Play" (A5.21) and "Not Fade Away" (A5.22). *A.V. Club.* Avclub.com. 25 May 2012.
Johnson, Derek. "Will the Real Wolverine Please Stand Up? Marvel's Mutation from Monthlies to Movies." *Film and Comic Books.* Ed. Ian Gordon, et al. Jackson: University Press of Mississippi, 2007. 64–85.
Jones, William. *History and Mystery of Precious Stones.* London: Richard Bentley and Son, 1880.
Joslyn, Daniel. "Looking Back on the Highs and Lows of Buffy Season 8." *PopCults* 11 Feb. 2011. http://www.popcults.com/looking-back-on-the-highs-and-lows-of-buffy-season-8.
Kaufman, Amy. "*Avengers*: Downey Says Whedon Brings 'Depths of Discovery.'" *Hero Complex. Los Angeles Times* 20 July 2011.
_____. "Scarlett Johansson: I Was 'Burdened' as My 'Avengers' Character." *Ministry of Gossip. Los Angeles Times* 12 Apr. 2012.
Kaufman, Peter, and Kenneth A. Feldman. "Forming Identities in College: A Sociological Approach." *Research in Higher Education* 45 (2004): 463–496.
Kaveney, Roz. "A Sense of the Ending: Schrodinger's *Angel.*" *Reading Angel: The TV Spin-off with a Soul.* Ed. Stacey Abbott. London: I.B. Tauris, 2005. 57–72.
_____. *Superheroes! Capes and Crusaders in Comics and Films.* London: I. B. Tauris, 2008.
Korsmeyer, Carolyn. "Passion and Action: In and Out of Control." *Buffy the Vampire Slayer and Philosophy: Fear and Trembling in Sunnydale.* Ed. James B. South. Chicago: Open Court, 2003. 160–172.
Kowalski, Dean. "'You're Welcome on My Boat, God Ain't': Ethical Foundations in the Whedonverse." *Joss Whedon and Religion: Essays on an Angry Atheist's Explorations of the Sacred.* Ed. Anthony R. Mills, John W. Morehead, and J. Ryan Parker. Jefferson, NC: McFarland, 2013. 102–122.
Kukkonen, Karin. "Comics and their History." *Studying Comics and Graphic Novels.* Malden, MA: Wiley-Blackwell, 2013. 99–122.
Labrecque, Jeff. "*Avengers* Premiere: Can You Have Too Many Superheroes?" *Inside Movies. Entertainment Weekly,* 12 Apr. 2012.
Lavery, David, and Cynthia Burkhead, eds. *Joss Whedon: Conversations.* Jackson: University of Mississippi Press, 2011.
Law, John. "Relax, Wolverine Won't be Dead Long." *Toronto Sun* 2014.
Leonard, Kendra Preston. "The Status is not Quo: Gender and Performance in Doctor Horrible's Sing-Along Blog." *Buffy, Ballads, and Bad Guys Who Sing: Music in the Worlds of Joss Whedon.* Ed. Kendra Preston Leonard. Lanham, MD: Scarecrow Press, 2011. 275–292.
"Lesbian, Gay, Bisexual, Transexual Orientation." *Psychology Topics.* American Psychological Association, 2014. http://www.apa.org/topics/lgbt/index.aspx.
Levy, Matthew, and Heather Mathews. "The Abyss Gazes Also: The Self-

Referential Cynicism of Watchmen." *ImageTexT* 7.2 (2013). Dept of English, University of Florida. http://www.english.ufl.edu/imagetext/archives/v7_2/levy.

Lewis, C. S. *The Abolition of Man*. 1944. New York: Harper Collins E-books, 2009.

Lo, Malinda. "Notes & Queeries: An Open Mind." *After Ellen* 13 Aug. 2008. http://www.afterellen.com/tv/35982-notes-queeries-an-open-mind.

Locklin, Reid B. *"Buffy the Vampire Slayer* and the Domestic Church: Revisioning Family and the Common Good." *Slayage: The Online International Journal of Buffy Studies* 2.2: (September 2002). http://www.slayageonline.com/essays/slayage6/Locklin.htm.

Lynch, Brian. "*First Night* Notes from Brian Lynch." *Angel: After the Fall: First Night Volume 2*. Joss Whedon, Brian Lynch, et al. San Diego: IDW, 2008.

_____. "Introduction." *Angel: After the Fall, Vol. 1*. Joss Whedon, Brian Lynch, and Franco Urru. San Diego: IDW, 2008.

_____. "Questions and Answers." *Angel: After the Fall, Vol. 3*. San Diego: IDW, 2009. Joss Whedon, Lynch, Runge, and Messina.

Madrid, Mike. *The Supergirls*. Ashland, OR: Exterminating Angel Press, 2010.

Makishima, Keiko. "'You're Not the Source of Me': Adoptive Identity and Child-Heroes in Buffy the Vampire Slayer." *Watcher Junior: The Undergraduate Journal of Whedon Studies* VI. 1 (July 2012). http://www.watcherjunior,tv/07/makishima.php.

Manning, Shaun. "Lynch Takes "Spike" to Sin City." *Comic Book Resources* 14 Sept. 2010. http://www.comicbookresources.com/?page=article&id=28308-title=Lynch.

Marano, Michael. "River Tam and the Weaponized Women of the Whedon-verse." *Serenity Found: More Unauthorized Essays on Joss Whedon's Firefly Universe*. Ed. Jane Espenson with Leah Wilson. Dallas: BenBella, 2007. 37–48.

Martin, Denise. "Joss Whedon: 'I Would Have Put "Dollhouse" on Fridays Too.'" *Los Angeles Times* 10 Dec. 2008. http://latimesblogs.latimes.com/showtracker/2008/12/joss-whedon-i-w.html.

Marvel Entertainment. "Marvel's The Avengers Featurette—Tension." Online video clip. *YouTube* 17 Apr. 2012.

McCloud, Scott. *Understanding Comics: The Invisible Art*. New York: Harper-Collins, 1994.

McRobbie, Angela. *Postmodernism and Popular Culture*. London: Routledge, 1999.

Melissa. "SXSW Drop-In: Joss Whedon Panel Liveblogged." *LeakyNews. The Leaky Cauldron* 10 Mar. 2012.

Meskin, Aaron, and Roy T. Cook, eds. *The Art of Comics: A Philosophical Approach*. Oxford: Blackwell, 2012.

Miller, Laura. "The Man behind the Slayer." *Salon*. 20 May 2003. http://www.salon.com/2003/05/20/whedon.

Mintz, Steven. "Placing Childhood Sexual Abuse in Historical Perspective." *The Immanent Frame* 13 July 2012. http://blogs.ssrc.org/tif/2012/07/13/placing-childhood-sexual-abuse-in-historical-perspective.

Mittell, Jason. *Complex TV: The Poetics of Contemporary Television Storytelling*, pre-publication edition, 2012–13.

Money, Mary Alice, with PopMatters, eds. *Joss Whedon: The Complete Companion*. London: Titan, 2012.

Moore, Matt. "The Human Torch Returns: Marvel Reignites Dead Comic Character in Latest Fantastic Four." *Huffington Post* 2011.

Morrison, Grant. *Supergods: What Masked Vigilantes, Miraculous Mutants, and a Sun God from Smallville Can Teach Us About Being Human*. New York: Spiegel & Grau, 2011.

Moss, Gabrielle. "From the Valley to the Hellmouth: "Buffy's Transition from Film to Television." *Slayage: The Journal of the Whedon Studies Association* 1.2–2 (2001). www.slayageonline.com.

Murray, Padmini Ray. "Behind the Panel: Examining Invisible Labour in the Comics Publishing Industry." *Publishing Research Quarterly* 29. 4 (2013). 336–343.

Muscat, Kat. "'Ain't Love Grand': The Erasure of Bisexuality in Buffy the Vampire Slayer." *Kill Your Darlings Journal* 19 Oct. 2014. http://www.killyourdarlingsjournal.com/?post_type=article&p=25751.

The Mythology of Superman. Warner Bros. 2006. Film.

natty. Weblog comment. Noel Murray.

Rev. of "Power Play" (A5.21) and "Not Fade Away" (A5.22). *A.V. Club.* Avclub.com. 25 May 2012.
Norton, Al. "411mania Interviews: James Marsters." *411mania* 10 Mar. 2012. http://411mania.com/movies/411mania-interviews-james-marsters-buffy-the-vampire-slayer-angel.
O'Brien, Susie, and Imre Sizeman. *Popular Culture: A User's Guide.* Toronto: Nelson Education, 2010.
Otto, Jeff. "Joss Whedon's Advice for a *Justice League* Movie & More from the Cast of The Avengers." *The Playlist. IndieWire* 3 May 2012.
Pappademas, Alex. "The Geek Shall Inherit the Earth." *GQ* May 2012.
PentaGon Pictures. "SDCC 2010—The Joss Whedon Experience Part 1." Online video clip. *YouTube* 29 Mar. 2011.
Persia. Weblog comment. Noel Murray. Rev. of "Power Play" (A5.21) and "Not Fade Away" (A5.22). *A.V. Club.* Avclub.com. 25 May 2012.
Pike, Mark. *Mere Education: C.S. Lewis as Ethical Teacher for our Time.* Cambridge: Luttherworth Press, 2013.
Place, U.T. "Is Consciousness a Brain Process?" *British Journal of Psychology* (47): 44–50.
Plato. "Phaedo." *Plato: Complete Works.* Ed. John M. Cooper. Indianapolis: Hackett, 1997. 49–100.
Pollefeyt, Didier. "The Morality of Auschwitz? A Critical Confrontation with Peter Hass's Ethical Interpretation of the Holocaust." *Good and Evil after Auschwitz: Ethical Implications for Today.* Ed. Jack Bemporad, John Pawlikowski and Joseph Sievers. Hoboken, NJ: KTAV, 2000. 119–138.
Posner RA. *Law and Literature.* Cambridge: Harvard University Press, 1998.
Pustz, Matthew J. *Comic Book Culture: Fanboys and True Believers (Studies in Popular Culture).* Jackson: University Press of Mississippi, 1999.
Reynolds, Richard. *Super Heroes: A Modern Mythology* (Studies in Popular Culture). Jackson: University Press of Mississippi, 1992.
Richardson, Amy. "Full Shadow & Act Report from Marvel Studios' *The Avengers* Press Junket." *Shadow and Act. IndieWire* 18 Apr. 2012.
Richardson, J. Michael, and J. Douglas Rabb. *The Existential Joss Whedon: Evil and Human Freedom in* Buffy the Vampire Slayer, Angel, Firefly, *and* Serenity. Jefferson: McFarland, 2007.
Ring, Trudy. "Exploring the Umbrella: Bisexuality and Fluidity." *Advocate* 11 Feb. 2014. http://www.advocate.com/health/love-and-sex/2014/02/11/exploring-umbrella-bisexuality-and-fluidity.
Rosenberg, Robin S. "Our Fascination with Superheroes." *Our Superheroes, Ourselves.* Ed. Robin S. Rosenberg. Oxford: Oxford University Press, 2013. 3–18.
Rubin, Lawrence C. "Are Superhero Stories Good for Us?" *Our Superheroes, Ourselves.* Ed. Robin S. Rosenberg. Oxford: Oxford University Press, 2013. 37–52.
Ryall, Chris. "IDWeek: Joss Whedon Talks *Angel: After the Fall.*" Newsrama.com. 27 Apr. 2007.
Sager, Christian. "Tense Proximities Between CCI's Comic Book Consumers, Fans and Creators." *It Happens at Comic-Con: Ethnographic Essays on a Pop Culture Phenomenon.* Ed. Ben Bolling and Matthew J. Smith. Jefferson, NC: McFarland, 2014. 153–168.
Salkowitz, Rob. *Comic-Con and the Business of Pop Culture.* New York: McGraw Hill, 2012.
Sanderson, Peter, Ed. *The X-Men Companion II.* Stamford, CT: Fantagraphic Books, 1982.
Schumacher, Lauren. "The Many Faces of Buffy: An Analysis of the Disharmonious Visual Representations of Buffy Summers in Primary and Secondary Texts." *Watcher Junior: The Undergraduate Journal of Whedon Studies* 4.2 (June 2010).
Sims, Chris. "Guns and the Batman: Why the Dark Knight Doesn't Use Firearms." *Comics Alliance* 2014.
Smith, Nigel M. "Joss Whedon: I Want to Make Things that are Small, Pure and Odd." *IndieWire* 12 Mar. 2012.
"The Spotlight Interview with Stan Lee." Stan Lee. Ed. Stan Lee, et al. New York: Marvel Comics, 2006.
Stanley, Marni. "Buffy's Season 8: Image and Text." Wilcox, Cochran, Masson, and Lavery 250–267.
Stuller, Jennifer K. "Feminism: Second Wave Feminism in the Pages of *Lois Lane.*" *Critical Approaches to Comics:*

Theories and Methods. Ed. Matthew J. Smith and Randy Duncan. New York: Routledge, 2011. 235–251.

Tantimedh, Adi, and Rich Johnston. "Alan Moore Speaks *Watchmen 2* to Adi Tantimedh." *Bleeding Cool* 9 Sept. 2010.

Tranter, Kieran. "'Come a Day There Won't be Room for Naughty Men Like Us to Slip About at All': The Multimedia Outlaws of Serenity and the Possibilities of Post-Literate Justice." *Law Text Culture* 16 (2012): 277–304. http://ro.uow.edu.au/ltc/vol16/iss1/12.

Tresca, Don. "Images of Paraphilia in the Whedonverse." Waggoner 146–172.

Turner, Victor. "Liminality and Community." *Culture and Society*. Ed. Jeffrey Alexander and Steven Seidman. New York: Cambridge University Press, 2000. 147–154.

Turnquist, Kristi. "Joss Whedon, Dark Horse Deliver 'Buffy' Eighth Season." Rev. of *Buffy the Vampire Slayer*, Season 8; Issue 12. *Oregonian* 10 Mar. 2008. http://oregonlive.com/entertainment/index.ssf/2008/03/joss_whedon_dark_horse_deliver.

Udry, J. Richard. "The Nature of Gender." *Demography* 31.4 (November 1994): 561–573.

Uidhir, Christy Mag. "Comics and Collective Authorship." Meskin and Cook 47–66.

Uwujaren, Jarune. "How Fluid Sexuality Fits into the LGBTQIA Spectrum." Editorial. *Everyday Feminism* 19 Oct. 2012. http://everydayfeminism.com/2012/10/fluid-sexuality-lgbtq-spectrum.

Vineyard, Jennifer. "Re-Buffed: New Comic Series Resurrects Vampire Slayer." MTV.com 31 Jan. 2007.

Von Franz, Marie Louise. *The Feminine in Fairy Tales*. Boston: Shambhala, 2001.

Waggoner, Erin B., ed. *Sexual Rhetoric in the Works of Joss Whedon: New Essays*. Jefferson, NC: McFarland, 2010.

Warn, Sarah. "Best. Lesbian. Week. Ever." *After Ellen* 18 July 2008. http://www.afterellen.com/tv/34904-best-lesbian-week-ever-july-18-2008.

Whedon, Joss. "Bronze VIP Archive—January 17, 1999." *Bronze VIP Posting Board Archives* 17 Jan. 1999. http://www.cise.ufl.edu/cgi-bin/cgiwrap/hsiao/buffy/get-archive?date=19990117.

Whedonesque.com. "Discuss Buffy Season 9 #5." 11 Jan. 2012. http://whedonesque.com/comments/27875.

Whedonesque.com. "Discuss Buffy Season 9 #6." 8 Feb. 2012. http://whedonesque.com/comments/28000.

Whedonesque.com. "For the Discussion of (the Rest) of Buffy #12." *Whedonesque* 5 Mar. 2008. http://whedonesque.com/comments/15685.

Whedonesque.com. "Some Buffy Season 9 Info from Dark Horse's Scott Allie." 28 Mar. 2015. http://whedonesque.com/comments/28309.

Wilcox, Rhonda V. "'I Don't Hold to That': Joss Whedon and Original Sin." Wilcox and Cochran 155–166.

____. "Much Ado About Whedon." Wilcox, Cochran, Masson, and Lavery 1–14.

____. *Why Buffy Matters: The Art of Buffy the Vampire Slayer*. London: I.B. Tauris, 2005.

Wilcox, Rhonda V., and Tanya R. Cochran, eds. *Investigating Firefly and Serenity: Science Fiction on the Frontier*. London: I.B. Tauris, 2008.

Wilcox, Rhonda, Tanya R. Cochran, Cynthea Masson, and David Lavery, eds. *Reading Joss Whedon*. Syracuse: Syracuse University Press, 2014.

"Will Dr. Horrible 2 Resurrect Penny? She Talks!" *Blastr* 13 Apr. 2010.

Wilson, Melanie. "She Believes in Me: Angel, Spike, and Redemption." *Buffy Meets the Academy: Essays on the Episodes and Scripts as Text*. Ed. Kevin K. Durand. Jefferson, NC: McFarland, 2009. 137–149.

Wilts, Alicia. "Evil, Skanky, and Kinda Gay: Lesbian Images and Issues." Edwards, Rambo, and South 41–56.

Woo, Benjamin. "The Android's Dungeon: Comic-bookstores, Cultural Spaces, and the Social Practices of Audiences." *Journal of Graphic Novels and Comics* 2.2 (2011): 125–136.

Wright, Bradford W. *Comic Book Nation: The Transformation of Youth Culture in America*. Baltimore: Johns Hopkins University Press, 2003.

Zeitchik, Steven. "Comic-Con 2010: Marvel Stages a Superhero Panel, and a Rock Concert Breaks Out." *Hero Complex, Los Angeles Times* 25 July 2010.

Zhang, Angela. "*Buffy* and *Dollhouse*: Visions of Female Empowerment and Disempowerment." Money 401–406.

About the Contributors

• • •

Christina L. **Blanch** is an educator, comics scholar, researcher, and writer. She is the force behind the online SuperMOOC courses, Gender through Comic Books and Social Issues through Comic Books. She produced her first comic series with co-writer Chris Carr and artist Chee for the digital publisher Thrillbent and the print publisher Dynamite; her work is also featured in Aw Yeah Comics.

Traci J. **Cohen** works with the ESL community and is an independent pop culture scholar. She has been a presenter at various conferences discussing topics ranging from gender to culture and materials such as Matantei Loki, iCarly and *Buffy the Vampire Slayer*.

Bryant **Dillon** is a co-founder and president of Fanboy Comics. He has served as a staff writer and reviewer for Whedonopolis.com and has been actor, director, writer and artist on a number of projects. He is an actor, writer, and executive producer on the popular fan-produced audio drama adaptation of *The Hunger Games* novels known as *The Katniss Chronicles*.

Valerie Estelle **Frankel** has written many books on pop culture; topics have included *Doctor Who* and *Game of Thrones*. Many of her books focus on women's roles in fiction, from her heroine's journey guides *From Girl to Goddess* and *Buffy and the Heroine's Journey* to books like *Women in Game of Thrones*, all from McFarland. She is a frequent speaker at conferences and lives in Sunnyvale, California, which really exists.

Lisa **Gomez** is a Los Angeles singer/songwriter in a duo with twin sister Gina called Gemeni. Gemeni has a song called "A Stake in My Heart," inspired by Buffy. In addition to the debut album *More Than Me*, Gemeni has a YouTube channel with more than 30,000 views, including the "YouTube Geek Week" hit video "Thorsday," which Marvel Entertainment featured on its channel.

Leora **Hadas** is a PhD candidate at the University of Nottingham, working on discourses of authorship and branding in the contemporary United States media industries, and a member of the Industrial Approaches to Media postgraduate initiative and the Media Mutations project.

Joel **Hawkes** is a lecturer in English literature at the University of Victoria, British Columbia. He is particularly interested in the practices and performances

237

that create the physical and literary spaces we inhabit. He has also written on such topics as William Blake, mental illness and *Buffy the Vampire Slayer.*

Mary Ellen **Iatropoulos** is the director of education at Spark Media Project, a media education nonprofit, where she develops media-rich interdisciplinary curricula, manages teaching teams, and teaches courses in media/digital literacies and multimedia production for colleges, secondary schools and libraries.

Melissa C. **Johnson** is an associate professor and chair of the Department of Focused Inquiry at Virginia Commonwealth University. Her areas of interest include poetry, gender studies, cultural studies, post-colonial literature and twentieth-century British literature.

Thomas **Johnson** is interested in film and television studies, speculative fiction, and the comparative study of print and visual media. He presented "One Gollum to Rule the Box Office" at the 9th Annual Conference of the Association of Adaptation Studies. His article "'Poor Unfortunate Souls': The Corporate Transformation of *The Little Mermaid*" is to be published.

Kristi Pope **Key** is Director of Academic Services at The Louisiana School for Math, Science, and the Arts in Natchitoches. While her research interests include Southern literature and women's writing, her favored areas of publication focus on Joss Whedon's work and his merry band of creative misfits.

David **Kociemba** is president of the Affiliated Faculty of Emerson College union and a member of the AAUP Committee on Contingency and the Profession. His interests focus on Joss Whedon and Jane Espenson, disability representation in *Glee* and the films of Todd Haynes, and paratexts like spoilers and opening title sequences. He has written for a number of journals and edited collections.

S. Evan **Kreider** is an associate professor of philosophy at the University of Wisconsin–Fox Valley. His areas of research include ethics, aesthetics and popular culture. He is a co-editor and contributor to a collection on Joss Whedon's philosophy and a contributor to collections on *The X-Files*, Jim Henson and philosophy and the Who and philosophy.

César Alfonso **Marino** is a professor of literature at the Universidad de Buenos Aires—Faculty of Philosophy and Letters (Argentina). He is a lecturer on popular culture in literature, film and videogames. He has published articles in *Luthor Magazine* and in the book *Dick Grayson, Boy Wonder* edited by Kristen L. Geaman (McFarland, 2015).

Tracy S. **Morris** holds degrees in communications and journalism from the University of Arkansas. Her work has appeared in *USA Today* online, the *Dallas Morning News* and the *Lexington Herald Leader*. She is the author of three novels and multiple essays on pop culture.

Thalia M. **Mulvihill** is a professor of social foundations and higher education and an affiliate faculty member in the Women's and Gender Studies Program and the Honors College at Ball State University. She also serves as the director of the Adult, Higher and Community Education Doctoral Program. She has produced more than 50 refereed journal articles and book chapters, 70 refereed conference research papers, and 80 invited presentations/training sessions.

About the Contributors

Fernando Gabriel **Pagnoni Berns** is a graduate teaching assistant of "Literatura de las Artes Combinadas II" at Universidad de Buenos Aires—Faculty of Philosophy and Letters (Argentina). He teaches seminars on American horror cinema and Euro horror. He is director of the research group on horror cinema "Grite" and has published essays in several books on comics.

Gail D. **Rosen** is an associate professor at Drexel University in the Department of English and Philosophy. She teaches courses in law and literature, mythology, the Broadway musical, and first-year writing, as well as a course entitled Our Vampires, Ourselves.

Don **Tresca** has a master's degree in English from California State University, Sacramento, where he specialized in 20th century American literature and film studies. He has previously published essays on a wide variety of pop culture subjects, including the works of Joss Whedon, J. K. Rowling, Stephen King, and Clint Eastwood. He is working on a book concerning found-footage horror films.

Index

• • •

abortion 4, 7, 33, 34
Abrams, J.J. 31, 187
academic criticism 4, 190
adolescent 148, 153, 179
"After These Messages" 2, 40
Agent Carter 226
Agents of S.H.I.E.L.D. 1, 2, 5, 6, 121, 133, 137, 140, 141, 197, 198, 209, 214, 224, 226
Alex Wilder 134
Alice in Wonderland 167
Alien: Resurrection 129
alienation 83, 147, 151
The Alliance 42, 43, 91, 96–98, 102, 155, 156, 161
Allie, Scott 34, 220
Alpha 107, 109, 111–117
Amy Madison 21, 39, 102–104, 213
Andrew Wells 5, 7, 28–30, 44, 64, 181, 184, 193, 213, 222
Angel (character) 16, 49, 52, 53, 54, 56, 59, 62–64, 71, 107, 116, 136, 138, 181, 183–187, 195, 196, 210, 213, 214; origin story 16
Angel (comics) 49, 60, 62, 65–67, 224, 226, 228
Angel (show) 4, 15, 43, 44, 55, 60, 64, 202
Angel: After the Fall 1–6, 35, 47, 49, 51, 53, 57–59, 66, 67, 163, 181, 187, 219, 220, 224, 226
Angel: After the Fall: First Night 2, 57, 58, 219
Angel & Faith 49, 64, 67, 68, 214, 220–225
Angel: Immortality for Dummies 184, 220
Angel: Long Night's Journey 2, 41, 49, 219
Angel/Spike 183, 186
Angelus 16, 68, 116, 174, 211, 212
Anne (episode) 155, 175
Anya Jenkins 181, 194, 211
Anywhere But Here 40, 213
archetypes 100, 150, 179
artists 37, 40, 44–46, 53, 59, 185
Astonishing X-Men 2, 3, 127, 128, 145, 147, 156, 166, 205, 222, 226; *see also X-Men*
auteur 2, 5, 31–34, 43- 46, 199, 200, 203–205, 208

The Avengers 1, 2, 4, 5, 121, 133, 193, 197-208, 210, 212, 214, 216, 218, 226, 228
Avengers Age of Ultron 1, 4, 197, 208

"Bad Eggs" 136
"Bad Girls" 20
Batgirl 127, 128
Batman 3, 15, 18, 119, 124, 126, 127, 163, 183, 188, 192, 222, 225
Batman Begins 199
Bea 98
Beck 44, 66, 67
"Becoming" 9, 11, 15–17, 87, 174
Bell, Jeff 51, 54
Benson, Amber 71, 83, 85
Betta George 35, 66, 67, 183
Billy Lane 29, 30
biological family 141–143, 216
"Birthday" 192
bisexual 20, 22, 25–27, 144
Black Widow 2, 100, 201
blood 13, 65, 87, 139, 152, 155
Blue Sun 156
"The Body" 2, 4, 111, 117
boy's club 184
Buffy (character) 20–22, 38, 47, 62–65, 68, 75, 79, 81, 89, 100, 111, 136, 137, 139, 141, 145, 147, 155, 156, 160, 161, 165, 167–176, 179, 194, 197, 209–213, 217, 218
Buffy (comics) 33, 62, 64, 68
Buffy/Angel 16, 20, 21, 25, 32, 38–39, 62, 141, 144, 210, 214
Buffy: Season Eight 1–5, 7, 19, 21, 26, 28–31, 34, 38, 40, 44–49, 52, 62, 65–67, 131, 168, 170, 193, 213, 220, 224, 226
Buffy: Season Nine 4, 7, 29, 32, 33, 49, 63, 64, 163, 165, 220
Buffy: Season Ten 1, 7, 29, 49, 63, 65, 68, 168, 221, 228
Buffy/Spike 20, 21, 25, 32, 38, 62, 63, 65
Buffy: The Animated Series 2
Buffy: The Origin 3–5, 7, 9–18, 41, 219
Buffy the Vampire Slayer 9, 15, 19, 38, 39, 43–47, 60, 63, 74, 78, 80, 82, 83, 90, 129, 136, 137, 140, 144, 160, 181, 191, 202,

203, 206, 209, 210, 212, 214, 217, 219–221
Buffybot 34
Buffyspeak 199
Buffyverse 11, 12, 17, 19, 22, 32, 34, 35, 41, 51, 52, 55, 59, 62, 63, 66, 67, 84, 151, 160, 219, 220, 222, 224–226
bully 29, 75, 126
bureaucracy 215

The Cabin in the Woods 187
California 29, 81
camera 2, 155
Campbell, Joseph 17, 89, 169, 174
canon 20, 31–35, 37, 41–46, 64–67, 69, 184, 186, 219, 220, 224, 226
Captain America 3, 35, 127, 193, 197, 199, 205, 225
Captain America: The First Avenger 207
Captain Hammer 119, 123, 124–126, 129
Captain Marvel 186
Chambliss, Andrew 63, 107, 220, 221
characterization 156, 201
Chase Stein 131, 134, 135, 141–143
"Choices" 13, 89, 210
"Chosen" (episode) 11, 12, 16, 19, 22, 55, 71, 166, 218
chosen family 5, 103, 131, 136, 139, 143, 160–161, 212–214, 217
chosen one 16, 165
Christianity 110, 181
Civil War (Marvel) 134
Claremont, Chris 3, 145, 149, 156, 157, 159, 160
Clark Kent 3, 13, 14, 15
Clem 211
Cloak and Dagger 134
closure 49, 52–57, 59, 137, 187
Colan, Gene 71, 78, 80
Colossus 128, 145, 170, 175
comic book culture 189
comic book dealer 181, 188, 189
Comic-Con 180–196, 204, 206, 225
Comic Con Episode IV 180
Comics Code 225
coming-of-age 3, 135
Commentary! The Musical 123
commercialism 195
Connor 66, 183
The Core 178, 221
Core Planets 95,
cosplay 181, 225
costumes 1, 3, 145, 147–149, 169, 185, 186, 196, 225
Coulson, Phil 140, 197, 214–218, 224
Council of Champions 123
cover 2, 28
creativity 1, 31, 41, 43, 65, 67, 89, 94, 110, 121, 167, 181, 200–208
crossover 49, 128, 199, 202, 225

cyborg 96
Cyclops 148, 149, 150, 158

"Damage" 28
Dandelion Naizen 163, 193–196
Dark Horse 7, 33, 34, 36, 39, 49, 60, 64–69, 74, 78, 80–84, 95, 147, 163, 181, 194, 219, 220, 222, 224–226
Dark Phoenix 5, 145, 149, 156
Dark Willow 172
Dawn Summers 13, 27, 38, 61, 63, 172, 213
DC 35, 121, 125, 127, 128, 163, 222, 225, 226
death 4, 11–17, 39, 54–57, 59, 63, 85, 99, 101, 110, 126–129, 134, 135, 141, 144, 163, 167, 168, 172, 174, 179, 190, 192, 211, 215
de Beauvoir, Simone 73, 75, 76, 82
deconstruction 122, 127, 130, 161, 183
Descartes 110
Disney 31, 185
Ditko, Steve 195
Dr. Horrible 1, 2, 5, 44, 119, 121–130, 133, 203, 222, 225
Dr. Horrible and Other Horrible Stories 119, 123, 222
Dollhouse 1, 5, 6, 26, 44, 107, 109–117, 133, 138, 141, 203, 222, 225
Doublemeat Palace 13, 184
Downey, Robert, Jr. 201, 202
dress 75, 81
Drusilla 10, 16, 61, 66, 71, 174
DuBois, W.E.B. 82
duel 188
dystopia 107, 122, 123, 163, 172, 225, 228

Echo 107, 115, 116, 117, 141, 165
Edna Giles 214
Emma Frost 145, 149, 150, 173, 177, 179
England 16, 152
epic 2, 51, 66, 165, 166, 168, 174, 183, 194
"Epitaph" 107, 115
"Epitaph 2" 107, 116
Epitaphs 5, 107, 109, 111–117, 222
Espenson, Jane 7, 29, 41, 44, 46, 71, 83, 86, 87, 162, 220
ethics 94, 107, 135, 147, 148, 150, 153, 209, 210–215, 217
ethics of care 209–215, 217
Evil League of Evil 119, 123
Eyghon 214

Faith Lehane 16, 20, 49, 64, 89, 160, 171, 173, 176, 213, 214
family 87, 94, 99, 100, 101, 124, 131, 133, 135–136, 139, 140–143, 202, 209, 212–214, 216–218
"Family" 20
fanboy 66, 155, 184, 187, 192, 200, 205, 225
fanfiction 45, 186, 226, 227

fans 4, 7, 19, 26, 29, 31–34, 37, 43, 46, 52, 53, 59- 69, 83, 121, 123, 127, 128, 144, 180, 181, 184, 185, 187, 192–196, 199, 202–206, 225, 228
Fantastic Four 127, 131, 188, 192, 197
Feige, Kevin 200–203, 207
femininity 11, 29, 73, 75–81, 95, 100–105, 156, 159, 167, 168, 170, 172, 174, 177, 209
feminism 3, 11, 23, 103, 129, 156, 160, 161, 199, 208
Firefly 1, 2, 4, 6, 34, 37, 43, 44, 91, 94–98, 100, 102, 104, 129, 133, 140, 141, 155, 156, 160–162, 191, 194, 202, 203, 222, 224
First Evil 10, 16
First Slayer 10, 13, 15, 71, 83, 84, 85, 151
Fitz, Leo 197, 215
"Five by Five" 17
flashback 9, 16, 43, 91, 172, 214, 219
fly 1, 101, 136, 178
"Fool for Love" 88
forgiveness 173, 211, 213, 216
fourth wall 123, 183, 186
Fox 4, 43
Fray 3, 5, 71, 84, 88, 145, 151, 159, 163, 165–179, 219, 225
Fred Burkle 5, 33, 54–58, 141
Free Comic Book Day 91, 95, 222
free will 59, 151
Freefall 220
friendship 63, 66
Fruity Oaty bars 157
functionalism 114, 117
Fury, David 51, 71, 83, 87

Gage, Christos 3, 29, 64, 67, 68, 165, 220, 221
gay 20–30, 134, 137, 226
Gellar, Sarah Michelle 40
gender 3, 5, 26, 29, 32, 71, 73, 75, 76, 81, 82, 86–88, 91, 94, 95, 100, 103, 117, 137, 156, 158, 171, 209
gender roles 91, 100
General Voll 214
Gertrude Yorkes 134, 142
"Get It Done" 15
ghost 1, 3, 55, 157, 170, 211, 212
Giant Dawn 1, 7, 36, 38, 46
Giant Size X-Men #3 163, 222
"The Gift" 13
Giles, Rupert 9, 12, 15, 18, 61, 71, 79, 139, 141, 167, 193, 210–214
Gischler, Victor 64, 67, 68, 221
The Glittering World 71, 87, 152
Glory 3, 13
Goddard, Drew 21, 24, 25, 44, 220
goddess 166, 167, 176
Goddesses and Monsters 4, 28
golden age 170, 225
good and evil 10, 147, 148, 150–152

good girl 171, 211
Graduation Day 20, 173, 210, 211
"Grave" 213
Green Lantern 128
Groo 66, 184–188, 196
groupies 123, 124, 181, 196, 225
Guarded 29, 220
gun 96–98, 100–102, 124, 157, 215
Gunn, Charles 52, 54, 56, 183
gutter 38, 56, 58, 226
Gwen Stacy 190–191

"Halloween" 1, 6, 79, 185, 186
Hamlet 13
Harley Quinn 35
Harmony Kendall 64
"The Harvest" 10, 211
"Helpless" 15, 79
Hemsworth, Chris 202
Hercules 17
heroine's journey 5, 145, 163, 165
hero's journey 11, 17, 18, 135, 169
Hollywood 1, 199, 203, 205, 207
homosexual *see* gay
The Hulk 3, 199, 226; *see also The Incredible Hulk*
Husbands 193
"Hush" 2

"I Only Have Eyes for You" 212
"I Robot, You Jane" 14
icon 40, 126, 169
identity 2, 5, 11, 13, 16, 21, 24, 51, 54, 73, 75, 78, 86, 91, 93–95, 99, 103–105, 109–117, 123, 127, 137, 139, 158, 165, 171, 175, 185, 186, 199–208
identity theory 112, 117
IDW 49, 51, 57, 58, 60, 65–68, 181, 182, 219, 224, 226
Illyria 52, 54–57, 66, 183, 220
"In the Dark" 138
In Your Eyes 130
Inara Serra 4, 91, 96, 101–104, 160
The Incredible Hulk 158, 197
initiation 173, 174
Inquisition 152
"Intervention" 13, 176
invulnerability 126, 134
Iron Man 193, 197–202, 206, 207, 226
It's Never Easy 91, 95, 97, 222
Ivy 107, 109, 111–114, 117

Jackson, Samuel L. 206
Japan 1, 25
Jayne Cobb 91, 99–101, 103, 156, 157, 194
Jean Grey 127, 150, 155–160, 210
Jeanty, Georges 19, 22, 36, 40, 95
Jenkins, Henry 42, 184, 192
Jenny Calendar 141
Jeremy Johns 66, 67, 184–188, 225

jewelry 77, 79, 185
Joyce Summers 16, 213
justice 10, 178, 209, 210, 215, 218

Karolina Dean 131, 133, 134, 137–143
Kaveney, Roz 2, 46, 51, 150, 155, 156, 160
Kaylee Frye 43, 91, 99–104, 156, 157, 160
Kendra 16, 18, 210
Kennedy 20, 26–28, 30, 193
"Killed by Death" 15
"The Killer in Me" 20
Kingpin 134, 135, 137, 140–142, 144
kiss 20, 21, 29, 66, 67, 113, 138, 178
Kitty Pryde 1, 3, 128, 145, 149, 150, 155–159, 166, 168, 177
Kitty Pryde and Wolverine 159
Klara Prast 131, 133, 138, 139, 143, 144

Las Vegas 66
Last Angel in Hell 163, 180–184, 219
Last Gleaming 63, 213, 220
Lavinia Giles 64
law 10, 97, 117, 121–124, 169, 209–217, 224
layout 45
Lee, Stan 5, 163, 180, 181, 188–192, 195, 196, 222
lesbian 4, 5, 7, 20, 24–27, 30, 129, 137, 138
Lex Luthor 126
library 9, 18, 88, 89, 174, 178
Lilah Morgan 17
liminality 147, 152, 156
L'Lihdra 163, 193, 194
loneliness 79, 84, 147, 151, 201, 205
The Long Way Home 21, 36, 38, 39, 220
Los Angeles 1, 49, 58, 59, 66, 131, 133, 183
Lothos 11, 14
love 5, 14, 19–22, 26–28, 41, 57, 61–68, 74, 79, 86, 101, 103, 104, 113, 119, 131, 133, 135–144, 157–159, 163, 170, 171, 175, 181, 196, 203, 205, 206, 209, 212–217
"A Love Supreme" 115
Lynch, Brian 49, 51–59, 65–67, 181, 182, 184, 187, 219, 220

"The Magical Place" 215
Magneto 145, 149, 179
Malcolm Reynolds 4, 42, 91, 96–104, 140, 157
marginalization 91, 95
Maria Hill 197
marketing 5, 31, 185, 200–203
Marsters, James 46, 61, 62, 68, 186
Marvel 3, 4, 5, 31, 121, 127, 128, 131, 133, 134, 136, 138, 140–145, 148, 150, 152, 156–158, 160, 162, 163, 188, 189, 190, 191, 197, 199–209, 214, 222, 224, 226, 228
Marvel Cinematic Universe 31, 197, 198, 201, 202, 206–208, 224, 226

masculinity 73, 75, 77, 79, 81, 95, 100–105, 161, 209, 215
materialism 109, 111, 113, 115, 117
The Matrix 42
Mayor Richard Wilkins 87
McCloud, Scott 37, 38, 41, 53, 56–59
Melinda May 197, 209, 214–217
mentor 11–16, 163, 167, 168, 170, 214
merchandising 181
The Merchant of Venice 211
Merrick Jamison-Smythe 4, 9, 11–18
metacomic 187
metacommentary 40, 121, 122, 123, 181, 186, 195
metalepsis 190, 195, 226
metanarration 193, 226
Mr. Fantastic 126–127
Molly Hayes 134, 135, 138–140, 143, 144
monomyth 135, 165
Moore, Alan 5, 45, 119, 121, 125, 127, 128, 130
moral 116, 160
Morrison, Grant 1, 2, 149, 180, 181, 186, 195
Mosaic Wellness Center 65
mother 75, 88, 101, 125, 138, 166–169, 176, 178, 192, 212
motion comic 2, 4, 7, 224, 226
Much Ado About Nothing 4, 130, 133
murder 15, 39, 114, 115, 122, 129, 141, 149, 210, 211
myth 10, 12, 14–18, 82, 85, 89, 109, 111, 112, 117, 151

narration 17, 38, 226
"Needs" 116
"Never Kill a Boy on the First Date" 14
New Rules 29, 65, 228
New York 1, 16, 88, 90, 129, 134, 137, 141, 142, 189, 191, 203
Nick Fury 197, 216
Nico Minoru 131, 134, 135, 137, 140–144
Nikki Goes Down 71, 77
Nikki Wood 33, 71, 77–81, 88
No Future for You 40, 131, 220
"No Place Like Home" 13, 17
noncanonical comics 40
"Normal Again" 15, 137
"Not Fade Away" 30, 51–59
"Nothing Personal" 216
nudity 3, 22, 25, 28, 29, 62, 159

"Objects in Space" 98, 157, 159
Omega 115
On Your Own 34, 220
"Once More with Feeling" 2
"The Only Light in the Darkness" 216, 217
origin stories 7, 9–11, 15, 17, 186
orphan 139, 216
Oswalt, Patton 94, 222

Otherness 5, 10, 32, 37, 71, 82, 85–90, 94, 96, 121, 160, 163, 166, 168, 170, 172, 174, 176, 178, 184, 186, 188, 190, 192, 194, 196, 222
"Our Mrs. Reynolds" 101, 157
Oz 167

panels 5, 32, 38, 45, 53, 55–57, 76, 87, 88, 226
"Pangs" 212
parody 7, 41, 160, 184, 185, 193
patriarchy 5, 76, 82, 85–89, 139, 160, 161, 174–177, 214
Paul Ballard 115, 141
pedophiles 138
Penny 119, 124, 127–129
Petrie, Doug 7, 41, 71, 78, 80, 83, 88
Phil the robot 163
"Pilot" (Agents of S.H.I.E.L.D.) 216
Plato 110
pop culture 4, 17, 24, 26, 93, 95, 160, 180, 224
"Potentials" 217
Power Girl 3, 11, 15, 18
Powers That Be 54, 62, 64
Predators and Prey 27, 213, 220
pregnancy 32–34, 63, 97
Presumption 71, 76, 86
Pride and Prejudice 76
privilege 35, 95, 169
prophecy 168
"Prophecy Girl" 13, 81, 168
prostitute 75, 76, 85, 99, 101, 103
The Punisher 144, 190, 193

Quentin Travers 12

race 35, 87, 122, 124, 134
racism 43
Rack 176, 177
rape 129, 144
relativism 147, 150, 153
religion 10, 11, 23, 91, 95, 98, 99, 110, 172
"Repairs" 215, 216
"Restless" 2, 4, 176
Retreat 193, 220
"Righteous" 2, 3, 71, 73, 74, 81, 84, 85, 152
righteousness 153, 161
Riley Finn 20
Rim Planets 95
River Tam 5, 91, 95, 97, 98, 100–104, 145, 155–162, 165
Robin Wood 20, 64, 88
Robot Phil 193
role models 123
romance 20, 22, 27, 62–65, 102, 104, 117, 131, 133, 135–137, 140–144, 194, 211
Romania 16
Rufallo, Mark 202
Runaways 2, 3, 5, 131–144, 222, 226

"Safe" 43
Saga Vasuki 28, 170, 177
St. Just 75
Satsu 21–27, 34
scholarship 4, 43, 45, 100, 156
Scoobies 16, 63, 136, 206
Scott Summers 145, 149, 151, 153, 169
scripts 45, 129, 202
scythe 155, 167, 170, 172, 174, 179
secret identity 11, 14, 16
"Seeds" 215, 216, 217
self-sacrifice 11, 13, 15–18, 62, 142
Serenity 2, 37, 42, 44, 91, 93, 94, 97, 99–104, 133, 140, 141, 155, 156, 159, 162, 199, 225
Serenity (comics) 5, 31, 42, 93, 95, 103, 158, 222
"Serenity" (episode) 156
Serenity: Better Days 2, 91, 94, 97, 100–103, 222
Serenity: Leaves on the Wind 91, 93–95, 98, 104, 158, 222
Serenity: The Shepherd's Tale 2, 31, 42, 43, 91, 93, 94, 97, 98, 101, 222
Serenity: Those Left Behind 91, 94, 96–98, 101, 222
Serenityverse 34, 35, 104, 160
sex 20, 22, 24, 25, 28, 39, 62, 66, 91, 101–103, 113, 139, 160, 171, 181, 192
sexual fluidity 22, 23, 26, 27
sexy 21, 24, 103, 166, 173
"Shadows" 217
Shepherd Book 2, 91, 93–101
shippers 21, 32, 186
sidekicks 3
silver age 226
Simon Tam 91, 97, 100, 102, 103, 119, 156, 157
Simone, Gail 128
The Simpsons 188
Singer, Bryan 148, 199
siring 16, 17
Skye 2, 136, 137, 141, 165, 197, 209, 215–218
Slayer Interrupted 32, 40
"Sleeping Beauty" 21
"Smile Time" 2
"Sonnenblume" 87, 88, 153
Sophronia Giles 64
soul 16, 25, 62–69, 76, 107, 109–111, 168, 170, 179, 214
space frak 39, 62, 66
spaceship 64, 67, 195
Spider-Man 3, 10, 13–15, 17, 126, 163, 190–192, 195, 197, 222, 226
Spike 5, 7, 10, 11, 16, 28, 33, 34, 46, 49–56, 58, 60–69, 71, 88, 111, 174, 183–187, 194, 196, 211, 219, 220, 225, 226
Spike (miniseries) 49, 66, 67
Spike: A Dark Place 7, 49, 63, 64, 67, 68, 220

Spike: After the Fall 66, 67
Spike and Faith 64
Spike: Asylum 35, 49, 51, 65, 66
Spike: Into the Light 68
Spike: Shadow Puppets 35, 49, 51
Spike vs. Dracula 49
splash page 38
spoilers 193, 228
Staff of One 131, 134
stake 75, 76, 81, 85, 98, 153
Stan Lee Meets the Amazing Spider-Man 5, 163, 180, 188–191
Star Trek 31, 183, 185, 187
Star Wars 31, 35, 171, 183, 185, 193, 224
stereotype 3, 26, 43, 161, 184
Steve Rennitz 188, 190–192, 196
"Storyteller" 28, 181
Strife 171–173, 175, 178, 179
students 93, 95, 100, 103–105, 148
Sugarshock 2, 3, 5, 46, 163, 180, 181, 193–195, 222, 225
Sunnydale 9, 13, 21
Supergirl 15, 18
superhero mythology 10
Superman 11, 13–15, 17, 35, 124–127, 185, 222, 224, 225
Superman/Batman 163, 225
supervillain 119, 121, 123, 126, 131, 135, 142
sword 74, 75, 141, 167, 178, 183, 185, 188
S.W.O.R.D. 2, 145, 174

Tales of the Slayers 2, 5, 71–90, 145, 147–152, 163, 219
Tales of the Vampires 71, 219
Tancharoen, Maurissa 119, 121, 180, 197
Tara Maclay 3, 26, 137, 140, 144, 167, 172, 213
"This Year's Girl" 20
Thor 197, 199, 202, 205
Thor (film) 207
tie-in novels 41
Time of Your Life 27, 28, 40, 89, 163, 171, 220
time travel 142, 143, 172
Topher Brink 111, 141
"Touched" 175
"Tough Love" 13
Toy Story 133
transmedia 1, 4, 31–34, 41–45, 228
Trio 171
tropes 2, 71, 119, 122, 161, 165, 168
Turner, Victor 147, 152
Twilight 3, 4, 26, 27, 168, 220, 225
"Two to Go" 28

Ultron 134
Uncanny X-Men 128, 149, 159
unconscious 174, 176
underworld 141, 174
UPN 4

Vaughan, Brian K. 3, 131, 220
Victor Mancha 67, 133–137, 140, 141, 143, 220
Victoria Hand 215
video games 41, 45
Villains 3, 47, 213
Viva Las Buffy 40

Wade 3, 163, 193, 194
"War Stories" 101, 156
Ward, Grant 136, 137, 141, 197, 215–217
Warren Mears 2, 28, 213
Wash 91, 100–102, 141
Watchers 9, 12, 16, 28, 29, 34, 54, 58, 64, 71, 76, 85–88, 139, 166, 167, 177, 178, 209, 210, 214
Watchers Council 12, 15, 85, 177, 209, 210–214
Watchmen 119–130, 193, 225
WB 4, 203
weaponized woman 161
"Welcome to the Hellmouth" 9, 13, 15
Wesley Wyndam-Pryce 3, 5, 12, 49, 54–59, 89, 141, 210, 211
"What They Become" 217
"What's My Line" 210
Whedon, Jed 119, 180, 197, 222
Whedon, Zack 42, 91, 94, 95, 107, 119, 121, 123, 222
Whedonesque 26, 34, 46
Wilcox, Rhonda 13, 18, 44, 90, 99, 162
Willingham, Bill 3, 220
Willow Rosenberg 1, 3, 9, 20, 21, 24, 26–28, 30, 32, 39, 49, 60, 61, 66, 137, 138, 140, 156, 160, 163, 165–167, 170, 172, 176–179, 181, 197, 209–213, 217, 221
Willow: Wonderland 7, 49, 163, 165–167, 221
"The Wish" 192
"Witch" 79
witches 71, 75, 85, 152, 161, 162, 171, 172
Wolfram and Hart 66
Wolverine 5, 91, 127, 141, 145, 148, 149, 155, 157–162; origin story 157
Wolves at the Gate 21–25, 40, 220
woman warrior 160–161
women in comics 128, 160
Women in Refrigerators 119, 127–129, 225
Wonder Woman 5, 129, 163, 165–175, 177, 179, 225

Xander Harris 3, 9, 10, 18, 21, 22, 27, 29, 60, 61, 65, 68, 138, 167, 181, 188, 212–214
Xavin 2, 131, 133–140
X-Men 1, 2, 3, 5, 91, 119, 129, 145–152, 155–166, 169, 170, 173–177, 197, 210, 222, 226
X-Men: Dangerous 175
X-Men: Days of Future Past 149
X-Men film 148, 199

X-Men films 155, 157
X-Men: Gifted 145, 148, 150, 153, 157, 166, 170, 173, 222
X-Men: The Last Stand 145, 150
X-Men: Torn 173
X-Men 2 158
X-Men: Unstoppable 175, 177

Young Avengers 134

0–8–4 215
Zoe Washburne 91, 96- 98, 100–104, 141, 160
zompire 34